MAGNA CARTA
Origins and Legacy

Tomb of King John before the high altar of Worcester Cathedral. © Peter Holzapfel.

MAGNA CARTA
Origins and Legacy

NICHOLAS VINCENT

Bodleian Library
UNIVERSITY OF OXFORD

For the two Susans

The Publisher gratefully acknowledges the generous support of Mr David Redden in the making of this publication.

First published in 2015 by the Bodleian Library
Broad Street
Oxford OX1 3BG

www.bodleianshop.co.uk

ISBN: 978 1 85124 363 1

Text © Nicholas Vincent, 2015

All images, unless specified © Bodleian Library, University of Oxford, 2015

Parts of this book previously appeared in *The Magna Carta* (Sotheby's, 2007) and are reproduced by kind permission of Sotheby's, Inc.

Every effort has been made to obtain permission to use material which is in copyright. The publisher would welcome any omissions being brought to their attention.

Cover image: Funeral effigy of King John, Worcester Cathedral. © Photo: Christopher Guy. Reproduced by permission of the Dean and Chapter of Worcester Cathedral.

Designed and typeset by Dot Little at the Bodleian Library in 10 on 14.5 Monotype Baskerville
Printed and bound in Italy by Printer Trento on Gardamatt 150 gsm

British Library Catalogue in Publishing Data
A CIP record of this publication is available from the British Library

CONTENTS

ACKNOWLEDGEMENTS

Eight years ago, and in light of the publicity generated by the sale of an original Magna Carta, the Bodleian Library contemplated what was intended as the present volume. Seven years later, and with that vision still unfulfilled, I was approached at extremely short notice and asked to write this book. The request came with Magna Carta's 800th anniversary celebrations fast approaching, and at a time when I was already engaged in writing two other books on the subject. I was approached because I had prior 'form' here, having written the catalogue commissioned by Sotheby's for the New York sale. The present book was intended as a adaptation of that catalogue. As things have turned out, it has been rewritten from the foundations upwards, including the insertion of six entirely new chapters. The years since 2007 have witnessed the discovery of new evidence, previously unreported, including one new Magna Carta and four new Forest Charters. Above all, they have enabled me to read far more widely on the document's post medieval history.

Thanks to a major research grant from the Arts and Humanities Research Council, since 2012 I have helped co-ordinate a 'Magna Carta Project', intended to assist with the celebration of the charter's 800th anniversary. To my colleagues on that project, I express my continuing gratitude: Sophie Ambler, Paul Brand, Claire Breay, David Carpenter, Andy Day, Hugh Doherty, Geoffrey French, Henry Summerson and Louise Wilkinson.

Sophie Ambler, in particular, was a tower of strength. Jim Holt, and more recently John Baldwin both died shortly before the present book went to press. I wish that they could have witnessed the great jamboree of 2015. For first asking me to write for Sotheby's, and for permitting various materials to be reused here, I am grateful to David Redden, as also to Christopher de Hamel and James Stourton. Others who have helped include John Baker, Bruce Barker-Benfield, Mark Bateson, Rosalind Caird, Cathie Carmichael, Tracy Deakin, Laura Fidler, Rhys Griffiths, Julian Harrison, Richard Helmholz, Felicity Hill, Steve Hobbs, Tony Howe, John Hudson, Martin Kauffmann, Thomas Otte, Matthew Payne, Nigel Saul, Richard Sharpe, Juliet Tyson, Rowan Watson, Cressida Williams and Gordon Wood. For prodding me into accepting the present commission, and for much delicate insistence thereafter, I am indebted to Samuel Fanous of Bodleian Library Publishing. Samuel also made a major contribution as pictures editor. Without him, this project could not have been completed.

To have written one book on Magna Carta might be accounted a privilege. To have written three was perhaps mere folly. Certainly, it has tested my powers of reinvention to the limit. If, as I hope, I have succeeded in making each book rather different from its predecessors, then this is thanks to the enduring fascination of a document central to our understanding of both the medieval and the modern world.

Nicholas Vincent
Norwich

PART One

❖

History

INTRODUCTION

What matters about Magna Carta?

Magna Carta is the most famous document in English history, arguably in the history of the English-speaking world. Together with the American Declaration of Independence it has become an icon of law and constitutionalism. The Declaration of Independence was printed on paper in relatively large numbers just over two hundred years ago. Magna Carta, by contrast, is nearly four times older, handwritten in medieval Latin on fragile parchment membranes. It is today a document not only world renowned but of surpassing rarity. Of the perhaps more than 200 original Magna Cartas produced in the Middle Ages, only twenty-four are today known to survive. Five of these are preserved in the Bodleian Library at Oxford. If we add to the Bodleian charters a further Magna Carta owned by Oriel College, then Oxford boasts six original Magna Cartas: more than survive in any other collection up to and including the British Library in London (which possesses four examples).

1 The Bodleian Library, where five of the 24 surviving thirteenth-century Magna Cartas are housed.
© Greg Smolonski

From the measures set out in Magna Carta emerged the concept of the rule of law as a proper and permanent challenge to the feudal tyranny of England's medieval kings. As trumpeted in clauses 39 and 40 of Magna Carta first issued in 1215, the sovereign was henceforth obliged to allow that 'No free man is to be arrested, or imprisoned, or disseised [i.e. be deprived of his lands or possessions], or outlawed, or exiled, or in any other way ruined, nor will we go against him or send against him, except by the lawful judgment of his peers or by the law of the land. To no-one shall we sell or deny or delay right or justice.' This is to define a principle of due process under law, today incorporated within the constitutions of most democratic (and many distinctly undemocratic) states. From Magna Carta 1215 clauses 39 and 40 we can trace a direct line to such foundational statements of modern democratic principle as the 1789 Declaration of the Rights of Man, or articles 9, 10 and 11 of the United Nations' 1948 Universal Declaration of Human Rights. No citizen or subject is to be imprisoned or punished without access to proper legal process and the right to a fair trial.

Magna Carta clauses 12 and 14 introduce a further limitation on royal power: 'No scutage or aid [in effect no taxation] is to be imposed in our realm except by the common counsel of our realm.' To obtain such counsel, the great men of the realm should be properly summoned to debate. From this stretches a direct connection to the American colonists of the 1770s and their demand for 'No taxation without representation'. More immediately, from Magna Carta's insistence that the king take counsel, we can trace the emergence of a body in England from the 1230s

onwards officially entitled 'Parliament'. From the 1250s, Parliament was deemed capable of meeting in the king's absence. By 1265, Parliament was expected to include not only the greater barons and bishops (the lords spiritual and temporal, the future 'House of Lords') but locally chosen representatives of each of the shires and principal boroughs of England (the future 'House of Commons').

Magna Carta is thus of profound constitutional importance. Many other books exist that explain the medieval circumstances in which it was written and its continuing modern significance. The present book is different. Having set out the context and legacy of the charter as a totem in world history, I have also attempted a comprehensive census of the surviving originals of Magna Carta. Until recently, the only such listing available was that made before 1810, for the Record Commissioners in their great folio edition of the laws of England, *Statutes of the Realm*. In 2007, thanks to Sotheby's and the sale in New York of a Magna Carta issued in 1297, I was able to attempt an updated census of manuscripts. The list that follows below nonetheless marks a great improvement upon that of 2007, and includes at least six Magna Cartas or Forest Charters

4 The sale in 2007 at auction of a Magna Carta issued in 1297.
© Sotheby's, Inc.

that in 2007 were still unknown. Together with this, I have listed a further series of documents issued in thirteenth-century England closely associated with Magna Carta: the various drafts from which the charter itself was made, the letters and charters that accompanied its issue and the other documents that helped to spread its fame within the first century of its existence. This in turn has allowed me to present new findings on the survival of manuscripts not previously known to survive (including four previously 'unknown' originals of the so-called Forest Charter, from 1217 onwards the essential accompaniment to Magna Carta and a document of almost equal constitutional significance). It has also prompted a study of the means by which laws and legislation, including Magna Carta, were proclaimed in the centuries before the invention of the printing press or the internet. I have attempted to explain below not only why Magna Carta mattered at the time of its issue in 1215, but how it survived thereafter, in a series of reissues that are, in many ways, far less well known than the 1215 charter, but of far greater legal and constitutional significance.

The document that was agreed at Runnymede in 1215, the instrument drafted in early summer and sealed on 15 June by King John, the 'original original' of Magna Carta, no longer survives. What we have instead are fair copies made from this document, intended for distribution around the shires of England, sealed with the king's seal. Each of these, officially issued by the king's chancery, deserves to be considered an 'original' Magna Carta. Four such originals from 1215 are today preserved, two of them in the British Library, the others in the cathedral libraries of Lincoln and Salisbury. Since 2009, they have been collectively enrolled on the UNESCO Register of World Heritage, where Magna Carta is described as 'the cornerstone of English liberty, law and democracy … an icon for freedom and democracy throughout the world.'

Yet as an attempt to bring peace between king and barons, the charter of 1215 was an utter failure, repudiated by the pope and practically redundant within only twelve weeks of its creation. It owed its survival thereafter to the desperate circumstances of 1216, the death of King John and the accession of his nine-year-old son, King Henry III (1216–1272). Keen to advertise their willingness to break with past misdeeds, King Henry's counsellors reissued Magna Carta in a revised form in November 1216. As a manifesto of future good government, it was reissued, further revised, on perhaps as many as a dozen occasions between 1216 and its last official reissue, by King John's grandson, Edward I, in 1300. As a result, we

ECCLESIÆ CATHEDRALIS
LINCOLNIENSIS
FACIES OCCIDENTALIS.

Vt præclaræ huius Ecclesiæ fama
amplius innotefcat, hoc pofuit,
MICHAEL HONYWOOD,
S. Th. D. ibidem Decanus,

5 Lincoln Cathedral, home to one of the surviving four originals of Magna Carta 1215. Wenceslaus Hollar, *Lincoln Cathedral from the West*, etching, published 1673 (Pennington 995; Turner, New Hollstein German, 2254). The Thomas Fisher Rare Book Library, University of Toronto, Hollar_k_0965. © University of Toronto.

have originals of the issues of 1215, 1216, 1217, 1225, 1297 and 1300, and copies of the issue made in 1265. At each of these reissues, changes were made to the substantive text of the charter. In the earliest reissues of 1216, 1217 and 1225, such changes were drastic, fundamentally altering the order and meaning of large sections of the document. Even after the 1225 text became the received version in English law, copyists continued to introduce minor modifications, so that the 1297 and 1300 reissues, for example, continue to represent a subtle evolution from the base text first published in 1215.

By the somewhat arcane rules according to which such matters are decided, the issue of 1297, being the first to be properly enrolled on the 'Statute Roll' of the royal chancery (the medieval office responsible for producing royal letters) is today considered the version of Magna Carta still binding under English law. Although written in Latin, this version of the charter is cited in the modern statute book from its semi-official English translation. Of the thirty-seven clauses of the 1297 charter, all but three have been repealed under subsequent reforming legislation, beginning in the 1820s with the repeal of the arcane clause 26 of the 1297 charter (clause 36 of 1215, requiring the royal chancery to issue writs of inquisition without demanding payment) and continuing with a series of further repeals, most notably under the Statute Law Revision Act of 1863. The last such clauses to disappear (clauses 8, 15–16, 22–3, 25 and 30 of the 1297 Magna Carta) were repealed as recently as 1969, under the Statute Law (Repeals) Act.

Even so, three clauses remain from this great sifting of redundant medievalism. According to the most recent online listing of English statute law (whose rather over-literal English translation I employ below) these are clauses 1 of the 1297 charter (substantially modified from clause 1 of the charter of 1215):

> We have granted to God, and by this our present Charter have confirmed, for us and our heirs for ever, that the Church of England shall be free, and shall have all her whole rights and liberties inviolable. We have granted also, and given to all the freemen of our realm, for us and our heirs for ever, these liberties under-written, to have and to hold to them and their heirs, of us and our heirs for ever.

Clause 9 of 1297 (clause 13 of 1215):

> The City of London shall have all the old Liberties and Customs [which it hath been used to have]. Moreover we will and grant, that all other cities, boroughs, towns, and the barons of the Five Ports, and all other ports, shall have all their liberties and free customs.

And clause 29 of 1297 (clauses 39 and 40 of 1215):

> No freeman shall be taken or imprisoned, or be disseised of his freehold, or liberties, or free customs, or be outlawed, or exiled, or any other wise destroyed; nor will we not pass sentence upon him, nor condemn him, but by lawful judgment of his peers, or by the law of the land. We will sell to no man, we will not deny or defer to any man either justice or right.

Since the 1297 issue is to all intents and purposes merely a reissue of the version of Magna Carta first promulgated in 1225, and since the clauses of 1225 were themselves in most cases adapted from those of 1215, the charter first issued by King John still enjoys a degree of legal currency. As such, it remains the very oldest legislation still in force in English law.

As a document, Magna Carta has to be set within both its historical and its archival context. How did this sheet of parchment – literally 'the Great Charter' – come into existence, and how did each of the particular originals of the charter come to be issued and thereafter to survive the accidents of time? Magna Carta itself has inspired an entire scholarly industry, with many dozens of books and academic articles devoted to its history and meaning. Rather surprisingly, much less work has been done on the charter's text, writing and physical appearance. Yet the story of the charter's writing and issue only further enhances the document's significance. In what follows, readers will find the latest and most comprehensive listing of Magna Carta manuscripts ever attempted, including the identification of new originals in English institutional collections and the demotion of purported originals now found to be nothing of the sort. Above all, I hope they will find a further contribution to the perennially fascinating story of the the modern world's evolution from the much more distant past.

REFERENCES

For the clauses of the 1297 Magna Carta still current under law in England and Wales, see the official site: legislation.gov.uk at http://www.legislation.gov.uk/ aep/Edw1cc1929. For the state of play to 2007, see the catalogue that I produced for Sotheby's as *The Magna Carta*, Sotheby's Sale Catalogue (New York, 18 December 2007). For general introductions, see David Carpenter, *Magna Carta* (London 2015); Nicholas Vincent, *Magna Carta: A Very Short Introduction* (Oxford 2012), and the collection of essays that I edited as *Magna Carta: The Foundation of Freedom, 1215–2015* (London 2015). The classic scholarly study remains that by J. C. Holt, *Magna Carta* (Cambridge 1965, 2nd ed. 1992, 3rd. edition forthcoming 2015). There is a wealth of new material available at the Magna Carta Project website: http://magnacartaresearch.org, sponsored by the Arts and Humanities Research Council. For twentieth-century approaches to the charter, see Nicholas Vincent, 'Magna Carta and the *English Historical Review*: A Review Article', *EHR*, cxxx (2015).

CHAPTER 1

King John and the making of the great charter

Today, the words 'Magna Carta' are assumed to apply to a text of just over 3,500 Latin words, setting out what many would agree to be fundamental liberties. From this document, it is supposed, spring the foundations not only of the British but of the American constitution. As law, Magna Carta does indeed have a long and distinguished history. It began, however, in its earliest form, as a peace treaty rather than as a legal statute. The intention of those who first made it was that it should put an end to a baronial rebellion that broke out in 1215 against the misrule of King John (1199–1216). As such, Magna Carta was intended to supply remedies to the abuses perpetrated not just by one bad ruler but by an entire dynasty of English kings. Of this tradition, King John was only the latest, though in many ways the most despised representative.

King John succeeded to lands and titles that had recently been assembled. His father, King Henry II (1154–1189), had been born merely the son of a count of Anjou, Geoffrey le Bel, albeit descended on his mother's side from the ruling dynasty of England and Normandy. At the death of Henry's grandfather, King Henry I, in 1135, Henry's mother had failed in her bid to be declared ruler of England as her father's heir. Instead, the Anglo-Norman realm on both sides of the Channel had been plunged into twenty years of civil war. Henry II grew up amidst this turmoil. From his father, Geoffrey, he inherited the county of Anjou on the river Loire. From his mother he inherited a claim to Normandy, made good in the 1140s only after military conquest. England eventually passed to him in 1154, on the death of the usurper, Stephen of Blois, who had seized the throne after 1135. Shortly before this, in 1152, Henry had married Eleanor of Aquitaine, heiress to a vast duchy that stretched from the Loire and the city of Poitiers southwards via Bordeaux and Gascony to the Pyrenees. To this assembly of lands, in due course, Henry himself added

6 Henry II (above left), founder of the Plantagenet dynasty, with his two sons, Richard I (above right), King John (below left) and his grandson, Henry III (below right). BL, Royal MS. 14 CVII, f. 9r. © The British Library Board.

7 From his grandfather, Geoffrey, King John inherited the county of Anjou. Funerary enamel, Le Mans Cathedral. Photo: S@bre

both Brittany (secured in the 1160s by the betrothal of its heiress to one of his sons), and Ireland (acquired by military conquest after 1172).

As a result, by a fortuitous accumulation of dynastic accidents, Henry II found himself from 1154 onwards in possession not only of the rich realm of England but of an 'empire' in France stretching from the Channel to the most southerly parts of Gascony. This constituted the greatest collection of French estates assembled under one single ruler since the fall of the dynasty of the emperor Charlemagne three hundred years before. This vast inheritance King John immediately proceeded to squander.

John has enjoyed a mixed reputation over the past eight hundred years. To the generation who lived immediately after his death, blackening his reputation was one means of explaining why England had undergone such extraordinary chaos under his rule. After 1216, there was no shortage of chroniclers, particularly those of the great abbey of St Albans north of London (led by the monk historian Roger of Wendover and his continuator, Matthew Paris), prepared to categorize John as a catastrophic, indeed semi-demonic failure. To Matthew Paris, writing in the 1230s, 'Black as Hell is, Hell itself is defiled by the presence of John.'

To the generations that followed, memory of the twelfth and thirteenth centuries was communicated chiefly through the rewriting and recycling of history as composed at St Albans. As a result, the later Middle Ages inherited an equally jaundiced view of John. Attitudes only began to alter under the Tudors. From the 1520s onwards, Henry VIII's struggles with the papacy put the English Church on a collision course with Rome. By a new generation of Protestant historians, John was reinterpreted as the first English sovereign bravely to have declared England independent from the papacy. John's attempt, it was acknowledged, had failed. He was forced, a few years before Magna Carta, to seal a surrender of England to the pope. But this was not held against him in such Tudor retellings of the story as Shakespeare's play of *King John* (probably of the 1590s).

Shakespeare constructed his play from a farago of historical details, derived via Foxe's *Book of Martyrs*, and Holinshed's *Chronicles*, from the St Albans chroniclers of the 1220s and 1230s. He used these materials to portray the king in generally positive terms, as proto-Protestant hero rather than as a semi-infidel villain. Wrongly accused by the false and perfidious French of the murder of his nephew, Shakespeare's John seeks

to defy both the king of France and the pope. The outcome is his murder
by a treacherous Catholic monk (an entirely fictitious denouement). The
play ends with a celebration of Englishness ('This England never did,
nor never shall, lie at the proud foot of a conqueror.'), itself quoted with
approval in Parliament, two hundred years later, at the time of England's
renewal of war against Napoleon Bonaparte.

As this suggests, Shakespeare's essentially positive approach to King
John persisted into the eighteenth century. Even David Hume (whose
History of England, first published between 1754 and 1762, enjoyed immense
influence) was not prepared entirely to condemn a king who had defied the
superstitions of the Church of Rome. For the reinstatement of the original
'black' legend of John we need to wait until 1819 and Sir Walter Scott's
Ivanhoe. Here, John was presented as a treacherous womanizer surrounded
by thugs and sycophants, the very model of everything that the Victorian
age came to despise in aristocratic indolence and greed.

8 Through diplomacy and
empire-building, the Plantagenet
kings came close to swallowing
the realms of both England and
France. Here King Philip of France
(left) sends a message to his sister,
betrothed to King John's elder
brother and held in custody by
John's father, King Henry II. BL,
Royal MS. 16 G VI, f. 343v. © The
British Library Board.

The life and death of King Iohn.

Actus Primus, Scæna Prima.

Enter King Iohn, Queene Elinor, Pembroke, Essex, and Salisbury, with the Chattylion of France.

King Iohn.

NOw say *Chatillou,* what would *France* with vs ?

Chat. Thus (after greeting) speakes the King of France,
In my behauiour to the Maiesty,
The borrowed Maiesty of *England* heere.

Elea. A strange beginning : borrowed Maiesty ?

K.Iohn. Silence (good mother) heare the Embassie.

Chat. Philip of *France,* in right and true behalfe
Of thy deceased brother, *Geffreyes* sonne,
Arthur Plantaginet, laies most lawfull claime
To this faire Iland, and the Territories :
To *Ireland, Poyctiers, Aniowe, Torayne, Maine,*
Desiring thee to lay aside the sword
Which swaies vsurpingly these seuerall titles,
And put the same into yong *Arthurs* hand,
Thy Nephew, and right royall Soueraigne.

K.Iohn. What followes if we disallow of this ?

Chat. The proud controle of fierce and bloudy warre,
To inforce these rights, so forcibly with-held,

K.Io. Heere haue we war for war, & bloud for bloud,
Controlement for controlement : so answer *France.*

Chat. Then take my Kings defiance from my mouth,
The farthest limit of my Embassie.

K.Iohn. Beare mine to him, and so depart in peace,
Be thou as lightning in the eies of *France* ;
For ere thou canst report, I will be there :
The thunder of my Cannon shall be heard,
So hence : be thou the trumpet of our wrath,
And sullen presage of your owne decay :
An honourable conduct let him haue,
Pembroke looke too't : farewell *Chattillion.*

Exit Chat. and Pem.

Ele. What now my sonne, haue I not euer said
How that ambitious *Constance* would not cease
Till she had kindled *France* and all the world,
Vpon the right and party of her sonne.
This might haue beene preuented, and made whole
With very easie arguments of loue,
Which now the mannage of two kingdomes must
With fearefull bloudy issue arbitrate.

K.Iohn. Our strong possession, and our right for vs.

Eli. Your strong possessiõ much more then your right,
Or else it must go wrong with you and me,
So much my conscience whispers in your eare,

Which none but heauen, and you, and I, shall heare.

Enter a Sheriffe.

Essex. My Liege, here is the strangest controuersie
Come from the Country to be iudg'd by you
That ere I heard : shall I produce the men ?

K.Iohn. Let them approach :
Our Abbies and our Priories shall pay
This expeditious charge : what men are you ?

Enter Robert Faulconbridge, and Philip.

Philip. Your faithfull subiect, I a gentleman,
Borne in *Northamptonshire,* and eldest sonne
As I suppose, to *Robert Faulconbridge,*
A Souldier by the Honor-giuing-hand
Of *Cordelion,* Knighted in the field.

K.Iohn. What art thou ?

Robert. The son and heire to that same *Faulconbridge.*

K.Iohn. Is that the elder, and art thou the heyre ?
You came not of one mother then it seemes.

Philip. Most certain of one mother, mighty King,
That is well knowne, and as I thinke one father :
But for the cerraine knowledge of that truth,
I put you o're to heauen, and to my mother ;
Of that I doubt, as all mens children may.

Eli. Out on thee rude man, ÿ dost shame thy mother,
And wound her honor with this diffidence.

Phil. I Madame ? No, I haue no reason for it,
That is my brothers plea, and none of mine,
The which if he can proue, a pops me out,
At least from faire fiue hundred pound a yeere :
Heauen guard my mothers honor, and my Land.

K.Iohn. A good blunt fellow : why being yonger born
Doth he lay claime to thine inheritance ?

Phil. I know not why, except to get the land :
But once he slanderd me with bastardy :
But where I be as true begot or no,
That still I lay vpon my mothers head,
But that I am as well begot my Liege
(Faire fall the bones that tooke the paines for me)
Compare our faces, and be Iudge your selfe
If old Sir *Robert* did beget vs both,
And were our father, and this sonne like him :
O old sir *Robert* Father, on my knee
I giue heauen thankes I was not like to thee.

K.Iohn. Why what a mad-cap hath heauen lent vs here ?

Elen. He hath a tricke of *Cordelions* face,
The accent of his tongue affecteth him :
Doe you not read some tokens of my sonne
In the large composition of this man ?

K.Ioh.

a

The 'facts' of *Ivanhoe*, however fictitious, fed into the Victorian presentation of John, not least in works such as Richard Thomson's *Historical Essay on the Magna Charta of King John* (1829), the first serious attempt to merge the political and legal history of the document, or Martin Tupper's best-selling romance of *Stephan Langton* (1858). Here the saintly Langton, archbishop of Canterbury, assisted by (the entirely fictitious) Robin Hood, contends against a black-masked King John, raping and pillaging his way across a background of French wars and baronial disgust. It was this view, albeit sobered with a strong dose of scholarship, that triumphed in the *Constitutional History* of William Stubbs, the greatest monument of Victorian medievalism, published between 1874 and 1878. Here John is portrayed as 'the worst of all our kings … polluted by every vice that could disgrace a man, false to every obligation.'

Since Stubbs, there have been attempts to rehabilitate John. Rejecting the unmediated prejudice of the chroniclers and instead relying upon the abundant administrative records of his reign, modern scholars have presented a portrait in greys and charcoals rather than the unforgiving black and white of Stubbs. As in many other things, the 1960s witnessed an attempt to overturn the accepted wisdom about King John. W. L. Warren's biography (first published in 1961 and still in print) sought to portray a king who combined deviousness with administrative genius. Warren suggested that the selfish impulses of John's baronial and ecclesiastical critics were more than matched by the king's political cunning. In recent years, nonetheless, the weight of opinion has come full circle. A volume of essays published in 1999, on the 800th anniversary of John's accession, far from exonerating John, charges him with crimes that even William Stubbs might have hesitated to specify: not just murder but infanticide, not just rape but child abuse.

What then was so wrong with John? What was it that provoked his barons against him, brought Magna Carta into being and helped blacken the king's reputation for all eternity? At the root of the chorus of disapproval lies an awareness that John, far from building an empire or conquering new land, not only failed in his military endeavours during his lifetime but died in the midst of civil war. Medieval kings were expected to perform two chief functions – they should preserve peace at home and they should defeat their enemies overseas. In both of these respects, John was an abject failure, standing in stark contrast to his father and elder brother, Henry II (who created the Angevin 'empire' that John

9 Shakespeare makes no mention of Magna Carta in his play *King John*. Instead the king defends the crown from rival claimants against a background of the threat of invasion by foreign powers and conflict with the papacy – themes which resonated with contemporary audiences. *King John, Mr. William Shakespeares comedies, histories, & tragedies* (1623) i.e. 'The First Folio'. Oxford, Bodleian Library, Arch. G c.7.

squandered) and Richard I (who performed heroic deeds on crusade in the East). In hindsight, therefore, it is hardly surprising that John was judged to be a 'bad' king. Thus is history written backwards, with Magna Carta presented as the crowning indictment of John's reign, and the howls of disapproval after his death serving as chief witnesses for his prosecution.

Even in John's lifetime, however, there seems little doubt that the king failed to impress his contemporaries either by his candour or his political cunning. Sent to govern Ireland in 1185 shortly after his eighteenth birthday, he outraged the Irish kings by mocking their long red beards. When things turned against him, he blamed not his own failings but his father's viceroy, Hugh de Lacy. Treated by his father as a favourite youngest son, he caused grief, and some suggested his father's death, when it was revealed in 1189 that his name came first on a list of conspirators against the ageing king.

Rewarded at his father's death with a vast trans-maritime lordship, extending from Ireland and Lancashire via Devon and Cornwall to the western seaboard of Normandy, he was obliged by his brother, the new King Richard, to swear only one undertaking: that he would not enter England during the king's absence on crusade. This oath John promptly broke, not only stirring up war in England but entering into alliance with

10 Sir Walter Scott, who cast King John in *Ivanhoe* as the antithesis of the British Victorian gentleman. British Museum, BH/FF10/Portraits British CVII P4 © British Museum Trustees.

King Philip of France, Richard's principal rival. When Richard returned in 1194, John was pardoned. But Richard's words on this occasion ('Forgive him, he is only a boy!') sat oddly with a younger brother already approaching thirty years of age. When Richard died in 1199, attempting to impose peace upon his lands in the French south-west, John promptly seized the throne, despite what many regarded as the superior claims of his nephew, the twelve-year-old Arthur of Brittany, born in 1186 a few months after the death of his father, Geoffrey, the elder brother of the new King John.

From this rivalry between John and Arthur of Britanny sprang one of the greatest crimes with which John was charged. In 1200, to forestall any alliance between Arthur and the French, John made peace with King Philip of France. His claims to the rest of Normandy were recognized in return for a surrender to Philip of the easternmost parts of the duchy, bordering Paris and the Ile de France. In the same year, putting aside his first wife, Isabella of Gloucester, who was apparently barren, John married a southern French heiress, Isabella of Angoulême, previously betrothed to the powerful southern lord, Hugh de Lusignan, count of La Marche. There were strategic justifications for this – John needed an heir.

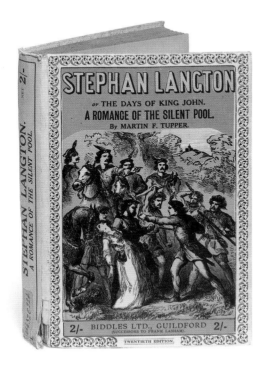

11 Martin Tupper's King John is a bone fide villain. *Stephan Langton: or The Days of King John* (London, 1863).

12 The royal clerk Gerald of Wales accompanied John to Ireland in 1185, drawing on his experiences for his *Topographia Hiberniae*. Typifying the views of the ruling elite, he depicted the Irish as a 'barbarous' people'. BL, Royal MS. 13 B VIII, f. 28r. © The British Library Board.

In due course, Isabella of Angoulême was to supply him with two sons and three daughters (indeed, remarried after John's death, she went on to produce at least a further nine children). The county of Angoulême straddled the main route between Poitiers and John's family lands in the far south, around Bordeaux. This was a region of crucial significance that, by marriage, John now at last brought under control. The problem was that Isabella's jilted suitor, Hugh de Lusignan, now made common cause with Arthur of Brittany against the Plantagenets. Hugh himself had been legitimately betrothed to Isabella but had deferred the consummation of their marriage, perhaps because Isabella herself was a mere eight or nine years old. King John had no such scruples.

As a result of their rebellion, in 1202, Arthur and his allies were taken captive in one of John's few real military victories: a lightning raid upon the besieged castle of Mirebeau north of Poitiers. Yet even here, John transformed victory into defeat. Sent into captivity at Falaise, Arthur of Brittany, the fifteen-year-old royal rebel, simply disappeared. His fate will probably never be known. By some it was rumoured that he died attempting to escape, perhaps falling into the river Seine from the castle battlements of Rouen. By others it was alleged that he had been secretly killed, either by John in person, or by executioners acting on the king's instructions.

Kings of the past had lived lives of less than blameless rectitude. John's own father, Henry II, had fathered a quiver of bastard children from a succession of mistresses. He had imprisoned his queen, John's mother, Eleanor of Aquitaine. In 1170, he had been directly blamed for the murder of his sainted archbishop of Canterbury, Thomas Becket, one of the most brutal acts of a brutal time, greeted with outrage across the whole of Christendom. But Henry II himself faced nothing worse than token penance, itself allowed to run on year by year unserved. By contrast, what Henry had done with impunity, John did only at the cost of public outcry and baronial rebellion. Hugh de Lusignan now re-emerged to demand what had become of Arthur. The Bretons and the Poitevins rebelled. The French king, Philip Augustus, summoned John to explain his actions, and when John failed to appear, publicly proclaimed that John and his heirs were deprived of all their lands in France.

13 To preclude his nephew Arthur's claim to the throne, John made peace with Philip, king of France. BL, Royal MS. 16 G VI, f. 362r. © The British Library Board.

Over the past twenty years, Normandy and Anjou had been transformed into frontier provinces, regularly contested by the kings of France and England. Rather than permit the continuation of such violence, the Normans themselves now abandoned John. The great Norman fortress of Château-Gaillard had been built above the Seine by Richard I as a permanent symbol of Plantagenet lordship, clearly visible from the neighbouring kingdom of France. In March 1204, it fell after only a few days of siege, some said as a result of treachery. Having seized Falaise and advanced on Caen, on 24 June 1204 King Philip took possession of the ducal capital at Rouen. In 1204, as during the D-Day campaigns of 1944, Caen and the Falaise 'gap' proved crucial strategic conquests. Normandy itself, for the previous 150 years united to the English crown, was now a French possession.

From Normandy, Philip's army moved south, seizing Angers and Poitiers, the ancestral homes of John's father and mother. Almost as a prophetic sign of what was about to unfold, John's mother, the eighty-year-old Eleanor of Aquitaine, died on the final day of March 1204, only three weeks after the fall of Château-Gaillard. The French empire that had first been established by Eleanor's marriage to Henry II, fifty years before, now stood on the brink of collapse. Only Gascony in the far south, and the great city of Bordeaux, remained as vestiges of Henry II's empire still effectively under English rule.

For the next four centuries, the geo-politics of northern Europe were to be dominated by attempts by the kings of England to recover what they

14 The funeral effigy of Isabella of Angoulême, wife of King John, Fontevraud Abbey, France. © Manuel Cohen Photography.

regarded as their ancestral lands in northern and south-western France. John himself, meanwhile, crept home to England. Taking ship from Barfleur, on the far northernmost tip of Normandy, on 5 December 1203, the eve of the feast of St Nicholas (patron saint of seafarers), he landed at Portsmouth. He spent Christmas in Canterbury, Becket's cathedral city and therefore in many respects a place of ill-omen for Plantagenet kings. When Normandy, Brittany, Anjou and most of Poitou fell to the French invaders, John himself was several hundred miles from the scene of battle. The St Albans chroniclers, indeed, imagine him lusting after his teenage bride, frolicking in his bed chamber whilst his cities and castles were betrayed. To a world that believed in God's omniscience, kings defeated in war necessarily revealed themselves as either tested or punished by God. For the next ten years, powerless to prevent the French occupation of his lands, John's chief priority became the organization of reconquest.

English kings of the past had survived military setbacks. Both Henry I (1100–1135) and Stephen (1135–1154) had, at various points in their reigns, lost control of Normandy. Stephen, for a brief while, had been captured in

15 The castle of Falaise, where John's rival to the throne, Arthur of Brittany, was imprisoned. Photo: Château Guillaume-le-Conquérant de Falaise.

battle and deposed as king of England. What was extraordinary about John's defeat in 1204 was its permanence and the effects that this had upon his government in England. John's father, Henry II, had spent less than half of his reign in England. John's elder brother, Richard I, had spent only a few weeks there after his coronation, followed by a few more on his return from crusade. For the rest of his ten years as king, Richard had been an absentee either in France or the Holy Land. English barons had grown accustomed to their own company and to shepherding their own resources, free from interference by a hyperactive French-speaking monarch. After 1204, all of this changed. From being a distant absentee, John became a daily presence in England, roaming the land from north to south, demanding entertainment, stabling for his horses and game for his hounds. Royal morals had never been good, but John's were worse than most. Rumours circulated that his lechery extended beyond the usual run of courtesans to include the daughters and wives of his greater barons. Above all, the king demanded money.

If John's lands in France were to be reconquered, then this could only be achieved at great expense. An already over-taxed realm of England was squeezed until the pips squeaked. The rot had set in here under Richard I, whose crusade, and whose subsequent kidnapping in Germany had cost England literally a king's ransom. As much as 100,000 marks (£66,000) had been sent overseas to pay for Richard's release.

16 Henry II and Eleanor of Aquitaine, as depicted in their funerary effigies in Fontevraud Abbey. © Manuel Cohen Photography.

Thereafter, there had been further massive expenditure on the defence and garisoning of Normandy. Ever since the great bonanza of the Norman Conquest of 1066, kings of England had never lacked for money. By 1204, all of this had changed. There were perhaps macroeconomic explanations here, beyond the costs of warfare and of John's lost territories in France. Northern Europe from the 1170 onwards seems to have experienced a period of sharp monetary inflation. Wages and prices rocketed. King John, whose income depended upon fixed rents from land, found himself with massively increased expenditure but with no compensating rise either in rents or the profits of war. In these circumstances, his only alternative was to impose heavier taxation on his barons, themselves victims of precisely the same economic pressures as the king.

Into this seething torrent of resentments and contingencies another ingredient was poured. Even before the murder of Thomas Becket in 1170, the Plantagenet kings of England had enjoyed less than easy relations with the English Church. Archbishops and bishops were in most cases nominated by the king, served at the royal court and held their lands from the crown. They nonetheless owed allegiance, in spiritual terms, to the pope in Rome. The Church taught that obedience to God came before service to mere earthly authorities, and that the contradictory

17 Château Gaillard, overlooking the Seine in Normandy, was built by Richard I in 1196–8 to protect the route to Rouen and to provide a foundation for the reconquest of territory taken by the king of France. A symbol of Plantagenet power, it was lost by King John to the French less than a decade after its completion. © Thomas Ulrich.

demands of God and king should be decided ultimately in favour of God. In particular, in the great University of Paris where many English churchmen were trained, a powerful strain of criticism had developed, very much to the disadvantage of kings who believed that the purpose of the Church was to ensure obedience to royal rather than divine will. Using a wealth of examples of good and bad kings drawn from the Old Testament, the masters of Paris now taught that kingship itself had been sent, not for the enlightment, but for the punishment of mankind. Kings must rule by God's law or face divine retribution. As in the Old Testament book of Leviticus, law itself should be written down and given precedence over royal will or command. Those subject to kings had rights as well as obligations. In particular, they should be taxed only in necessity and for the greater public good.

In 1205, a year after John's defeats in France, the archbishop of Canterbury, Hubert Walter, died. For twenty years he had been a leading figure in royal administration, as justiciar (chief minister) and

18 *above* The coronation of Richard I. A few weeks later, Richard left England and spent the vast majority of his ten-year reign commanding armies abroad. London, BL, Royal MS. 16 G VI, f. 374. © The British Library Board.

19 *right* King John, as depicted in a fourteenth-century manuscript. His demands for game for his hounds and stabling for his horses were the least of his excesses. BL, Royal MS. 20 A II, f. 8v. © The British Library Board.

20 *opposite* Richard I was imprisoned and ransomed for the unheard of sum of £66,000. BL, Cotton Vitellius MS. A. XIII, f. 5. © The British Library Board.

Apres Henry le secund regna Richard sun fiz. x. aunz e
demy sl entrepaysand de la terre seynt fuist pris del dutz
de Ostriz par eyde del Roy Phylippe de Fraunce. e fuist reynt hors
de prison pur cent mil lyuers de argent. e pur cel tauncun fu
rent les chalitz de Engleterre pris. des Eglyses e venduz. Puis
fuist tret de vn quarel de Ablast al Chastel de Chalezun. dit
ceste vers su fet: Xpe tui calicis: predo fit preda caliccis.

later, royal chancellor (head of the king's writing office). John proposed to replace him as archbishop with another royal servant, John de Gray, bishop of Norwich. The pope objected. With the compliance of the monks of Canterbury, the pope then engineered the election of a very different candidate. Master Stephen Langton had for thirty years taught in the University of Paris. There he was recognized as a leading theologian, expounding precisely that tradition of Biblical criticism in which the bad kings of the present were contrasted with good kings of the past. Although an Englishman born in Lincolnshire, as a long-term resident of Paris he had been subject to the French King Philip. As a former teacher of the pope, Innocent III, Langton had more recently been promoted as a cardinal in Rome. For all of these reasons, so far as King John was concerned, Langton was obnoxious. John refused to recognize his election, and forbade him entry to England.

The outcome was an open breach between king and Church. Langton was forced to remain in exile in northern France. He spent much time there in the great Cistercian abbey of Pontigny, deliberately imitating the fate of Thomas Becket who had lived in exile at Pontigny in the 1160s. In 1208, after repeated threats, the pope imposed a sentence of Interdict upon the English church. The sacraments were denied to the faithful, no church bells were to be rung, no masses said. The king himself was pronounced excommunicate. The vast majority of English bishops left the

21 *opposite* Even before the murder of Thomas Becket, relations between the Crown and the Church were difficult. BL, Harley MS. 5102, f. 32. © The British Library Board.

22 *above* A lead papal seal (*bulla*) of Pope Innocent III, 1198-1216. Portable Antiquities Scheme, SF-75C3F8.

23 *left* The Old Testament provided examples of kings whose rule was a blight upon their people, such as Saul, who ordered the slaughter of priests whom he suspected of conspiring against him. BL, Royal MS. 2 B VII, f. 52. © The British Library Board.

realm, seeking refuge in Scotland or France. The full extent of their exodus is revealed by the fact that the activities of the king's own chancery or writing office, previously staffed by clergymen, were drastically curtailed. From John's accession in 1199 to the imposition of the Interdict in 1208, the king's chancery had kept detailed copies of all outgoing correspondence, today our chief source of knowledge for royal administration. From 1208, these enrolments ceased. For each year from 1199 to 1208 we have several hundred, sometimes more than a thousand royal letters. After 1209, the survival rate slows to less than half a dozen.

Dark rumours circulated. Many of the estates of the church were now seized by the crown, with the king making vast profits from their exploitation. Timber was felled, land was pillaged, the peasantry forced to pay heavier rents. Further taxes were raised by blackmailing the monastic orders, such as the Cistercians, and by threatening to deprive the parish clergy of their concubines. In particular instances, clergymen themselves felt the king's violent temper. An exchequer official, Geoffrey of Norwich, accused of speaking treason against the king, was supposedly crushed to death under a leaden cope, a legend that perhaps owes more to the vivid imagination of the chroniclers than it does to reality. Even so, not all rumours were unfounded. Peter of Wakefield, a Yorkshire hermit who prophesied that the king's impiety would be punished, was executed by dismemberment, his body pulled apart between two galloping horses. According to Matthew Paris, writing in the 1230s, the king toyed with the idea of converting to Islam. Certainly he entered into a military alliance with the heretic count of Toulouse, in league with the king of Aragon, himself an ally of the Muslims of north Africa.

Even the king's closest companions had cause for fear. William de Braose, lord of Bramber in Sussex, had been one of John's most intimate friends. Privy to many of the darker secrets of the reign, he had been richly rewarded with lands in Wales and Ireland. He was now hounded into exile. It has been suggested that he or his wife had spoken too openly of the circumstances of Arthur of Brittany's disappearance. William's wife and eldest son were incarcerated and reputedly starved to death, either in Windsor Castle or in the great state prison at Corfe in Dorset. The chroniclers report the gruesome details here, including allegations of cannibalism. William himself died in 1211, some claimed of grief at the news of his wife's death. He was buried with full honours in the French capital, Paris. These were crimes (today we might refer to them as 'crimes

24 *above* Statue of Stephen Langton, (1852), previously on the Clock Tower of the Palace of Westminster, now displayed at Person Hall, University of North Carolina at Chapel Hill. © Duane Dial.

25 *opposite* In a conscious echo of Thomas Becket's exile, Stephen Langton lodged at the Cistercian Abbey of Pontigny in northern Burgundy during his exile. Photo © lrp392.

26 *above* The papal interdict imposed on England in 1208 forbade the celebration of sacred rites. Across the land church bells, which ordinarily summoned the faithful, remained silent, represented in this marginal drawing of an upturned (silent) bell. BL, Royal MS. 14 CVII, f. 90r. © The British Library Board.

27 *below* Writing two decades after the monarch's death, the chronicler Matthew Paris imagined the oppressions committed under King John. Cambridge, Corpus Christi College, MS. 16, f. 48v. © Corpus Christi Library, Cambridge.

against humanity') that were widely whispered about, but with which no-one as yet dared openly charge the king. Like Arthur of Brittany, the Braoses were henceforth presented as martyrs to Plantagenet tyranny.

In 1212, whilst John was preparing to campaign in Wales, rumours spread of a plot against his life. John, so it was said, would be deliberately betrayed to the Welsh, his wife and his sons would be murdered. The barons would then place a Frenchman, Simon de Montfort, hero of the crusades, on the English throne. When this plot was exposed, the two barons most closely implicated, Robert Fitz Walter, lord of Dunmow in Essex and hereditary constable of Baynard's Castle within the city of London, and Eustace de Vescy, lord of Alnwick, fled into exile in France. There they made common cause with the exiled English bishops. As a result a new and highly significant alliance was forged between the baronial and ecclesiastical critics of John's government.

In the following year, 1213, to forestall the threat of a French invasion, John made his peace with the Church. In a diplomatic masterstroke, copied from the kings of Sicily and Aragon, he declared England itself to be a papal fief. His realm was placed under the pope's feudal overlordship in return for an annual rent or 'census' of 1,000 marks (£666), 700 marks for England and 300 for Ireland. The exiled clergy were invited to return. Stephen Langton was at last permitted to take up residence as archbishop of Canterbury. As yet, however, the Interdict remained in force, pending the payment of full monetary compensation to the Church.

This was eventually set at 100,000 marks (£66,000), the same sum that in the 1190s the German emperor had extracted as ransom for King Richard I.

As this vast sum suggests, John had made full use of his power over Church and barons to extract profit from the Interdict. By 1213, he had amassed more treasure than even his vastly wealthy father, Henry II. All of this was intended to pay for his long dreamed of reconquest in France. The king sailed for Poitou in February 1214. Simultaneously, a second English army, commanded by the king's half brother, William Earl of Salisbury, joined the German emperor and the count of Flanders, north of Lille. The intention was to crush Philip of France within a great pincer movement, converging upon Paris from north and south. The outcome was a fiasco. In June 1214, John himself was forced to withdraw from the river Loire, following an ill-executed attack upon the fortress of La Roche-aux-Moins, just to the west of Angers. Three weeks later, on Sunday 27 July 1214, his northern allies were annihilated near Lille at the Battle of Bouvines.

28 *above* Corfe Castle, where the wife and son of William de Braose, formerly one of John's closest companions, may have been imprisoned and starved to death. Photo: Dafinka/Shutterstock.

29 *left* Simon de Montfort, hero of the Albigensian Crusade, was named in a plot against King John as a possible candidate to lead the country. BL, Royal MS. 16, G VI f. 374v. © The British Library Board.

30 *overleaf* John's Irish coinage, showing the king's portrait. In making himself a vassal of the pope, John promised to pay 1,000 marks per anum to the papacy in exchange for protection. Portable Antiquities Scheme, GLO730921.

From Bouvines, the road to Runnymede was both straight and swift. In October 1214, John slunk back to England, his vast fortune all spent, his planned reconquest transformed into yet further humiliating defeat. Many of his leading barons, already reluctant to serve in Poitou, now began to whisper amongst themselves of the possibility of rebellion.

REFERENCES

For King John, there are good modern biographies by Stephen Church, *King John and the Road to Magna Carta* (London 2015); Marc Morris, *King John: Treachery, Tyranny and the Road to Magna Carta* (London 2015); W.L. Warren, *King John* (London 1961, still in print) and R.V. Turner, *King John* (London 1994). Amongst the older studies, still classic is Sidney Painter, *The Reign of King John* (Baltimore 1949), for which see W.L. Warren, 'Painter's "King John" - Forty Years On', *Haskins Society Journal*, I (1989), 1–9. For recent collections of essays, see *King John: New Interpretations*, ed. Stephen Church (Woodbridge 1999), and *Magna Carta and the England of King John*, ed. Janet S. Loengard (Woodbridge 2010).

31 *below* King John's campaign against the forces of King Philip of France ended in disaster at the Battle of Bouvines, where the English army was routed. BL, Royal MS. 16 G VI, f. 379r. © The British Library Board.

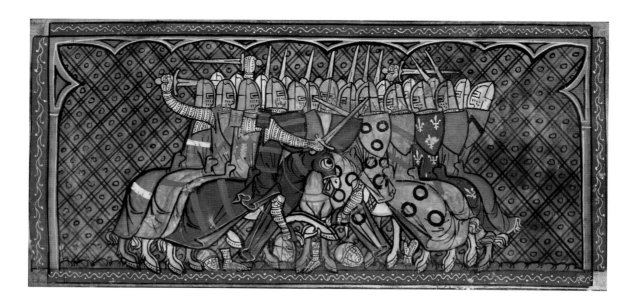

CHAPTER 2

Runnymede

1215

HERTFORDE SHIRE

Cheſhm̄

Kinges Langley
Abbottes Langley
A̶ldbm̄

latimers
Mauſlayne
Elſtre

Cheynes
Serret
Watforde

Amershm̄
Rickmanſworth
Buſſhye

Hertfordſe Pats
Edg

PARTE
Pen
Stannerſpua als whitchurch

OF
Chalfunt Sct: gyles
Stanner magna

Beaconfelde
Riſhp
Pinner

Chalfunt Sct peters
Pinner
Harrowe

SVCKINGHM̄
Derhm̄
Hayfeld
Iſelnhm̄
Twiforde

SHIRE
Helhydon
Northold
Pernale

Vxbridge
Heais
Grinforde
Hanwell

Cowley
Southold
Horn od

Burnhm̄
W: Draton
Harlingeo
Oſterley

Thames flu:
Warmeſwerth
Heſton

Madenhead
Granforde
Cranforde
Sion
Bra

Colbrot
Stanwell
Houſley
Shen

PARTE OF
Eaton
Datcher
Bedſunt
Thiſtle worth
R

Wrayſburye
Aſhforde
Felthm̄

Windſor
Stanes
Hanworthe
Twickinhm̄

Old Windſor
Litleton
Twickinhm̄

BERKE
Lalam̄
Sunbury
Tuddaton Hamptocourt

The great Pke of Windſor
Eghm̄
Sheperton
Hampco

Sunyng hill
Thorp
Walton
W: Mouſlay
Mouſ

Cherſey
Oteland Waybrigdge
Duton

The forreſt of
Eſshere

SHIRE
Winſhm̄
Byſlet
Cheſing

Bagshot
Horſhill
Winſley
Couchm̄

Windſor
Chobhm̄
Pirford
Stoke

Blackwater
Biſley
Newark
Lech

S
Woking
Ockhm̄
Feechm̄

On 15 June 1215 at Runnymede – a meadow on the banks of the river Thames, half way between Windsor and Staines – King John gave his assent to a charter of liberties devised following discussions between king and barons. He had been forced into negotiations first of all by his defeats in France, and thereafter as the result of a concerted baronial and clerical rebellion already stirring as early as 1212. Even before his return to England, in October 1214, the king had begun to draft in mercenaries from Gascony and Ireland, clearly in anticipation of civil unrest.

The chroniclers allege a series of meetings between king and barons. Beginning almost immediately after Archbishop Langton's return from exile in 1213, Langton had demanded that the king swear obedience to the good laws of the English past, referring in particular to the laws of King Edward the Confessor (who had died in January 1066, the last of his Anglo-Saxon royal dynasty to rule England). In November 1213, Langton is said to have shown the barons, assembled at St Paul's in London, a copy of a charter of King Henry I, more than a century old, undertaking the reform of English government. This, Henry I's so-called Coronation Charter, issued in 1100, thereafter formed the basis for negotiation between John and the barons. According to the chronicler Roger of Wendover, as early as the autumn of 1214, meeting at the great abbey of Bury St Edmunds, the barons had leagued together, swearing that as soon as the time was ripe they would rise in arms against the king and force him to follow the ways of his ancestors, upholding the laws of King Edward Confessor and the Coronation Charter of Henry I first shown to them by

32 *left* Sixteenth-century map showing the area of Runnymede, lying at the conjunction of four counties, on the south bank of the river Thames midway between Windsor and Staines, by Christopher Saxon, Oxford, Bodleian Library, EC 17:8 (313).

33 *below* Edward the Confessor, shown in The Bayeux Tapestry. Photo: Myrabella.

34 *above* The liberties of the Church, especially the right to elect freely its abbots and bishops, was a key point in the discussion between King John and the barons in 1214–15. BL, Royal MS. 6 E VII, f. 19r. © The British Library Board.

35 *opposite* St Augustine's Gospels, made in the sixth century and brought to England as part of the mission led by St Augustine sent by Pope Gregory the Great. Christian tradition encouraged kings to set down laws in writing. Cambridge, Corpus Christi College, MS. 286, f. 125r. © Corpus Christi College, Cambridge.

Archbishop Langton in 1213. This Bury meeting was perhaps a figment of the chronicler's imagination. Even so, there is no doubt that John himself came to Bury early in November 1214, and that discussions there turned upon the king's obligation to observe the liberties of the English Church, above all to allow free election of abbots, and by extension bishops. Resistance was already in the air, with claims and counter-claims focused upon the validity of laws written down, in charter form, in the far distant past.

The problem remained that, however united the opposition, there was no accepted or generally acceptable means of forcing a bad king to behave better in future. Kings of the past had faced baronial rebellion. Theologians and historians had acknowledged the justice of such rebellions and even sanctioned the removal of tyrants. The English

36 As a result of Henry I's failure to keep his coronation oath, in which he promised to do away with the corruption and abuses that oppressed the people in the reign of William II, the king suffered a series of nightmares, according to the chronicler John of Worcester (1095–1140). He saw himself reproached by representatives of the three orders of society: the peasants, knights and clerics. On wakening, Henry vowed to do penance for his sins. The final image depicts the king in a stormy sea-crossing, where in fear of death he vows to suspend the Danegeld tax. Oxford, Corpus Christi College, MS. 157, pp.382-3. © Corpus Christi College, Oxford.

writer, John of Salisbury, secretary to Archbishop Thomas Becket, writing in the late 1150s, had gone so far as to argue that 'it is right to kill a tyrant'. What he had in mind here was not baronial conspiracy but God's judgement working through human agency. Kings, however bad, were sent by God for the government (and if necessary the chastisement) of their people. The greatest recent rebellion against an English king, launched by the wife and sons of Henry II in 1173–4, ended not in the king's defeat but in the humiliation of his foes, the imprisonment of his wife and a vast increase in the extent of royal authority over the English people. Wiser then to allow events to take their course and to hope for better days. Kings were powerful – their resources vastly outweighed those of even the most powerful barons. Their private annual income alone exceeded that of twenty or more barons. Their castles, their powers of taxation, their military households, all of these protected them against rebellion and in the longer term suggested that, short of regicide, it was almost impossible to bring the king to any long-term redress. Hence, no doubt, the decision of the baronial conspirators against King John in 1212, that it was better to betray the king to death at the hands of the Welsh than to rise in open rebellion against him.

There was a yet further reason for caution. To demand redress for wrongdoing was all very well. But how was correct royal behaviour to be defined? Kings stood at the head of the body politic, appointed by God to decree laws and rule their subjects' lives. No law made by man could bind a king, or so it was generally supposed. As the legal tradition of the Roman emperors, transmitted to the lawyers of the twelfth century, had long decreed: 'What pleases the prince has the force of law'. In other words, just as kings could make laws, so they could break laws once made. For a solution to this conundrum, the rebels against King John turned to remedies long tried in England and elsewhere. A demand that the king respect custom and age-old liberties would now be backed by the threat of armed rebellion should the king resist.

By the reign of King John, law was long established in England. The Anglo-Saxon peoples who had invaded Roman Britain from across the North Sea, from the fourth century onwards, found there a colony already living under Roman imperial law. The Anglo-Saxons' own Germanic traditions of law were unwritten but nonetheless powerful. The conversion of the Anglo-Saxons to Christianity, from the 590s onwards, not only introduced a further legal tradition (from the laws of God in the Bible and the laws of the Church as regulated by the popes) but encouraged the kings of Anglo-Saxon England to set down their laws in writing. The resulting law 'codes', stretching from that attributed to Aethelbert King of Kent in the 590s, to the laws of King Cnut, only forty years before the Norman Conquest of 1066, lacked much that we would now expect of modern statutory law. To a large extent, they focused upon the regulation of feud and the maintenance of public peace. Kings themselves, lacking the administrative machinery to impose the routine of law, depended upon the chief men and kinship networks of the localities to enforce the law. Even so, the assumption that law was something decreed by kings, to be written down and obeyed, reinforced the idea that the king's subjects could expect a degree of public service from their rulers. The king must protect them, ensure their peace, and respect their local 'liberties'. In particular the 'liberties' of the Church (to govern its own estates, to avoid the consequences of violence and to regulate the morals of its own members) became an increasing concern in charters solicited from kings by the various great churches and monasteries of England. Liberties in this context were conceived of more as privileges than as what we would today consider 'freedoms'. Nonetheless, their protection and observation were already obligations expected of kings, long before the reign of King John.

The Norman Conquest had disrupted but in no way eradicated the tradition of English law. In the decades around 1100, concerted efforts were made to gather together records of the Anglo-Saxon past. Without such post-conquest collections, including the so-called *Textus Roffensis* preserved in the cathedral archives of Rochester, our knowledge of the pre-conquest law codes would be virtually non-existent. As early as 1100, in promising to eradicate 'all of the evil customs by which the realm of England is unjustly oppressed', Henry I's Coronation Charter had set out a series of traditions in respect to inheritance, marriage and taxation that he now promised to observe. The charter was issued at a desperate moment. Henry needed baronial support for his coronation and to defend England against the claims of his elder brother, the duke of Normandy. Promising to reinstate the laws of the past, his charter looked back to the supposedly 'good' practices of the reign of King Edward the Confessor. It was precisely this 'law' of King Edward that Henry I now promised to restore.

This was neither the first nor the last occasion when an English king, placed in a tight spot, would make vague appeals to ancient customs as a means of buying present concessions. In 1100, there is little to suggest that

37 The coronation charters of King Stephen and King Henry II (both kings pictured here) might have influenced negotiations in 1215. BL, Cotton Vitellius MS. A. XIII, f. 4v. © The British Library Board.

Pres henry regna Este
uen sun neuou. xix. anz
e morust. e gyst a fauers
ham.

Apres Esteuen regna
le secund henry fiz
de sa sorour lemperice le
quele henry lors estoyt
dunkz de Normudye en
son tes su sept thomas
martyrize. e regna. xxxv.
ou. xxxv. aunz. puis mo
rust e gist a srin Guard.

the laws of Edward the Confessor even existed as a recognized code. None of this prevented lawyers, over the next forty or so years, from seeking out the laws of King Edward, if necessary by inventing a series of laws that could be attributed to the last great Anglo-Saxon king. By the 1140s, a text calling itself the *Leges Edwardi Confessoris* ('The Laws of King Edward') was in circulation. Clearly a post-conquest production, it nonetheless attracted notice as one of the more comprehensive statements of what the laws of the past were supposed to have been. A London lawyer, writing in the reign of King John, considered the *Leges Edwardi* sufficiently important not only to preserve but to embellish. It was in London, only a few years before Magna Carta, that a series of additions were introduced to Edward's laws, including a highly significant claim that kings were instituted by God to rule and defend God's people and Church. Should a king fail to discharge this duty, 'then he loses the name of King'. No wonder that in 1213, the archbishop of Canterbury, Stephen Langton, is said to have persuaded King John to swear to uphold 'the laws of King Edward', or that a year later, these same 'laws of King Edward', together with the Coronation Charter of Henry I were presented as the best blueprint then available for the concessions that barons and bishops wished John to make.

In all of this, the barons had the precedent of Henry I's Coronation Charter of 1100. They also had the subsequent, even vaguer coronation charters issued by Henry's successors, King Stephen in 1135–6 and Henry II in 1154. A copy of all of these charters, today surviving in the British Library in London, furnishes not only their Latin texts but translations into the Anglo-Norman French vernacular (below no.26, pp.257–8). This itself may well have been drawn up in 1214 or 1215 and played a part in negotiations at Runnymede. Another document, today surviving in the French national archives in Paris (known as the 'Unknown Charter' although in reality rediscovered as long ago as the 1830s) supplies a text of Henry I's Coronation Charter followed by a series of clauses headed with the words 'The King (John) has conceded ...' (below no.25). This too must have been part of the dossier of one or other of the chief negotiators of 1215, perhaps of the archbishop of Canterbury, Stephen Langton. The new provisions set out here open with a promise that the king 'will arrest no man without judgement nor accept any payment for justice nor commit any unjust act'. Herein lay the origins of two of the most important clauses of Magna Carta.

Besides manipulating the records of the English past, the barons could also look beyond England to European precedents. In Germany

38 Issued in southern France three years before Magna Carta, the Statute of Pamiers addressed many of the same issues as John's Charter, such as the sale of justice, inheritance rights and military service. Paris, Archives nationales, ARCHIM, AE/II/207. © Archives nationales, Paris.

39 The north of England, home of many of the barons who rebelled against King John, from the fourteenth-century Gough Map. *The Gough Map*, Oxford, Bodleian Library, MS. Gough Gen. Top. 16.

from the 1150s onwards, in Spain, in Sicily and in southern France, kings had already been obliged to offer written concessions based upon the supposedly good practices of the past. King Pedro II of Aragon had, in 1205, drafted (but apparently not issued) a charter of liberties promising an end to new or excessive taxes, and the appointment only of local men as royal officials to administer 'common justice' according to the right and custom of the land. Even closer to home, in December 1212, Simon de Montfort, leader of the pope's crusade against the heretics of southern France, had issued laws known as the 'Statute of Pamiers'. Approaching the scale of the 1215 English Magna Carta, this document amongst other things outlawed the sale of justice, regulated inheritance and the rights of widows, and forbade the exaction of military service save by grace and at the ruler's pay. By 1215, the Statute of Pamiers was almost certainly known in England, not least because many of the greater barons, including Stephen Langton, had brothers or cousins fighting in Montfort's crusade in France. In 1212, we should remember, it was to Simon de Montfort that the English barons are said to have turned as a potential replacement for the despised King John.

Modern lawyers seeking to frame a constitution would produce a document very different from the clauses of Magna Carta that began to be discussed in 1215. In particular, they would look for a general statement of sovereignty and right; they would want a detailed division and limitation of powers, specific regulation of administrative practice and almost certainly a degree of control over the administration's disposal of patronage. None of these features is explicit in Magna Carta, even though, if we search hard enough, some can be found there in embryo. The political programme articulated by the barons in 1215 was necessarily conservative: more a demand for the restoration of a vanished (and largely mythical) golden age of right and justice, than a blueprint for any brave new future. Its provisions were piecemeal and in many instances severely limited in scope or application. As incentive, the barons could offer nothing save the threat of armed rebellion, the seizure of the king's castles and resources, and ultimately the physical compulsion of the king himself. Even so, and despite the crudity of aims and sanctions, this deserves to rank as one of the earliest occasions in English history when a political programme, rather than simple self-interest, animated rebellion. In this, the convergence since 1212 of Church and barons was of crucial significance.

The precise process by which the barons drew together in conspiracy is to a large extent concealed from us. Their negotiations were potentially treacherous and therefore secret. Certain characteristics can nonetheless be discerned. Many of the rebel barons came from the north of England. As a result, and despite the fact that many others were drawn from East Anglia or the south, they were known collectively as 'The Northerners', arguably the first party political label in English history. The north was a region of forests and great baronial estates. It had suffered disproportionately as a result of John's determination to impose his will upon parts of England previously left more or less to their own devices. Most of the barons, the Northerners included, had personal grievances against the king beyond the fact that he had exploited them for financial gain, depriving them of land or inheritances. In many instances he had allegedly inflicted more personal injuries.

Amongst the baronial leaders, Robert Fitz Walter claimed that the king had attempted to seduce his eldest daughter, herself married to another baronial leader, Geoffrey de Mandeville. Rumours later circulated (almost certainly embellished) of a similar lapse by the king involving the wife of Eustace de Vescy. In 1213, Geoffrey de Mandeville, Fitz Walter's former son-in-law, offered the king 20,000 marks to marry (as his second wife) Isabella of Gloucester, John's former queen. The price was absurdly high, not least because Isabella herself was beyond child-bearing age. When even the first instalment of the money proved impossible to raise, Geoffrey faced the confiscation of his estate. Amongst the same circle of cousins and close acquaintances, Robert Fitz Walter's brother, William, served as archdeacon of Hereford under Bishop Giles de Braose, himself the son of the disgraced William de Braose and brother of the Braose heir, starved to death by the king.

40 It was at tournaments that the barons first began to discuss their misgivings against the rule of John. BL, Royal MS. 14 E III, f. 125r. © The British Library Board.

41 In May 1215, the barons gained control of London, forcing King John to the negotiating table. BL, Royal MS. 16 F II, f. 73r. © The British Library Board.

Es nouuelles dalbion

42 During the interdict, there had been rumours that Innocent III intended to depose King John here pictured. BL, Royal MS. 14 CVII, f. 9r. © The British Library Board.

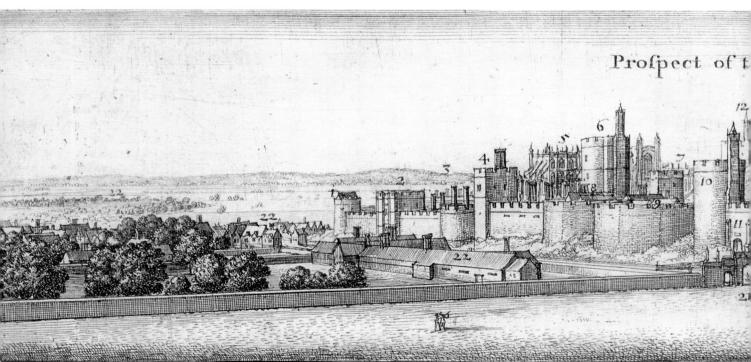

Prospect of t

These, and many others of the baronial leaders were closely related by marriage. In particular, the alliances fostered by the great Norman and East Anglian dynasty of the Clare earls of Hertford meant that a high proportion of the rebel barons were cousins or brothers-in-law. As a result of the Clare connection, the northern element to the rebel party was matched or outnumbered by contingents from Essex and East Anglia. Saher de Quincy was a key figure here, related to the Clares yet also linked to the northern rebel, Eustace de Vescy. Like Eustace, Saher was closely in touch with the court of the king of Scotland. All of this ensured that the rebels were well known to one another: an army in waiting.

The links between them went beyond kinship. For example, two of the rebel leaders, Saher de Quincy, earl of Winchester, and Robert Fitz Walter, were not only closely related (they shared a grandmother) but had served together as keepers of the great Norman fortress of Le Vaudreuil. When Le Vaudreuil fell to the French in 1203, both Saher and Robert had been imprisoned. They were released only after paying a heavy ransom, negotiated via yet another cousin, William de Aubigny, lord of Belvoir, himself later amongst the rebels. King John meanwhile refused to contribute to their ransom.

43 Windsor Castle, where King John chose to reside during the negotiations of June 1215. Wenceslaus Hollar, *Windsor Castle*, etching, published 1672 (Pennington 1072; Turner, New Hollstein German, 2165). The Thomas Fisher Rare Book Library, University of Toronto, Hollar_k_2497. © University of Toronto.

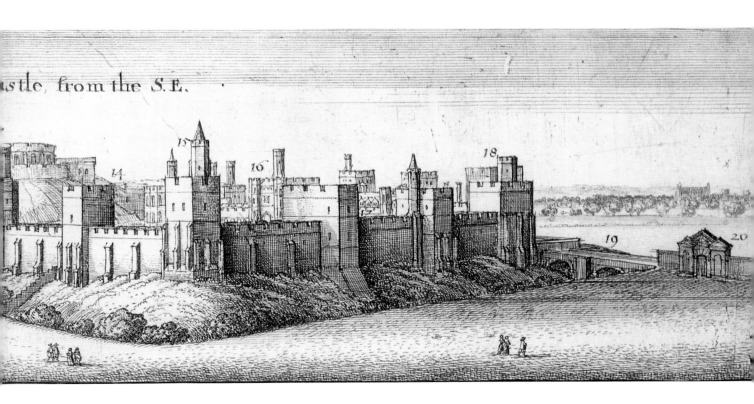

Some indication of the bond between Saher and Robert is revealed from the seals they used to authenticate their own letters and charters. Robert's shows not only his own heraldic arms but those of Saher, displayed inside a small shield. The seal that Saher used before 1208 likewise displays Robert's arms alongside those of the de Quincys: clear signs of a pact of friendship. As this in turn suggests, the emerging science of heraldry was itself testimony to the class loyalties that had emerged amongst the newly wealthy English aristocracy, bound together by a common devotion to sport (hunting) and warfare (either the tournament or the crusades). Both the Fitz Walter and the Quincy seals show their owners as mounted and heavily armoured warriors, charging into battle, in Robert's case with a dragon, symbolizing wickedness or heresy, trampled beneath his feet. The back of the seal used by Saher further shows its owner grappling in single combat with a lion. The lion, it should be remembered was very much the symbol of Plantagenet kingship. As rebel leader, Robert Fitz Walter assumed the title 'Marshal of the Army of God', presumably to proclaim that he was fighting for a holy cause, tantamount to a crusade. What we have here is a combination of class and family solidarity mingled with bravado. Those mocked by John in 1203 for their failure to make war would not repeat the mistake in 1215, now making war against the king.

Heraldry, as plastered across the seals of Fitz Walter, De Quincy or others of the rebel barons, had itself first emerged on the tournament field as a means of telling apart one force from another. It was no doubt during their meetings at tournaments that the barons first began to discuss their misgivings about the rule of John. The great tournament fields of England thereafter played a prominent role in discussions throughout the spring of 1215. It was at Stamford and then at Northampton, both of them places of tournament, in April 1215, that the barons first came together to declare their united stand against the king. They subsequently converged upon Brackley, site of another great tournament field and Saher de Quincy's chief residence. There, on 3 May 1215, the rebels repudiated their homage to John, in effect declaring public warfare.

A week later, on Sunday 17 May, whilst the city's chief men were at Mass, a baronial force entered London. The Londoners had their own good reasons for opposition to John – they had long sought freedom from the king's tolls, taxes and other impositions. Over the past decade, their wealth, dependent upon foreign trade, had been hard hit by restrictions imposed upon French shipping. In 1212, the London suburbs south of the Thames had been burned in a great fire. This was judged by many to demonstrate divine approval for the papal Interdict imposed against the king, with John's capital now cast in the role of Sodom or Gomorrah. London was a city, then as now, seething with both ambition and resentment. On 17 May 1215 it fell into rebel hands, transformed from royal capital into chief rebel stronghold. The barons themselves referred to it as their '*receptaculum*' or point of safety. To draw knights to its defence, they summoned a tournament to the region between Hounslow and Staines. Once again, tournament and rebel solidarity went hand in hand.

From 17 May onwards, the king had little choice but to negotiate. London and Westminster, the site of his Exchequer and chief treasure houses, were crucial to royal finances. Worse still, there was a risk that the barons would go further. By summoning an alternative ruler, most obviously the eldest son of the king of France, they could now hope to crown a rival king in England's traditional coronation church, Westminster Abbey. Deposition had long been a threat looming over King John. In 1203, Philip of France had declared John deposed as duke of Normandy and Aquitaine. During the Interdict, after 1208, there had been persistent rumours that the pope was about to depose John from the throne of England. The threat was never fulfilled. Even so, king and barons were aware that bad rulers in the past had been deposed. Biblical kings had lost their thrones, as had many emperors in the history of Rome, Kings Aethelred and Harold in Anglo-Saxon history and most recently King Stephen of England (following defeat in battle in 1141). What was to prevent a similar fate befalling the equally despised King John?

Hence the change in John's tactics after May 1215 from defiance to negotiation. The campaigning season was at hand. Given the uncertainties of harvest, and the disastrous state of roads, little improved since the departure of the Romans, only in summer could armies be supplied and manoeuvred. If peace were to be restored it must be now, before the harvest, and before much blood had been spilled. The barons were ensconsed in London. The king came to Windsor Castle, thirty or so miles up the Thames. A meeting place was agreed between them, where tents could be pitched and a degree of neutrality could be guaranteed. Runnymede, a meadow on the Thames, was the site selected. Neither entirely land nor water, dotted with islands and lying at the junction

45 The seal matrix of Robert Fitz Walter below the seal of Saher de Quincy. Both barons had the other's arms depicted on their seal, reflecting their close friendship. Seal of Robert Fitz Walter, British Museum 1841,0624.1, © British Museum Trustees. Seal of Saher de Quincy, Oxford, Magdalen College, Brackley D247 © Sophie Amber.

between four counties, Runnymede had perhaps already served as a place of meeting. Its name, literally interpreted, means 'the meadow where counsel takes place'. Perhaps this was already an Anglo-Saxon meeting place. Perhaps it owes its name not to earlier negotiations but to those specifically of 1215, the first time that the name is recorded. In any event, what was transacted at Runnymede early in June 1215 was to echo down the ages.

As Rudyard Kipling was to phrase it, nearly seven hundred years later:

> And still when Mob or Monarch lays
> Too rude a hand on English ways,
> The whisper wakes, the shudder plays,
> Across the reeds at Runnymede.
> And Thames, that knows the moods of kings,
> And crowds and priests and suchlike things,
> Rolls deep and dreadful as he brings
> Their warning down from Runnymede!

REFERENCE

For law before 1215, see my chapter in *Magna Carta: The Foundation of Freedom* (2015), and (for a scholarly audience) John Hudson, *The Oxford History of the Laws of England. Volume II: 871–1216* (Oxford 2012). For the rebellion of 1215, Holt, *Magna Carta* (1992) and Carpenter, *Magna Carta* (2015) both depend heavily upon the classic account by J.C. Holt, *The Northerners* (Oxford 1961, 2nd ed. 1992). For the tournament and aristocratic culture, David Crouch, *Tournament* (London 2005); Nigel Saul, *For Honour and Fame: Chivalry in England, 1066–1500* (London 2011). For a new narrative of events in the year leading to Magna Carta, see my ongoing blog 'King John's Diary', at http://magnacartaresearch.org.

CHAPTER 3

The great charter 1215–1300:
From defeat into victory

hit his ylðran mid feo ⁊ mid freoðe wihte begeatan. ⁊ letan. ⁊ læf ðan ðam to geƿealde ðe hy ƿel uðan. ⁊ sƿa ic hit hæbbe sƿa hit sesealde ðe to fyllanne ahte unbryde. ⁊ unforboden. ⁊ ic agnian ƿylle to agenne æhte ðæt ðæt ic hæbbe. ⁊ næfre ðæt yntan ne plot. ne ploh. ne turf. ne toft. ne furh. ne fot mæl. ne land. ne læse. ne fersc. ne mersc. ne ruhne rum. ruðes ne feldes. landes ne strandes ƿealtes. ne ƿæteres. butan ðæt læste ða hƿile ðe ic libbe. for ðam unse tinan on life ðe æfre gehyrde ðæt man cƿydde oððon crafode hine on hundrede oððon ahƿar on gemote on ceapstoþe oþþe on cyrce ƿare ða hƿile ƿe he lifde unsac he ƿæs on life beo on legere sƿa sƿa he mote. do sƿa ic lære beo ðe be þinum. ⁊ læt me be minum. ne gyrne ic ðines ne lædes ne landes. ne sace ne socne. ne ðu mines ne ðærfst ne mynte ic ðe nan ðing.

Institutiones henrici regis.

Anno incarnationis dominice .M.C.I. Henricus filius Willelmi regis post obitum fratris sui Willelmi. dei gratia rex anglorum omnibus fidelibus salutem. Sciatis me dei misericordia et communi consilio baronum totius regni anglie eiusdem regem coronatum esse. Et quia regnum oppressum erat iniustis exactionibus; ego dei respectu et amore quem erga vos habeo. sanctam dei ecclesiam inprimis liberam facio. Ita quod nec vendam nec ad firmam ponam. nec mortuo archiepiscopo. sive episcopo. sive abbate. aliquid accipiam de dominio ecclesie vel de hominibus eius. donec successor in eam ingrediatur. Et omnes malas consuetudines quibus regnum anglie iniuste opprimebatur. inde aufero. Quas malas consuetudines ex parte hic pono;

Siquis baronum comitum meorum. sive aliorum qui de me tenent mortuus fuerit: heres suus non redimet terram suam sicut faciebat tempore fratris mei. sed iusta et legitima relevatione relevabit eam. Similiter et homines baronum meorum iusta et legitima relevatione relevabunt terras suas de dominis suis;

Et siquis baronum vel aliorum hominum meorum

On 15 June 1215, following negotiations over several preceding days, the king put his seal to a document later known as 'the great charter' ('Magna Carta'), intended to restore peace between king and barons. Judged on the basis of most of its sixty-three or so clauses as agreed and sealed at Runnymede, Magna Carta remained a highly conservative affair. Citing the good customs and practices of the past, it attempted to return to a halcyon era of peace and justice. Drawing upon precedents set out in Henry I's Coronation Charter, already more than a century old, it sought to regulate the excesses of King John and his predecessors by defining proper procedures, many of them related to the king's jurisdiction over inheritance or taxation.

Rather than pay the exorbitant fines that King John had sought to impose, the son of an earl or baron should inherit his father's estate on payment of a standard relief of £100. The son of a knight should inherit for a mere £5 (100 shillings). Widows were to be assigned a reasonable competence from their late husband's estate, and were not to be compelled to marry against their will. Justice was to be made regularly and easily available to those who sought it, rather than being purchased by the highest bidder. The king was no longer to persecute widows and orphans by wasting their estates, handing them over to cruel or rapacious guardians, or by acting as middle-man for the collection of debts, especially debts to the Jews (one of the few communities in medieval England that could lawfully lend money to Christians and charge interest upon the repayment, such usury being theoretically forbidden in dealings between Christian and Christian, as indeed between Jew and Jew).

In these respects, and others, Magna Carta sought to enforce the king's age-old obligation to serve as protector of the vulnerable, the widow and the orphan. Here Christ's law became the law of England. Similar impulses informed the entirely Christian prohibition of usury.

46 The twelfth-century *Textus Roffensis* contains Anglo Saxon law codes and the Coronation Charter of Henry I (shown here, fol.96r and following). Strood, Medway Archives and Local Studies Centre, MS DRc/R1. © Dean and Chapter of Rochester Cathedral.

This same idea of God's law is to be found articulating the very opening clause of the charter, promising to uphold the liberties of the English Church, itself staffed by men whose clerical orders made it impossible for them defend their rights by the sword. In all of this, God's peace was guaranteed and the long-established obligations of Christian kingship were reinforced. Peace was likewise the subject of those clauses dealing with the settlement of John's disputes with the Scots and the Welsh, and of other clauses (unusually specific in naming a series of French captains and constables) that demanded the expulsion from England of John's mercenary knights. Peace was indeed one of the chief leitmotifs informing the charter as a whole. No wonder, perhaps, that nineteenth- and twentieth-century historians were sometimes inclined to belittle Magna Carta as too much a product of its own time: too 'feudal' a document, too concerned with procedures and practicalities, too bound up with the circumstances of June 1215 and the 'selfish' interests of earls, barons and the feudal elite.

What were lawyers of the age of Queen Victoria to make of such 'feudal' phenomena as the writ of '*Precipe*', or the prohibition of fines and exactions that deprived a peasant of his '*waynagium*' or a free man of his '*contenementum*'? Here we find Latin terms that, even by the seventeenth century, were judged so obscure that lawyers and historians bickered over their meaning. No wonder that, from the 1820s onwards, the vast majority of Magna Carta's clauses were repealed or stripped away from English statute law as so much redundant medievalism. As the *pièce de résistance* of such archaism, commentators are fond of citing that clause of Magna Carta forbidding the construction of '*kiddels*' (generally translated as 'fish weirs') on the Thames, the Medway or any other of the rivers of England. What, they might ask, have fish weirs on the Medway to do with any broader questions of right and justice?

And yet even here, in the technical terminology of fish weirs, we find ourselves confronting principles far less conservative or archaic than superficially they may appear. Fish weirs were forbidden in Magna Carta because they interfered with river navigation and hence, in the longer term, threatened river-borne trade. They had long been a particular target of criticism from the men of London who depended upon the navigation of the river Thames. The silting up of the Thames was by 1215 a very present reality. The rise of the University of Oxford from the 1180s itself bears witness to this. Oxford became England's first university, in part because it had no local ecclesiastical authority capable of discouraging its growth, in part because masters and students were drawn to a city no longer thriving as a port, where rents were falling and property could be purchased relatively cheaply.

What was at stake in Magna Carta's condemnation of 'kiddels' was not some archaic concern for fish farming, but the 'liberty' of free navigation and economic imperatives that obliged the king to act as guardian of the public good. We find the same issues at stake, for example, in the clause of Magna Carta that deals with weights and measures. Here it was no doubt the Londoners who took the initative in insisting that the king declare nationally agreed measures for wine, ale, corn and dyed cloth, both 'russet' (coarse) and 'haberject' (high quality). From the fish weirs

47 The silting up of the river Thames partially accounts for the attraction of scholars to the town of Oxford, which ceased to be a bustling port city with high rents and property prices. *Oxford: General views, topographical prints, elevations, photographs, etc. of buildings* (1700). Engraved by N. Whittock for James Ryman. Oxford, Bodleian Library, G.A. Oxon. a.42, f. 77.

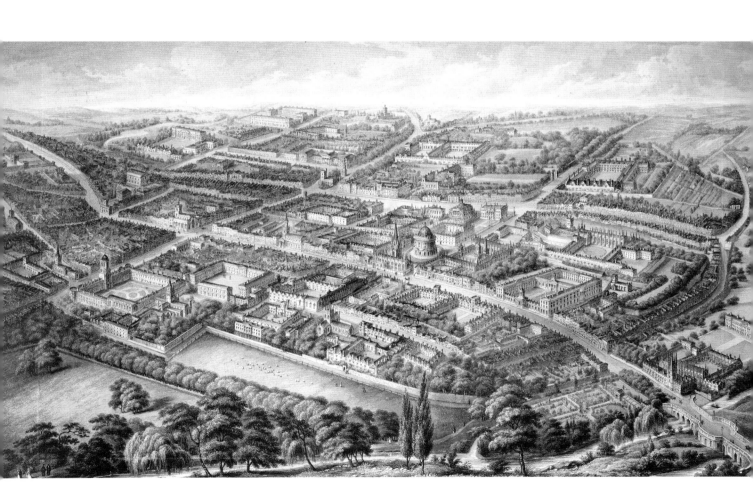

or *haberjects* of Magna Carta 1215 to the Welfare State may stretch an apparently unbridgeable gulf. Yet the protection of confidence in trade, like the freedom of navigation, assumes a responsibility for *res publica*, the public good, that the lawyers of ancient Rome or Victorian England would immediately have recognized. Such responsibility is still to be found today in the state's protection of its citizens' welfare. This and other such provisions helped transform Magna Carta from something narrowly or 'selfishly' motivated into a far more abiding definition of the relations between ruler and the ruled.

Viewed in this perspective, there is a great deal in Magna Carta that was not conservative but in practice highly radical. We have already cited those clauses that forbid the sale of justice and demand speedy and proper judgement by a man's equals (his 'peers') or the law of the land. The sale

of justice had been forbidden in classical Athens and ancient Rome. Judas had betrayed the innocent Christ for thirty pieces of silver. Ever afterwards the connection between money and judgement had been tainted with a sense of sin. Church councils regularly declared that neither judgement nor ecclesiastical office should be sold. Simon de Montfort had forbidden such things again, in his Statute of Pamiers of 1212. Stephen Langton followed suit in legislation for the Church of Canterbury, issued only a few months before the meeting at Runnymede. But Magna Carta 1215 went further than this. It not only defined what was forbidden but insisted upon what was licit ('judgement by peers or the law of the land').

In doing so, the charter did not (as is sometimes supposed) invent the concept of trial by jury. The jury was a more ancient institution, and in this period its role in trials was very different from that assumed today. Juries themselves are never once referred to explicitly in Magna Carta. Nor did Magna Carta introduce the concept of '*Habeas Corpus*' (a name derived from the opening Latin words of a writ used to order the trial of prisoners held in captivity, not incorporated within statute law by act of Parliament until 1640). In the same way, Magna Carta's insistence that the king impose taxes only after advice from his subjects and with their consent invented neither the concept of counsel nor the institution later known as Parliament. Magna Carta did, nonetheless, set down aspirations by which the performance of such later institutions could be judged.

All of this may seem very imprecise. Magna Carta is indeed in many ways a mixture of the infuriatingly vague and the anachronistically concrete. Fish weirs, '*haberjects*' and the names of long-forgotten French mercenaries jostle here with such woolly good intentions as those of its closing admonition, that the liberties and customs granted by the king to his men, be extended by the charter's beneficiaries to their own subjects. Who precisely was intended to benefit here? Freemen? Peasants? Did the category of 'men' include women or children such as the widows and orphans of earlier clauses? What precisely were the 'liberties and customs' according to which the king should rule?

We can quibble over the details. Lawyers have done so for the past eight hundred years. What we cannot deny is that Magna Carta enshrines certain basic concepts of right and justice that stand apart from the particular disputes of 1215 or the particular tyranny of King John. More than this, it was most impressive not just in terms of depth but length. Its division into numbered clauses is a modern refinement, but even so,

with its more than sixty clauses, John's charter of June 1215 far exceeds the mere fourteen clauses of Henry I's Coronation Charter of 1100. Hence the fact that within only two years of its issue it was being referred to as the 'big' charter, not least to distinguish it from the smaller charter concerning the king's jurisdiction over forests (the so-called 'Forest Charter') to which it subsequently gave rise. Contemporaries were as yet undecided whether it should be known as the 'bigger' (in Latin '*maior*') or simply as the 'great' ('*magna*') charter. It had not yet acquired a definitive title. Even so, at more than three times the length of Henry I's Coronation Charter, and far longer than any new law or assize issued by a twelfth-century king, it was a physically impressive thing.

In some respects Magna Carta as issued in 1215 was so revolutionary that its survival was doomed from the start. Law was made by kings. But it could also be broken by them. How then were the barons and bishops of 1215 to prevent King John from repudiating the document that he had been persuaded to seal at Runnymede? One means was for the charter to be phrased as a grant by King John not to his fellow men but to God Almighty. As the opening clause of Magna Carta reads: 'In the first place we have granted to God and by this our present charter have confirmed for ourselves and our heirs in perpetuity.' Liberties granted to God could not be rescinded at the king's merely human whim. Another means of enforcement was to seek to rob the king of his military and financial advantages. Hence the insistence upon consent for taxation, and upon the expulsion of the king's foreign mercenaries.

But the charter went even further than this. In its final clauses, as drafted in 1215, it attacked the very foundations of royal sovereignty. It ended with a so-called 'securities clause' decreeing that, should the king attempt to evade any of its terms, a committee of twenty-five barons be empowered to seize the king's estates and in effect to wage war upon the king until amends were made. How, it might be asked, could the king in one and the same document both claim to act as a sovereign authority, granting liberties and privileges, and at the same time state that neither he

49 By addressing the Great Charter as a grant from the king to God, it became more difficult for King John to repudiate the document he had sealed. Oxford, Bodleian Library, MS. Douce 180, p.21.

nor his successors might take away the privileges thus conferred by royal charter? How could the king place himself under the supervision of twenty-five rebels? Hence the joke that apparently circulated amongst John's foreign mercenaries. By issuing Magna Carta, it was suggested, John had condemned himself to a role as 'the twenty-fifth king in England'. Viewed in this context, Magna Carta 1215 represented the most radical programme of restrictions that had ever been imposed by written settlement upon a reigning English king. As a result, it became unenforcable.

King John had no intention whatsoever of holding to its terms. Nor could God's vicar on earth, Pope Innocent III, be expected to accept an award that institutionalized rebellion and imposed limititations upon a sovereign's God-given authority. Meanwhile, in England the king refused to expel his alien constables. The barons refused to surrender the city of London. Archbishop Langton, caught in the middle of these disputes, and commanded by the king to surrender Rochester Castle, was powerless to comply. The pope, informed in August of Magna Carta's

50 Innocent III, on learning of Magna Carta, annulled the document. Fresco from Sacro Speco, Monastery of St. Benedict, Subiaco, Italy. Photo: Soerfm.

terms, pronounced it annulled and anathematized. His letters of 24 August took several weeks to travel to England. Meanwhile, at Dover, early in September 1215, the king's clerical supporters published a papal letter, excommunicating the rebels and declaring Archbishop Langton suspended from office (below no.30). The peace agreed at Runnymede only twelve weeks earlier was now dead. Magna Carta should have died with it.

51 The rebel stronghold of Rochester Castle was besieged by royal forces in the autumn of 1215, with many barons taken as prisoners. Photo: Rui Saraiva/Shutterstock

52 Henry III, from his funeral effigy in Westminster Abbey. © Dean and Chapter of Westminster Abbey.

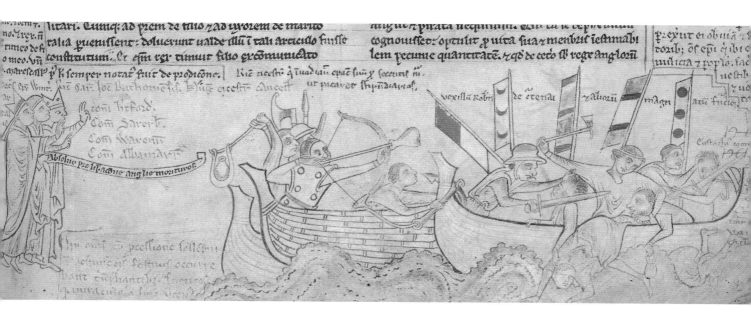

The medieval illustration contains Latin marginal text including: "litari. Cumq: ad prem de filio 7 ad uxorem de marito", "cognouisseo optulit p uita sua 7 menbris iestimabi", "vexilla Robin... de etenai... 7 aliozu... magn...", and other inscriptions.

It did not. Its survival owed nothing to King John and very little to the barons. The outbreak of civil war in September 1215 was followed by a siege of Rochester Castle, commanded by the king. Many rebels were taken prisoner but rebellion itself did not end. Desperate for aid, the barons now sought an alliance with John's enemies overseas. Louis, son of the French king, Philip Augustus, was invited to cross to London, to lay claim to the English throne. There followed a year of civil war, fought out across southern England. Winchester was taken by the rebels. Dover was besieged. In October 1216, after a disastrous crossing of the Wash, the river estuary dividing Norfolk and Lincolnshire, in which much of his baggage and perhaps a considerable quantity of his treasure was lost, John himself fell ill at Newark on Trent where he sickened and died. The chroniclers, as ever eager to catalogue the king's misdeeds, attributed his death to over indulgence in peaches and new cider. John's nine-year-old son, Henry III, was now crowned king.

The coronation took place at Gloucester, in the greatest haste, clearly for fear that if the royalists did not move swiftly, then Louis of France would be crowned in the rightful coronation church, Westminster Abbey, still under rebel control. The Gloucester coronation was conducted by an Italian cardinal, acting as the pope's 'legate' or local representative, attended by a rump of the late king's councillors. To advertise their

intention to rule differently from King John, and to demonstrate their
determination to abandon John's more arbitrary and controversial ways,
the guardians of Henry III now revived the great charter of June 1215,
reissuing it at Bristol in November 1216, no longer as an assault upon royal
privilege but as a manifesto of future good government. The cause of
Henry III, the pope's legate proclaimed, was to be fought as a crusade, a
sacred war against the enemies not just of the king but of God.

Almost miraculously, over the next twelve months, the royalist regime
inflicted a series of military defeats upon the rebels, most notably in a great
battle fought in the streets of Lincoln in May 1217. This was followed by a
naval engagement off the Kent coast, at Sandwich, defeating reinforcements
sent to Louis from France. As a result, it was the rebels rather than the
royalists who sued for peace. In token of royal magnanimity and of the boy
king's determination to rule in harmony with his repentant barons, Magna
Carta was once again reissued, in November 1217.

Far from being strangled at birth in the summer of 1215, Magna Carta
thus lived on. In both November 1216 and November 1217 it was reissued
with considerable modifications, and in particular without various of
the clauses of the 1215 charter that had posed the greatest threat to royal

54 In 1224, Louis VIII of France seized La Rochelle, forcing Henry III to grant a new version of Magna Carta in return for the taxation he would need to preserve his continental inheritance. BL, Royal MS. 16 G VI f. 388r. © The British Library Board.

sovereignty: the insistence that the barons control the king's patronage of foreigners, for example, and above all the securities clause that had effectively licenced the barons to make war on the king should the king not implement the barons' wishes. Not all of Henry III's courtiers were enthusiastic supporters of Magna Carta. The leading royal official, William Brewer, suggested that the charter would be best consigned to oblivion. The immensely powerful bishop of Winchester, Peter des Roches, was to spend much of the next twenty years attempting to restore royal government to the arbitrary sovereign powers that it had boasted under King John. Nevertheless, in the country at large, Magna Carta had already, by 1220, begun to acquire totemic status as a touchstone of communal liberties, guaranteeing the king's free subjects against any revival of royal tyranny.

Even in those parts of England only loosely attached to English law and the English crown, the local authorities could not ignore the great charter. Magna Carta undoubtedly reached the bishopric of Durham, which preserves copies of the reissues of 1216, 1225 and 1300. In Cheshire, the jurisdiction of the earls of Chester in effect excluded that of the crown. Here an entirely different text circulated, known as the 'Cheshire Magna Carta'. Issued in the name of the earl, this was almost certainly composed during the summer of 1215 and was intended to remedy particular local abuses drawn to the earl's attention by the men of his lordship. It remained significant in the administration of Cheshire law through to the 1290s and beyond.

In the meantime, Henry III's reissues had immediate and very practical effects. They put an end to the extortions by which John had raised revenue before 1215. The fines that were imposed upon the king's subjects declined in magnitude. Barons paid the standard £100 for their estates, knights the agreed £5. Widows and orphans enjoyed a degree of special protection. Taxation, when taken, was generally imposed only after consultation between king, councillors and barons. The problem here was that this, in turn, left the crown financially weakened. Henry III lacked the means to pay for his own administration in England, let alone for the defence of what lands remained to him in France. In 1224, whilst Henry was preoccupied with putting down civil disturbance in England, Louis of France seized the port of La Rochelle. The whole of southern France appeared doomed to French conquest. Desperate to raise money, the king and his councillors traded off a further reissue of Magna Carta in return for a grant of taxation from his subjects. Henry III once again confirmed the charter, sending exemplifications into each of the counties of England. It was this fourth, 1225 issue that was to become the standard legal instrument thereafter. Magna Carta was thus transformed from a failed peace settlement into a permanent legislative statute, jealously protected by those whose rights it was believed to guarantee.

Pressure from the county communities, from the knights of the shire and from those whose careers were passed largely outside the confines of the royal court led to yet further reissues. In 1234, for example, after a period in which Peter des Roches had threatened to restore royal government to many of the arbitrary devices of King John, Henry III guaranteed to uphold Magna Carta as a means of signalling his breach with the controversial policies of his minister. Three years later, in 1237, the king made similar promises, this time themselves distributed in charter form and county by county. This was done in return for a grant of taxation intended to pay for the king to campaign in France. All told, between 1225 and Henry III's death in 1272, the king promised on several further occasions to uphold the terms both of Magna Carta and of the briefer document, known as the Forest Charter. First enacted in 1217, this was intended to curb arbitrary methods of government within the vast tracts of land, extending into most English counties, known as the royal forests. Here the ordinary law of the land did not run.

The sense that both Magna Carta and the Forest Charter now conveyed was that England was a land of chartered liberties, in which the rights of the subject were protected against the arbitrary powers of the king. No matter that the individual terms of the great charter became increasingly remote from the realities of later thirteenth-century government. Scutage, for example, was no longer nearly so significant an imposition as it had been in the reign of John. The law courts in Westminster operated so effectively, and at such a profit, that there was no real fear for their survival as there had been under John. Moreover, Henry III himself was increasingly resident in Westminster Palace, so that the risk that pleas would be held before the king in out-of-the-way places became increasingly remote. Baronial courts were no longer so sensitive to the writ of 'Precipe' (prohibited by Magna Carta when it drew business away from the barons and into the king's own jurisdiction). By the 1230s, and despite what was written in Magna Carta, the honour of Wallingford was no longer in the king's own hands, and nor, from the 1260s onwards,

was the honour of Lancaster. Earls and barons continued to be amerced or fined at the king's discretion rather than at the command of their fellows or peers. The annual judicial visitation of the counties, envisaged in Magna Carta, was never effectively enacted. In all of these respects, and more, the text of Magna Carta 1225, although regularly renewed and popularly invested with the authority of holy writ, diverged increasingly from the realities of local and central government.

Taxation, however, and the king's financial needs remained pressing concerns. The politics of thirteenth-century England were dominated by the gulf between royal ambitions and the king's ability to pay for his wars, his luxuries and his court. Henry III, in particular, not only poured a fortune into the rebuilding of Westminster but squandered vast sums on failed attempts to recover his father's lands in France. Ever since its first issue in 1215, Magna Carta had been linked to the principle that taxation could only be granted with consent. To obtain such consent, councils were

55 Sicily, the conquest of which Henry III was determined to accomplish, as depicted in the earliest extant map of the island, from the thirteenth-century Arabic Book of Curiosities. Bodleian Library, MS. Arab. c. 90, ff. 32b-33a.

summoned. By the 1230s, these had come to be known as parliaments ('speakings together'), although in essence their existence can be traced back much further, to the great councils of the twelfth century and indeed to the meeting (the '*witan*') that had counselled, warned and advised earlier Anglo-Saxon kings. After 1253, whilst the king himself was in Gascony, Parliament was judged capable of meeting even in his absence. It remained, nonetheless, an occasion rather than an institution.

By this time, Henry III had not only committed himself to crusade in the Holy Land but to the conquest of the island of Sicily. When the Welsh rebelled in 1258, the king lacked the financial means to pay for defense against them. The barons were summoned to agree taxation. Instead, they insisted upon a root and branch reform of the king's government. In effect, the king was placed under the executive authority of a committee of barons. The earl of Leicester, Simon de Montfort, son of that Simon who in 1212 had issued the Statute of Pamiers, emerged as the most radical of the reformers. In 1264, when King Henry III attempted to overthrow baronial constraint, Simon defeated him in battle at Lewes. Desperate to widen the basis of his support, Montfort summoned a parliament, bringing together not only the barons (or 'lords') but 'the commons', via

56 Defeat and death of Simon de Montfort at the Battle of Evesham. BL, MS. Cotton Nero D ii, f. 177r. © The British Library Board

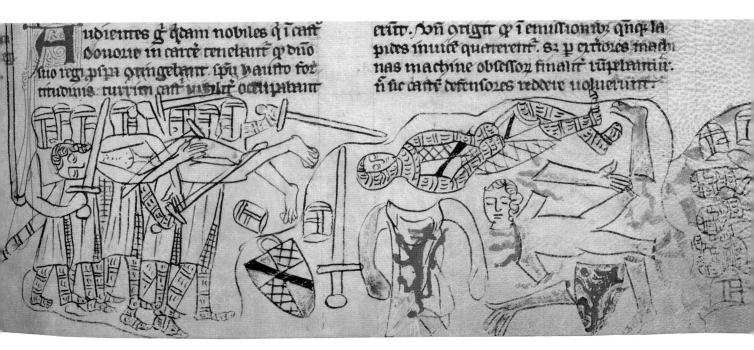

representatives sent from each of the English shires and from each of the greater towns. The Parliament of 1265 was crucial in the emergence of the future 'county and borough' franchise for the parliamentary House of Commons, still going strong, albeit in modified form, 750 years later. As part of its propaganda campaign, Parliament in 1265 once again reissued Magna Carta.

This did little to salvage Montfort's regime. Within a few months, the king's son had defeated Montfort in battle at Evesham. Montfort himself was killed, and Henry III was restored to full command over his resources. Parliament itself, over the next thirty years, returned to its role as an obedient theatre of kingship in which royal magnanimity could be displayed and justice be seen to be done. As with Magna Carta, the kings of England very swiftly transformed what had been intended as a shackle into a tool of royal control. Even so, the events of 1265, the linking of Magna Carta to counsel taken in Parliament and parliamentary consent to taxation, established a future posterity for Parliament as a means not only of counselling but, if necessary, of restraining or compelling kings.

The regularity with which Magna Carta was reissued during the thirteenth century ensured that by the reign of King John's grandson, Edward I (1272–1307), it enjoyed totemic status as a symbol of good government. Edward's conquests in Wales, Scotland and France, were largely financed by taxation granted by obedient parliaments in return for promises of justice and peace. In the late 1290s, this virtuous circle collapsed. The pressures of war in Gascony and Flanders placed impossible burdens upon public finance. In Scotland, the revolt of William Wallace (1272–1305) led to a crushing defeat for the English at the battle of Stirling Bridge (11 September 1297). With the king absent on campaign in Flanders, and with popular protest mounting against the emergency taxes imposed to deal with the crisis, on 12 October, the king's son (the future Edward II) reissued Magna Carta. This 1297 reissue, intended to buy popularity, was the first officially to be copied onto the royal roll of statutes. As a result, it is the 1297 issue that today enjoys currency under English law. In theory, the 1297 charter merely rehearsed the terms of the charter as granted in 1225. In practice, because it was taken from an unofficial or inferior copy of 1225, it introduced a number of minor variants. The most important of these was that henceforth earls would pay the king £100 to inherit their lands whereas barons would pay only 100 marks (£66). Because it was issued

57 While Edward I was on military campaign in Flanders in 1297, Magna Carta was re-issued by his son, the future Edward II, here shown in his funeral effigy in Gloucester Cathedral. © Nick Barton.

by the regency government rather than by the king in person, the 1297 charter was reissued three years later under the great seal of Edward I. This 1300 issue was the last occasion on which Magna Carta was officially sealed by a king and distributed to each of the thirty or so shires of England.

In 1225, 1265, 1297 and 1300 the full text of Magna Carta was sent into the counties under the king's own seal. For the rest, royal commitment to uphold Magna Carta involved not the physical distribution of full texts, but the issue of letters promising renewal and respect for the charter's terms. Nonetheless, even as early as the 1260s, so many such promises had been extorted from the king that it was virtually inconceivable that Henry III or his successors could repudiate the charter or contravene what were by now understood as its underlying principles. As principle, even more than as law, Magna Carta was now hard-wired into England's sense of identity.

REFERENCES

For the text of Magna Carta in its various issues, see Holt, *Magna Carta* (1992), and Carpenter, *Magna Carta* (2015), with an ongoing and entirely new clause-by-clause commentary, by Henry Summerson, at http://magnacartaresearch.org. Amongst the more important studies of the first century of the charter, Faith Thompson, *The First Century of Magna Carta* (Minneapolis 1925); J.R. Maddicott, 'Magna Carta and the Local Community, 1215–1259', *Past and Present*, 102 (1984), 25–65; Maddicott, *The Origins of the English Parliament, 924–1327* (Oxford 2010); David Carpenter, *The Minority of Henry III* (London 1990); Carpenter, *The Reign of Henry III* (London 1996). For the 1297 and 1300 issues, there is much new material in my Sotheby's catalogue, *The Magna Carta* (Sotheby's New York, 18 December 2007). For the Chester Magna Carta, see Graeme White, *The Magna Carta of Cheshire*, Cheshire Local History Association (Chester 2015).

CHAPTER 4

The charter ancient and modern

Throughout the later Middle Ages, English kings and parliaments regularly paid lip service to Magna Carta, undertaking to observe its terms. Yet even as early as 1300, much of the charter had been rendered archaic by the onward march of events and by changes in the application of feudal law. The political crisis of 1297, for example, was marked not just by the reissue of Magna Carta but by the negotiation of a further series of 'Articles upon the Charters', offering suggestions not only on how Magna Carta was best interpreted but on what else needed to be done for the realm to be reformed (below nos.38–42).

Lawyers continued to debate the meaning of the charter's individual clauses. The charter itself, often in the version promulgated in 1300, continued to appear at the head of the many hundreds of books of statutes sold and distributed as a standard part of the educational system of the Inns of Court (England's 'third university'). Most discussions nonetheless pursued only arcane points, skirting the greater principles of due process and the rule of law set out in clause 29 of the 1225 and 1297 reissues ('No free man is to be taken or imprisoned or deprived of his free tenement or of his liberties or free customs … save by lawful judgment of his peers or by the law of the land.')

For an exception here, we can cite the works of John Wycliffe (*c.*1330–1384), theologian, philosopher and controversialist, regarded after his death as founder of that sect of religious dissidents or heretics known as 'Lollards'. Wycliffe cited Magna Carta on several occasions. For the most part, he used the charter to argue for the feudal dependence of the clergy upon king and realm. This formed part of his wider attempt to detach the English Church from its theoretical obedience to the popes in Rome or Avignon. To this, however, Wycliffe added a further dimension, arguing that Magna Carta rather than the laws of the Roman empire or Church, should be taught to lawyers. Under Roman law it was accepted

58 Magna Carta acquired a preeminent status in books of statutes read and studied at the Inns of Court. Eighteenth century engraving of Lincoln's Inn, from Samuel Ireland, *Picturesque views, with an historical account of the Inns of court, in London and Westminster* (London, 1800). Oxford, Bodleian Library, G.A. Lond. 4° 78.

that 'what pleases the prince has the force of law'. By championing 'the great charter' as an alternative to Roman law, Wycliffe to some extent anticipated the future uses of the charter, as a brake upon the brute exercise of royal sovereignty.

Magna Carta was widely supposed to have placed the king under the rule of law. The tyranny of King John should in theory have become a thing of the past. Communal consent for taxation, and proper administration of justice, should ensure peace and harmony between king and subjects. Reality, of course, diverged from such wishful thinking. England continued to suffer under tyrannical kings. Warfare and public display, rather than *res publica* or the subject's protection remained kingship's principal concerns. From 1327 onwards, the English developed so regular a habit of deposition (of Edward II in 1327, of Richard II in 1399, of Henry VI in 1461 and again in 1471, of Richard III in 1485) that they became notorious as a people who killed their kings. In the late 1380s, there is evidence from the circle of Thomas of Woodstock, duke of Gloucester, that the so-called securities clause of Magna Carta 1215, instituting a committee of 25 barons over and above the king, was keenly read by the Lords Appellant seeking sanctions and a degree of control over King Richard II. In all of this, the English continued to proclaim their adherence to 'liberty', whilst their kings were regularly encouraged to issue promises that Magna Carta would be upheld.

59 Bronze statue of Caesar Augustus near the Trajan Forum in Rome. Roman law held that 'what pleases the prince has the force of law'. Photo: Mattia Mazzucchelli/ Shutterstock.

Despite being manipulated in favour of the king, late medieval English law did to some extent offer protection against arbitrary arrest and imprisonment. Death sentences could in theory only be imposed after lawful judgement. Slavery had no recognition in the courts. Torture remained an extra-legal resort, at odds with legal principal. By contrast to all this, clause 1 of Magna Carta, guaranteeing the liberties of the English Church, not only proclaimed a degree of compulsion in adherence to Christianity and the Catholic faith but, in effect, placed the church courts in a privileged position outside the mainstream of English legal procedure. Especially in cases of heresy, church courts could receive evidence extracted under torture, not least in the inquisitorial procedures used against the Lollards and later followers of John Wycliffe.

With the coming of the Tudor dynasty after 1485, even that great defender of the liberties of the Church, St Thomas More (1478–1535), was prepared to accept all manner of injustices in the prosecution of heretics by perjured witnesses, hearsay and the use of torture. Only from the 1580s onwards did lawyers, most notably Robert Beale (1541–1601), clerk of the Elizabethan Privy Council, begin to challenge the prosecution of heresy as a crime. In doing so, they cited the 1225 Magna Carta, clause 29, arguing that Magna Carta recognized 'rights' as freeholds of which individuals could not lawfully be deprived. To this extent, in the fight for religious toleration Magna Carta served as a witness both for the prosecution and the defence.

By this time, Magna Carta itself had been transmitted to the new medium of the printing press. The first popular edition was that published by Richard Pynson in 1508. By the 1580s, this had passed through no less than twenty-seven reprints. In the meantime, works such as George Ferrers' *Boke of Magna Carta* (1534) offered the first attempt at a full English translation of the charter, placed here at the head of all other statutes and with only minimal commentary. One peculiarity of these Tudor editions was their insistence upon printing the charter of 1225 (often from Edward I's 1300 reissue of the 1297 charter) as if it represented the charter issued by King John at Runnymede. In this way, a fundamental confusion arose as to the identity of John's Magna Carta. The charter issued at

60 In 1508, Richard Pynson published a collection of the earliest statutes, including the 1225 Magna Carta at the start of the book. This work was reissued no less than 27 times by the 1580s and spawned similar works by competing printers. Pynson, *Paru[us] codex qui Antiqua Statuta vocatur.* Oxford, Bodleian Library, 8° B 3 Med. Seld. (2), here showing the start, now bound up with other tracts.

THE GREAT CHAR= Fo.f.

(woodcut title page and printed text of the charter — as shown)

61 *above* George Ferrers' first translation of Magna Carta, published in 1534. *The great Charter called i[n] latyn Magna Carta with divers olde statutes.* Oxford, Bodleian Library, Douce C 391.

62 *right* Sir Edward Coke (1552–1634) tirelessly championed the constitutional role of Magna Carta and used it as a hedge against royal excesses of power. Serving as the attorney general for Queen Elizabeth I, chief justice of King's Bench for King James I, solicitor general and later speaker of the House of Commons, he had an enormous influence on the interpretation of Magna Carta. TC Oils P 40. © Trinity College, Cambridge.

Runnymede was more or less forgotten, only to be rediscovered and properly compared with its later reissues by William Blackstone, in 1759. Meanwhile, Tudor and Stuart debates over the charter depended upon the text of 1225. As a result, much of the charter's original radicalism, its establishment of a committee of twenty-five barons, its insistence upon the rights of 'the commune of the whole realm', its insistence that taxation be imposed only after properly convened discussion, went unnoticed by its modern readers.

Despite its publication and its significance in religious affairs, Magna Carta played only a limited role in Tudor political debate. For its revival as a political manifesto we must look to the early seventeenth century, and in particular to the writings of the Stuart Chief Justice, Sir Edward Coke (1552–1634). As early as 1608, Coke could be found arguing that no ecclesiastical court should examine a man on the secrets of his heart, 'for thought is free'. Thereafter, in opposition to the attempts made by the Stuart kings to revive medieval feudal taxes and to exalt the king as 'absolute' sovereign, Coke championed Magna Carta as chief

AMBVLASTI IN VIIS MEIS ET FECISTI
QVOD RECTVM EST IN OCVLIS MEIS
ET PERFECISTI CVRSVM TBI
PROPOSITVM CVM
PATIENTIÂ ET
SVSPICIENS
D ME. TOTAM IN ME
FIDVCIAM COLLOCAS-
TI REPOSITA EST
BI CORONA
GLORIÆ.

63 Coke interpreted Magna Carta as the continuation of Anglo Saxon law and hence a cornerstone of English common law. His treatise on Magna Carta became basic reading for lawyers in Britain and America for over two centuries. *The Second Part of the Institutes of the Lawes of England* (1642). Oxford, Bodleian Library, Vet. A3 C.154.

embodiment of what he presented as an 'Ancient' English Constitution. Magna Carta, he argued, was not so much a novel or revolutionary settlement forced upon a reluctant King John, but a restatement of an existing body of rights. Like earlier writers, most notably Sir John Fortescue (d. *c.*1480), Chief Justice under King Henry VI, Coke argued that Englishmen were by nature born to freedom and liberty, their constitution entirely set apart from that of continental monarchies where the absolute power of the king held sway. England, according to Fortescue, was ruled by 'political' rather than 'regal' monarchy, with the sovereign power of the monarch 'restrained by political law'. Fortescue's view of the past was undoubtedly warped. Nonetheless, as early as the thirteenth and fourteenth centuries there are sufficient signs of English exceptionalism, not least the existence of a freeholding peasantry across much of eastern England, able to buy and sell land, to suggest a fundamental divergence between the English experience of law and government and that of other parts of northern Europe. In all of this, the same events that had set Philip Augustus and his kingdom on the road to autocracy and Versailles may, even before 1500, have determined that England would become a land of limited monarchy, free peasants and constitutional liberty. To this extent, the view of English exceptionalism encouraged by Fortescue and Coke,

although rose-tinted, may correspond rather more closely to underlying realities than has sometimes been allowed.

Like Fortescue, whose chief works were only published sixty or more years after his death, Coke had long to wait before his more controversial political doctrines could be printed. His thoughts here were set out at greatest length in his *Institutes of the Lawes of England*, of which publication began in 1628 but was only completed in 1644, eight years after Coke's death. Meanwhile, Coke's championing of Magna Carta brought the charter to centre stage in the political debates that preceded the English Civil War. Magna Carta was widely cited in the controversies over the Petition of Right (1628), passed by Parliament in open defiance of King Charles I and intended to restrict the king's powers to impose non-parliamentary taxes, to billet troops or to imprison his subjects without trial.

The irony here is that Coke and his contemporaries cited Magna Carta, not as an innovation of the reign of King John but as the embodiment of an entirely mythical 'Ancient Constitution' stretching back to the time of the equally mythical King Arthur, and thence to the dim and even more

64 In 1628, a committee of the House of Commons, chaired by Sir Edward Coke, drafted a petition of right to oppose the methods used by Charles I to raise funds without parliamentary approval. The Petition of Right became a cornerstone of English constitutional law, reaffirming the liberties set out in Magna Carta and prohibiting taxation without Parliament's consent and extra-legal imprisonment. W Prynne, *The petition of right of the free-holders and free-men* (1648). Oxford, Bodleian Library, Wood 609 (13).

mythical past. Key here was the sense that liberty was something inherent to the British Isles: a genetic right passed down from distant antiquity, in due course, as in Magna Carta, recognized by English kings, but in no way king-made. The role of the king was to uphold the law, not, as in an absolutist system, to serve as law maker. Meanwhile, it was as a result of the contemporary excitement over Magna Carta that the politician and manuscript collector, Sir Robert Cotton (1570–1631) went to such lengths to acquire the charter as artefact. Thanks to this, two of the four surviving originals of the 1215 Magna Carta are today amongst the Cotton collection of manuscripts in the British Library. Cotton collected the charter itself. He did not, however, resolve confusion between the text of 1225 and the document issued by King John.

This was the England of Sir John Denham, whose *Cooper's Hill*, begun in the late 1630s and completed just before the outbreak of the Civil War in 1642, reimagines the view from Cooper's Hill near Egham in Surrey as a vista both of England's pastoral beauty and England's past. Denham attempts a compromise between the nascent republicanism of Coke and the absolutist tendencies of the Stuart kings. Scanning the view of Windsor and the Thames, Denham glimpses Runnymede in the distance:

> Here was that charter seal'd, wherein the Crown
> All marks of arbitrary power lays down:
> Tyrant and slave, those names of hate and fear,
> The happier style of king and subject bear:
> Happy, when both to the same centre move,
> When kings give liberty, and subjects love.

This is a distinctly 'royalist' view of Magna Carta. It nonetheless celebrated the same chartered liberty later referred to in James Thomson's *Masque of Alfred* (1740), set to music by Thomas Arne and supplying generations of Englishmen with an alternative National Anthem:

> When Britain first at heaven's command,
> Arose from out the azure main,
> This was *the charter of the land*.
> And guardian angels sung this strain:
> 'Rule Britannia! Britannia rule the waves,
> Britons never, never, never will be slaves!'

65 *left* The politician and antiquary, Sir Robert Bruce Cotton (1571–1631), acquired two of the four surviving exemplars of the 1215 Magna Carta, one of which was badly damaged after the disastrous fire of 1731 at Ashburnham House. Portrait by Cornelius Johnson. TC Oils P 43. © Trinity College, Cambridge.

66 *above* This image from the frontispiece to the first edition of his *Tryall* shows John Lilburne reading at the proceedings from Sir Edward Coke's commentary on Magna Carta from his *Institutes*. Portrait of John Lilburne, British Museum, BH/FF10/Portraits British CIII P2. © Trustees of the British Museum.

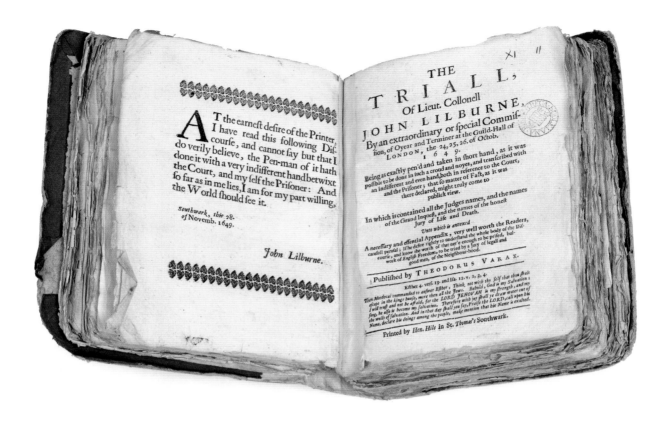

AT the earneſt deſire of the Printer, I have read this following Diſ-courſe, and cannot ſay but that I do verily believe, the Pen-man of it hath done it with a very indifferent hand betwixt the Court, and my ſelf the Priſoner: And ſo far as in me lies, I am for my part willing, the World ſhould ſee it.

Southwark, this 28.
of Novemb. 1649.

John Lilburne.

THE
TRIALL,
Of Lieut. Collonell
JOHN LILBURNE,
By an extraordinary or ſpecial Commiſ-
ſion, of Oyer and Terminer at the Guild-Hall of
LONDON, the 24, 25, 26. of Octob.
1 6 4 9.

Being as exactly pen'd and taken in ſhort hand, as it was
poſſible to be done in ſuch a croud and noyes, and tranſcribed with
an indifferent and even hand, both in reference to the Court,
and the Priſoner; that ſo matter of Fact, as it was
there declared, might truly come to
publick view.

In which is contained all the Judges names, and the names
of the Grand Inqueſt, and the names of the honeſt
Jury of Life and Death.

Unto which is annexed
A neceſſary and eſſential Appendix, very well worth the Readers,
carefull peruſal; If he deſire rightly to underſtand the whole body of the Diſ-
courſe, and know the worth of that ne'r enough to be priſed, bul-
work of Engliſh Freedom, to be tried by a Jury of legall and
good men, of the Neighbour-hood.

Publiſhed by THEODORUS VARAX.

Either 4. verſ. 13. and Iſa. 12. v. 2, 3, 4:
Then Mordecai commanded to anſwer Either; Think not with thy ſelf that thou ſhalt
eſcape in the kings houſe, more then all the Jews. Behold, God is my Salvation;
I will truſt and not be afraid, for the LORD JEHOVAH is my ſtrength, and my
ſong, he alſo is become my ſalvation. Therefore with joy ſhall ye draw water out of
the wells of ſalvation. And in that day ſhall you ſay, Praiſe the LORD, call upon his
Name, declare his doings among the people, make mention that his Name is exalted.

Printed by *Hen. Hils* in St. *Thomas's* Southwark.

In the meantime, the Civil War of Charles I's reign returned England to a state of political turmoil unknown since the Wars of the Roses. Sir John Denham, of Cooper's Hill fame, entered the Civil War as royalist sheriff of Surrey and constable of Farnham Castle, offices that had already been of significance in the war between King John and his barons, after 1215. No wonder that contemporaries continued to look to Magna Carta both as totem and as precedent. Sir Simonds D'Ewes, for example, a Warwickshire landowner and keen collector of medieval manuscripts, specifically cited Magna Carta in debates in the Long Parliament, from 1640 onwards, upholding Parliament's duty to receive petitions as consistent with the principle of Magna Carta clause 40 that 'to no-one shall we deny justice'.

Other writers of the English Revolution used Magna Carta to even more radical effect. Imprisoned in the Tower of London, John Lilburne employed the charter's defence of liberty as ammunition not only against the king but against Parliament's claims to sovereignty. Parliament,

67 John Lilburne (1614–57), the pamphleteer and Leveller, held that the Charter was founded upon natural law and invested sovereignty in the people. He appealed successfully to Magna Carta at his trial for high treason. *The triall of Lieutenant Collonell John Lilburne* (1649). Oxford, Bodleian Library, Wood 368 (11).

Lilburne argued, was potentially just as much a tyrant as the king. Magna Carta, he suggested, being based upon the principle of natural law, instead invested sovereignty in the people as the birthright of all 'free-born Englishmen'. In his tract *By law and reason. Being a collection of the marrow and soule of Magna Charta* (1648), Lilburne asserted that English liberties derived not from king or Parliament but from the law itself, here reimagined as a 'natural' entity, predating even the Anglo-Saxon law codes, in time transmitted via such foundational texts as the Laws of Edward the Confessor or Magna Carta. As late as 1667, and fearing that the 'very high language' of the times portended a return to the strife of the 1640s, Samuel

68 Thomas Jefferson's copy of King James I's charter to the Virginia Company, which granted the privileges and liberties enjoyed by English subjects to the inhabitants of Virginia and their descendants. Washington D.C., Library of Congress, Rare Book and Special Collections Division, Thomas Jefferson Library Collection (022.00.01).

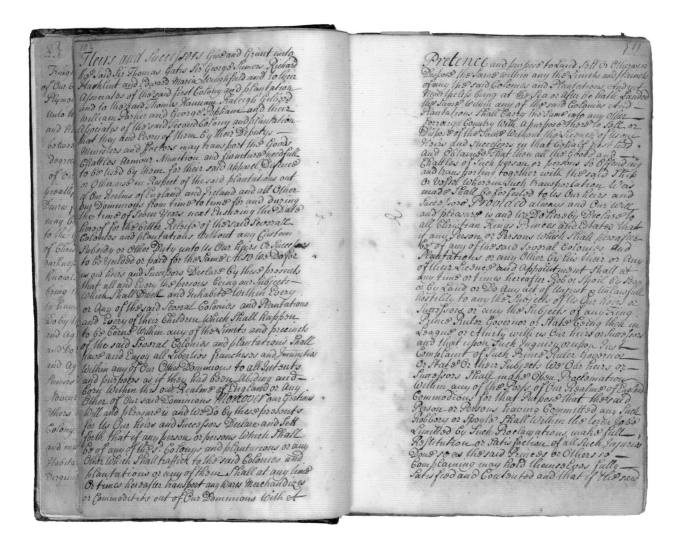

69 In 1619, Virginia was the first English colony to hold a representative assembly, the external sign of English liberties enjoyed by the colony's members. Similar bodies – established in Bermuda, Massachusetts, Maryland, Connecticut and Barbados – rank as some of the oldest democratic bodies outside of Britain. *The Historie of Travell into Virginia Britania* (1612). Oxford, Bodleian Library, MS. Ashmole 1758, ff. 13v-14r.

VIRGINIA

Massaw-Massawomeck omecks

Signification of these markes.
To the crosses hath bin discouerd
what beyond is by relation
Kings houses
Ordinary houses

14

The Sasques=ahanougs
are a Gyant like people and
thus a=tyred

SEA

Discouered and Discribed by Captayn John Smith
Grauen by William Hole

Scale of Leagues

Chesapeack Bay

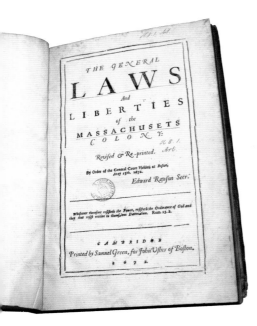

70 The first law code of Massachusetts, enacted in 1648, includes a paraphrase of clause 29 of Magna Carta 1225, forbidding unlawful imprisonment, execution and seizure of property, and guaranteeing due process of law. *The General Laws and Liberties of Massachusetts* (1672). Oxford, Bodleian Library, Arch. G d.52 (1).

Pepys is to be found referring to Magna Carta as 'the great preserver of our lives, freedoms and properties'.

Thus far Magna Carta can be regarded principally as an English phenomenon. This is to some extent misleading. It had long ago reached Ireland, to which the 1216 issue was sent within a few months of the coronation of Henry III. A copy of the 1215 charter, translated into Anglo-Norman French, was circulating in Normandy by the 1230s. Thereafter, the Normans undoubtedly came to know the Magna Carta of 1225 issued by Henry III. This was copied into a series of books of Norman law, albeit misattributed there as a charter of King Henry II (1154–1189) granted not to England but to Normandy. This 'Norman' Magna Carta played a part in late thirteenth-century defences of Norman legal privilege. In 1315 (exactly a century after Runnymede), the arguments here were enshrined in Louis X's 'Charte aux normands': a promise to uphold Norman rights against encroachments by Paris or the laws of France.

By the seventeenth century, however, it was no longer France but the New World that served as chief focus of English ambitions overseas. According to the theories of Fortescue and Coke, England was by nature a land of liberty. It necessarily followed that Englishmen carried liberty in their very bodies when they travelled outside the realm. In particular, when they established colonies for themselves in Ireland, North America or the Caribbean, they brought to these places a right to be tried by due process of law, an immunity from arbitrary arrest or punishment and the right to make, or at least to assent to, the legislation by which they were governed. The royal charter of 1606 authorizing the foundation of Virginia was drafted under the guidance of Sir Edward Coke, who had a financial stake in the colony and therefore an interest in its success. The charter extended to the colonists and their descendents the privileges and liberties of English subjects. Thereafter, it became standard practice for colonists to be offered the liberties and protections of English common law. Clauses to this effect were inserted in the charters offered by Charles I to Massachusetts (1629), Maryland (1632), Maine (1639) and by the rulers of Britain to other colonies thereafter. Since the jury and the representative assembly were the chief outward signs of English liberty, these too were eagerly adopted wherever English settlements were planted. Beginning with Virginia in 1619, the colonies produced a whole series of such assemblies, with those of Virginia, Bermuda,

Anno nono HENRICI III. 7.

CAP. XXVIII

CAP. XXIX

Nullus liber homo cap-
vel impriſonetur aut

R. E. Pine Pinx.ᵗ   Jaˢ. Watson Fecit.

Arthur Beardmore

Common Council-man of the City of LONDON. Teaching his Son Magna Charta.

Theſe words which I command theе this day, ſhall be in thine heart. And thou ſhalt teach them diligently unto thy children. DEUT. CHAP. VI. ver. 6. 7.

London, Printed for Robert Sayer, at the Golden Buck in Fleet Street. As the Act Directs May 20.ᵗʰ 1765.

71 *previous page* Arthur Beardmore's (1719–71) victory in his lawsuit against the government for wrongful arrest was commemorated in an engraving by James Watson (1739–90), portraying him at the moment of his arrest, teaching his son Magna Carta. His finger points to the opening words of clause 29 (Magna Carta 1225) forbidding wrongful arrest and imprisonment, while the Charter as a whole is imbued with a quasi-scriptural stature through the quotation from Deuteronomy at the bottom of the print, 'These words which I command thee this day, shall be in thine heart. And thou shalt teach them diligently unto thy children.' *Arthur Beardmore, Common Council-man of the City of London Teaching his Son Magna Charta*, mezzotint, by James Watson, after Robert Edge Pine. As republished 20 May 1765, printed for John Smith and Robert Sayer, British Museum, (1902,1011.6373). © British Museum Trustees.

72 *above right* Arrested in 1763 for seditious libel, John Wilkes (1725–97) fully grasped the figurative power of Magna Carta. Here he is depicted surrounded by documents proclaiming English liberties, including the Bill of Rights. In the background Hercules fights the hydra, metaphor for tyranny. *John Wilkes Esqr*, mezzotint, published for Carrington Bowles, 1768, British Museum, 1902,1011.761. © British Museum Trustees.

Massachusetts, Maryland, Connecticut and Barbados ranking amongst the oldest continuously functioning parliamentary bodies outside of Britain itself. By the 1770s, England had twenty-nine colonies in North America (eleven in the islands, and eighteen on the mainland). Of these only one (Quebec) remained without representative institutions. Magna Carta thus became a part of colonial as well as of English law.

Those sceptical of the benefits of British rule, and in particular those in flight from religious persecution, were by no means confident that Magna Carta offered the best defence of American liberty. Did not Magna Carta invest sovereign authority in a king? Was it not witnessed by bishops? Was not its opening clause a ringing defence of the privileges of the Church in England, ever since the sixteenth century generally interpreted as the Anglican Church establishment? To the heirs of William Penn and other exiles from Anglican persecution, Magna Carta was a far from easy pill to swallow. The Mayflower pilgrims who settled the Plymouth Colony in 1620 were religious separatist hounded out of England and then out of the Netherlands. Eschewing Anglican 'tyranny', they wished to govern themselves not under a parliamentary constitution but in accordance with the theology of Calvin and the Geneva congregation. Here, the Bible and the traditions of the early apostles triumphed over those of Magna Carta.

Elsewhere, arguments based upon natural law appeared more attractive to many colonists than those founded upon the 'Gothic' constitution of a mother country only recently emerged from feudal tyranny. If historic precedents were to be sought, then they were better sought in ancient Judea or Rome than in the squalor of medieval England. In such a telling, the rebellious colonists were proud republicans or defiant Christian martyrs, new Catos contending against the tyranny of George III, a Hanoverian Nero. Hence the later building of the federal capital at Washington along strictly classical Athenian or Roman lines. Hence the foundation of the Society of the Cincinnati amongst veterans of the War of Independence, and the establishment of Cincinnati Ohio, named in honour of the Roman consul who had assumed dictatorial powers only in time of crisis, thereafter handing rule back to the Senate. Hence the way in which Biblical or classical images of Moses, Augustus or Julius Caesar rub shoulders somewhat incongruously with images of Magna Carta and King John in the state capitols and supreme courts of many great American cities.

Even so, before independence, not all Americans were inclined to spurn English precedents. As early as the 1640s, the Puritan clergyman Nathaniel Ward had attempted to establish principles of liberty and justice dervied from Magna Carta and the common law, incorporated in his *Body of Liberties* (1641). In December 1641, Ward's *Liberties* were adopted by the General Court of the Massachusetts Bay Company, in effect as the first code of laws newly promulgated in New England. They open with a paraphrase of clauses 39 and 40 of King John's Magna Carta:

No mans life shall be taken away, no mans honour or good name shall be stayned, no mans person shall be arested, restrayned, banished,

...inerian Professor of the
Laws of England
Solicitor General to the Queen
& Member for Hindon
Wilts.

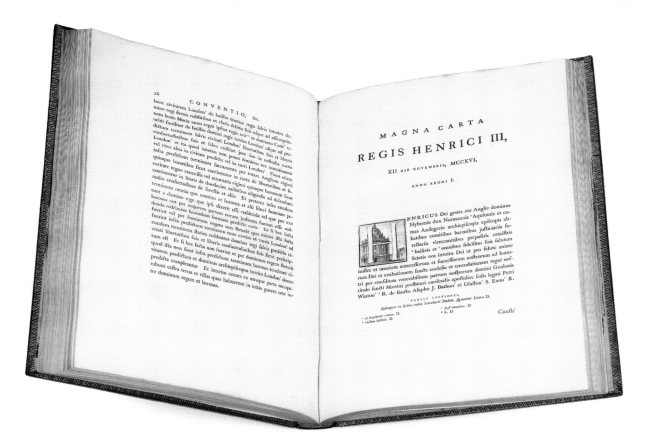

dismembred, nor any wayes punished … unlesse it be by vertue or equitie of some expresse law of the Country waranting the same, established by a generall Court and sufficiently published.

Even earlier than this, in 1636, the Plymouth settlers had codified their regulations into a document known as the 'General Fundamentals' insisting that no law be imposed upon them save 'by consent according to the free liberties of the State and Kingdome of England'. Such laws and liberties included regulations on weights and measures and the rights of widows derived ultimately from the terms of Magna Carta.

In 1683, it was to Magna Carta that the settlers of New York turned in devising for themselves a draft 'Charter of Liberties and Privileges'. In part modelled upon Magna Carta, in part upon the 1628 Petition of Right, this was presented to (although in the event never ratified by) the future King James II. For a brief period through to 1691, a group of rebel militiamen seized power in New York. With their overthrow, the New York assembly re-enacted the 'Charter of Liberties and Privileges' as the price of their continued adherence to British government.

73 *left* As the first Vinerian Professor of English Law at the University of Oxford, Sir William Blackstone (1723–80) advanced the study of English law in universities. His extensive work on Magna Carta helped not only to identify the various issues of the charter but also led to greater veneration of the document. Oil painting by Tilly Kettle (1735–86). Oxford, Bodleian Library, LP 265.

74 *above* William Blackstone's ground-breaking work, *The Great Charter and Charter of the Forest* (1759), was the first attempt to identify and transcribe the numerous issues of Magna Carta issued between 1215 and 1297. Here is the opening page of his edition of the 1216 charter, issued in the first year of the reign of Henry III. Oxford, Bodleian Library, Broxb. 49.7.

In eighteenth century England, Magna Carta continued to be cited in defence of the immunity of the king's subjects from arbitrary imprisonment. This at a time when politicians and lawyers were acutely sensitive to any sign that English or British liberties were being eroded by the absolutist tendencies of monarchy. Britain, so the theorists had long argued, was a land of political rather than regal or absolutist monarchy. Having executed a tyrant king in 1649 and forced his Catholic son to flee the realm in 1688, the British were not about to allow any resurgence of either absolutism or its correlative, Catholicism. In this defence of liberties, Magna Carta once again played a leading role.

Accused of seditious libel in 1762, the London lawyer, Arthur Beardmore, arranged to be arrested in the act of teaching Magna Carta to his son. This abuse of liberty was swiftly advertised in print by the engraver Robert Pine. Two years later, Pine's portrait of the London radical John Wilkes depicts Wilkes seated amidst the icons of his political creed, including a copy of Magna Carta. Reacting to events across the Atlantic, the Whig parliamentarian, Edmund Burke, demanded that America's settlers should 'sit down … to the feast of Magna Charta'. In all of this, Englishmen now had the use of William Blackstone's 1759 edition and commentary on Magna Carta, for the first time properly distinguishing between the charter as issued by King John and the later reissue of 1225 (albeit misdated by Blackstone to 1224). In personal and political terms, Blackstone was poles apart from John Wilkes and those other radicals who sought to use Magna Carta in the defence of liberty. As a Tory MP, patronized by George III, he was amongst those who in 1769 voted for Wilkes' expulsion from the House of Commons. He later expressed hostility to the American demand for independence. He remained ambivalent on the question of slavery, retreating from an early conviction that any slave, once landed on English soil, became emancipated from all obligations to his supposed 'owner'. His great edition of the charter in 1759 coincided with his first suffering from gout, that great malady of reactionaries. Blackstone nonetheless cited the charter as a model of constitutional balance, in which the sovereignty of Parliament emerged from the necessity to keep all competing authorities in check. Here we are not far from the Victorian constitutionalists and their conception of the British constitution as the most perfect form of government towards which all previous or competing systems were merely striving.

This, the so-called 'Whig Interpretion of History', was evident not only in British but in American approaches to Magna Carta. In Britain, Blackstone's commentaries led to an even greater veneration of the charter as artefact and totem. So much so that great excitement was expressed in 1765, when the original Articles of the Barons, agreed at Runnymede and sealed by the king as an early draft of the terms later granted by Magna Carta, re-emerged for sale. Looted from Lambeth Palace in 1640, following the impeachment of Archbishop Laud, this document had since passed through the hands of Bishop Burnet of Salisbury and his immediate heirs. In 1769, the document was purchased by the second Lord Stanhope for 50 guineas (£52 10s). Stanhope intended it for presentation to the newly established British Museum as a gift from the king. Thereby, Stanhope rather optimistically believed, honour would be reflected both upon George III and his ancestor, King John, whose own role in the events of 1215, it was supposed, had been cruelly misrepresented.

To the British colonists in North America meanwhile, protesting against arbitrary taxation and the 1765 Stamp Act, the principle of 'No taxation without representation' could itself claim roots in clause 14 of the 1215 Magna Carta, itself only recently rediscovered by Blackstone. The

75 In this popular satirical print celebrating the repeal of the Stamp Act, a funeral procession bears a small coffin containing the remains of the bill. The sign above the vault declares it the resting place of all unjust acts that would alienate Englishmen. *The repeal, or the funeral procession of Miss Americ-Stamp*, etching with engraving, 1766 or later. Washington, D.C., Library of Congress, Prints and Photographs Division (PC 1 - 4140b).

Seven Years War (1756–63) had been fought by Britain at least in part on the justification of maintaining the 'liberty' of navigation and trade, itself one of the many such liberties included in Magna Carta. The war brought Britain new conquests, both in America and in India. When the costs of war came to be reckoned, however, and the British Parliament demanded contributions from the colonies themselves, tensions between colonists and the home government reached boiling point. In the ensuing disputes over such matters as taxation, arbitrary arrest, the billeting of troops and the searching of private property, Magna Carta was widely cited in the colonists' support. As the local assembly of Virginia phrased it, in 1765, Virginia's charters from James I entitled the colonists to all liberties, privileges and immunities 'as if they had been abiding and born within this our realm of England'. Such privileges necessarily included the liberties guaranteed by Magna Carta.

There were problems here, nonetheless. Magna Carta was a document intended to curb the tyrannical impulses of monarchy. For more than a century, both in the disturbances leading to the English Civil War and in the Glorious Revolution of 1688, Magna Carta had been adopted as the totem of those arguing that sovereignty resided in the English Parliament rather than at the royal court. Yet so far as the North American colonies were concerned, it was Parliament rather than the king whose tyranny was most in need of restraint. It was Parliament, not the king, that passed the Stamp Act. Not only this, but by the 1760s Parliament itself appeared to the colonists to be in league with the hereditary proprietorial claims of those families, the Penns of Pennsylvania and the Baltimore family of Maryland, whose titles derived from chartered liberties granted to the first colonial settlers. The New World's first printing of the text of Magna Carta had been undertaken in 1687 at the direct prompting of the Penn family.

It was in order to escape from the tyranny both of Parliament and of Thomas Penn that Benjamin Franklin proposed, in the 1760s, that the colonies be placed directly under the authority of King George III. Even when this scheme evaporated as so much moonshine, it remained difficult to imagine how Magna Carta, itself conceived of as a 'parliamentary' act, could be used to contest other such acts, the Sugar Act (1764), the Stamp Act (1765), the Declaratory Act (1766), the Townshend Acts (1767) or the Coercive Acts (1774), all of which seemed to emanate from Parliament rather than the king. To most native-born Englishmen, the idea of defying Parliament in the name of liberty and Magna Carta appeared a logical absurdity.

76 Thomas Paine, holding a copy of his best-seller, *Common Sense*, which promoted democratic beliefs in natural law and the rights of man. *Thomas Paine*, by Peter Kramer, Published by F. W. Thomas, no.172 Nth. 4th St.; 1851. Washington, D.C., Library of Congress, Prints and Photographs Division, PGA - Krämer–Thomas Paine.

Only by re-imagining Magna Carta not as an act of Parliament but as a written contract between king and people, were the colonists once again able to invoke it in defence of what they now conceived of as their historic rights. It was thus that John Adams invoked the Massachusetts charter of 1691 as a form of miniature Magna Carta protecting the liberties and rights of the people of Massachusetts. It was thus that, in 1776, the framers of the Declaration of Independence scrupulously avoided any mention of Parliament, stating only that their grievances lay against King George III and 'others' who had conspired with him to do them harm. Amongst the leaders of colonial opinion, Tom Paine grounded his democratic beliefs in natural law and the rights of man, entirely rejecting monarchy and the privileges of a hereditary peerage. Even so, he suggested, the means used to control the monarchy in 'the dark and slavish' circumstances of medieval England could be just as easily used to establish constitutional democracy in America. Paine's *Common Sense* (1775–6) was an immediate best-seller. More than 100,000 copies were sold within the first three months of its publication. It proposed a 'Continental Charter' to serve as North America's equivalent to Magna Carta, composed by elected representatives. On the paper money issued by the rebels of Massachusetts in 1775, Paul Revere is depicted as a Minuteman carrying a sword in one hand and a copy of Magna Carta in the other. This same image was adopted on the Massachusetts state seal, from 1775 to 1780. During the War of Independence, after 1776, Magna Carta was regularly cited in the colonists' defence, portrayed in political cartoons showing the American revolutionaries seated under the great tree of liberty from whose branches Magna Carta hung. Calls were heard in London for a new committee of twenty-five to sit in judgement upon King George III. In due course, a paraphrase of Magna Carta clauses 39 and 40 (clause 29 of the 1225 and all subsequent reissues) found its way into the constitutions of all of the newly independent states of America, in essence demanding 'due process' under law before any citizen could be deprived of life, liberty or property. Similar clauses were adopted in the Fifth, Sixth and Eighth amendments to the United States federal constitution, known collectively as 'The Bill of Rights' (1791). By conceiving of the constitution as something greater and higher than a mere act of the legislature,

77 On the eve of the Revolution, the province of Massachusetts adopted a new seal, depicting a militiaman with sword in one hand and Magna Carta in the other. Designed by Paul Revere, the seal bears the motto, *Ense petit placidam sub libertate quietem* ('By the sword we seek peace, but peace only under liberty'), still in use today. Photo: Massachusetts State House.

Congress of the United States.

begun and held at the City of New York, on

Wednesday the fourth of March one thousand seven hundred and eighty nine.

THE Conventions of a number of the States, having, at the time of their adopting the Constitution, expressed a desire, in order to prevent misconstruction or abuse of its powers, that further declaratory and restrictive clauses should be added: And as extending the ground of public confidence in the government, will best ensure the beneficent ends of its institution.

RESOLVED by the Senate and House of Representatives of the United States of America, in Congress assembled, two thirds of both Houses concurring, that the following Articles be proposed to the Legislatures of the several States, as Amendments to the Constitution of the United States, all or any of which Articles, when ratified by three fourths of the said Legislatures, to be valid to all intents and purposes, as part of the said Constitution — viz.

ARTICLES in addition to, and amendment of the Constitution of the United States of America, proposed by Congress, and ratified by the Legislatures of the several States, pursuant to the fifth Article of the original Constitution.

Article the First. After the first enumeration required by the first Article of the Constitution, there shall be one Representative for every thirty thousand, until the number shall amount to one hundred, after which, the proportion shall be so regulated by Congress, that there shall be not less than one hundred Representatives, nor less than one Representative for every forty thousand persons, until the number of Representatives shall amount to two hundred, after which the proportion shall be so regulated by Congress, that there shall not be less than two hundred Representatives, nor more than one Representative for every fifty thousand persons.

Article the Second. No law varying the compensation for the services of the Senators and Representatives, shall take effect, until an election of Representatives shall have intervened.

Article the Third. Congress shall make no law respecting an establishment of Religion, or prohibiting the free exercise thereof; or abridging the freedom of Speech, or of the Press, or the right of the people peaceably to assemble, and to petition the Government for a redress of grievances.

Article the Fourth. A well regulated Militia, being necessary to the security of a free State, the right of the people to keep and bear arms, shall not be infringed.

Article the Fifth. No Soldier shall, in time of peace, be quartered in any house, without the consent of the owner, nor in time of war, but in a manner to be prescribed by law.

Article the Sixth. The right of the people to be secure in their persons, houses, papers, and effects, against unreasonable searches and seizures, shall not be violated, and no warrants shall issue, but upon probable cause, supported by oath or affirmation, and particularly describing the place to be searched, and the persons or things to be seized.

Article the Seventh. No person shall be held to answer for a capital, or otherwise infamous crime, unless on a presentment or indictment of a Grand Jury, except in cases arising in the land or naval forces, or in the Militia, when in actual service in time of war or public danger; nor shall any person be subject for the same offence to be twice put in jeopardy of life or limb; nor shall be compelled in any criminal case, to be a witness against himself, nor be deprived of life, liberty or property, without due process of law; nor shall private property be taken for public use without just compensation.

Article the Eighth. In all criminal prosecutions, the accused shall enjoy the right to a speedy and public trial, by an impartial jury of the State and district wherein the crime shall have been committed, which district shall have been previously ascertained by law, and to be informed of the nature and cause of the accusation; to be confronted with the witnesses against him; to have compulsory process for obtaining witnesses in his favor, and to have the assistance of Counsel for his defence.

Article the Ninth. In suits at common law, where the value in controversy shall exceed twenty dollars, the right of trial by jury shall be preserved, and no fact, tried by a jury, shall be otherwise re-examined in any Court of the United States, than according to the rules of the common law.

Article the Tenth. Excessive bail shall not be required, nor excessive fines imposed, nor cruel and unusual punishments inflicted.

Article the Eleventh. The enumeration in the Constitution, of certain rights, shall not be construed to deny or disparage others retained by the people.

Article the Twelfth. The powers not delegated to the United States by the Constitution, nor prohibited by it to the States, are reserved to the States respectively, or to the people.

Attest.

John Beckley, Clerk of the House of Representatives.
Sam. A. Otis, Secretary of the Senate.

Frederick Augustus Muhlenberg, Speaker of the House of Representatives.

John Adams, Vice-President of the United States, and President of the Senate.

---

he General Assembly of Delaware Having taken into their consideration the above Amendments proposed by Congress to the respective Legislatures of the several States, Resolved, that the First Article be postponed. Resolved, that the General Assembly do agree to the Second, Third, Fourth, Fifth, Sixth, Seventh, Eighth, Ninth, Tenth, Eleventh and Twelfth Articles; and We do hereby assent to, ratify, and confirm the same, as Part of the Constitution of the United States. In Testimony whereof We have caused the Great Seal of the State to be hereunto affixed this twenty eighth Day of January in the Year of our Lord One thousand seven hundred and ninety, and in the Fourteenth Year of the Independence of the Delaware State.

Signed by Order of Council.

Geo. Mitchell Speaker

Signed by Order of the House &c. Generally.

the founding fathers including Paine and Thomas Jefferson, ensured that American conceptions of law increasingly diverged from those held in England. In England, with no written constitution, the concepts of what was constitutional and what was legal went hand in hand. Parliament, or the sovereign acting through Parliament, made law that in turn became part of unwritten constitutional tradition. To Blackstone, indeed, law was synonymous with command, so that statutes made by the King-in-Parliament must be obeyed even if they conflicted with natural law. In America, by contrast, the constitution was conceived of as something distinct, set apart from any mere legislative act. From this sprang the idea of judicial review – the tradition by which judges in the ordinary courts of law have the authority to determine the constitutionality of acts of the state or federal legislatures. From this also sprang calls for a Bill of Rights, presented, like Magna Carta itself, as a means of controlling what would otherwise be the undirected power of a constitution lacking either morality or reason.

As a result, even today, Magna Carta commands a reverence in the United States greater than that which it has achieved in the land of its birth. There is irony to this. Magna Carta seeks to guarantee the liberties of free men, extending these to the subjects not just of the king but of all English lords. In doing so, it enshrines ideas of lordship, of the sanctity of property and of free men as a group set apart from the majority of their dependent subjects. Inequality between independent and dependent citizens was thus hard-wired into the British constitutional tradition. Liberty and inequality were paired in ways that made the American and later French claims to liberty and equality very hard for free-born Englishmen to stomach. In Britain and in many British colonies, property ownership came to serve as a necessary qualification for the right to vote. Even in those colonies that brought a high proportion of their settlers within the franchise, there remained a tendency to exclude indigenous populations from liberties granted to colonists. This was accentuated all the more in North America, whose settlers not only deliberately expelled the native inhabitants but imported African slaves to work their land.

To the defenders of slavery, Magna Carta and its tacit division of society between freemen and villeins or dependent peasants, served to justify the exclusion of black slaves from the liberties otherwise afforded to those living under British law. The plantation owners of Jamaica had celebrated their right to hold their own assemblies and make their own

78 Paraphrases of Magna Carta articulating essential liberties, including the need for due legal process before an individual could be deprived of life, liberty or property, appear in the constitutions of all of the newly independent states of America. Similar clauses were adopted in the US Bill of Rights (1791). *Delaware's Ratification of the Bill of Rights*, 01/28/1790. Washington D.C., National Archives and Record Administration.

laws, first conceded in 1729, as Jamaica's 'Magna Carta'. Yet at this very time Jamaica, a land of free-born British settlers, was fast developing into an island worked by slaves. With the persistence of slavery in the United States, the pairing of liberty and inequality was transmitted from Britain to the newly independent America. Indeed, by upholding the right of Americans to make their own laws under autonomous state legislatures, the American constitution more or less guaranteed the right of such legislatures to perpetuate the institution of slavery.

Nor was it only in America that such inequalities persisted. The experience of defeat in America inclined the British authorities in what remained of their Empire to the amelioration of religious (Ireland) and civil liberties (West Indies, India), not least through the abolition of slavery. To preserve the exceptional rights of settlers against those of native populations, various colonial legislatures, beginning with Ireland in 1801 and continuing with Jamaica and the other West Indian colonies after 1865, deliberately abolished themselves, taking refuge under direct crown colony status, rather than extend full liberty to the majority of native subjects. This, as in the division between free and unfree in the United States, perpetuated a two-tier system of liberty. In India, for example, adopting the metaphors of parent and child, the colonists continued to be governed by English law whilst extending to the natives a system of laws supposedly modelled upon more ancient (and thereby reputedly authentic) native traditions. Similar distinctions between the rights of settlers and those of indigenous peoples informed the subsequent constitutions of Canada, Australia, New Zealand and South Africa. Magna Carta and the Common Law were thus allowed to settlers who carried liberty in their bodies as genetic inheritance, but disallowed to natives who enjoyed no such birthright.

None of this necessarily tarnished the reputation of Magna Carta as a guarantor of liberty. Nor did the fact that, as early as the 1820s, the text of Magna Carta was coming to seem increasingly archaic, as codification and the repeal of redundant law swept away large swathes of 'feudal' legislation from a self-consciously post-feudal world. Beginning in 1828 with a tentative repeal of clause 36 (clause 26 of the 1225 Magna Carta, on payments for writs of inquisition), larger and larger chunks of Magna Carta began to be chipped away from the statute book. Since the seventeenth century, it had been apparent that English law was a tangled thicket of statute and precedent. Successive royal charters or acts of Parliament had altered or replaced earlier legislation without any attempt to repeal or codify the laws thus rendered obsolete. Not until 1810, and even then only as a result of competition with the French, was there an official attempt to publish the laws of England. The nine vast folios of these *Statutes of the Realm* began, naturally enough, with Magna Carta 1215. They also revealed the degree to which the laws of England were inconsistent, self contradictory, riddled with textual confusions and weighed down with anachronisms from the medieval past. From 1828 onwards, Magna Carta itself came under scrutiny.

Seventeen of the thirty-seven clauses of the 1225 Magna Carta were repealed by Parliament in 1863, chiefly relating to 'feudal' incidents. Between 1879 and 1892 a further five clauses went. Clause 18 (clause 7 of the 1225 Magna Carta) was removed in 1925, and clause 26 (clause 18 of the 1225 charter, on debts and testamentary bequests) in 1947. The clauses relating to amercements and fines owed to the king, first heard of as long ago as 1100, in Henry I's Coronation Charter, enshrined in clauses 20–22 of the 1215 Magna Carta (clause 14 of the 1225 charter), were repealed in 1966. Attempts to repeal the remaining eight clauses then stalled, partly as a result of fears that the entire substructure of English law should not be so entirely scraped clean. As a result, four clauses of the 1215 Magna Carta (clauses 1, 13, 39 and 40, represented by clauses 1, 9, 29 and part of 37 of the 1225 charter) still remain in English law. Ironically, at precisely the same time that law reformers were repealing large parts of Magna Carta as redundant feudal legislation in Great Britain, seventeen of the states of America, beginning with South Carolina in 1836 and most recently with North Dakota in 1943, voted to embody Magna Carta fully within their statute books. As a result, far more of Magna Carta survives in American than in British law.

Law reform was itself a British response to a process of codification and rationalization of law already long familiar on the continent. Although most often portrayed as a distinctively English or Anglo-Saxon statement of liberties, Magna Carta had long ago been introduced to Europeans. The pope himself, via his legates, had confirmed the charter as early as 1216. It was known in France, where it enjoyed a role in constitutional debates of the fourteenth century. It played a small but significant part in the French Revolution of 1789. Its principal message, that kings must rule under law and that the law itself must be applied with 'due process'

was echoed in the French revolutionary Declaration of the Rights of Man. Thereafter, once the turmoil of revolution and Napoleonic war had subsided, the restoration of the Bourbon kings was made conditional upon their acceptance of a Charte Constitutionelle (1814). This was a document drafted in circumstances of British military conquest, with Magna Carta very obviously as archetype. It was accepted after Waterloo (1815) as the principal guarantee of the liberties of the French people.

A similar constitutional charter was drafted to establish Belgium as an independent kingdom following the Belgian revolution of 1830. Thereafter, the French and Belgian charters informed the revolutionaries of 1848 attempting to impose constitutional law across Europe. Meanwhile, in America a 'due process' clause directly derived from Magna Carta, was incorporated into constitutional law, promising that 'no person shall be … deprived of life, liberty or property without due process of law'. Words to this effect appear in the Fifth Amendment to the United States Constitution (1789, amended 1791), again in the Fourteenth Amendment passed in 1868 after the American Civil War, and again in articles 9, 10 and 11 of the United Nations' 1948 Universal Declaration of Human Rights.

In the meantime, the scene of King John granting Magna Carta to his barons became one of the stock images of Victorian history painting. Artists and engravers showed the king sometimes with pen in hand 'signing' the charter, sometimes holding the charter, sometimes pensive,

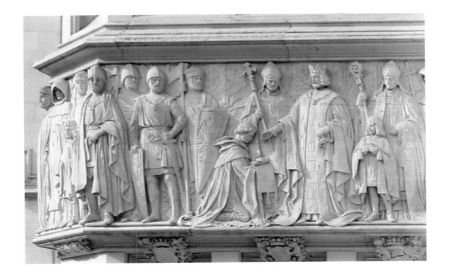

79 Several key clauses in the *Declaration of the Rights of Man*, penned by French revolutionaries, echoed Magna Carta: article III proclaimed that sovereignty lay within the nation and not within any individual, while article VII demanded due process in the application of the law. *Declaration of the Rights of Man and of the Citizen in 1789*, by Jean-Jacques-François Le Barbier. Photo © SteveStrummer.

80 The stone frieze to the Middlesex Guildhall depicting an Edwardian interpretation of events at Runnymede, carved by Henry Fehr *c*.1906. The building, opposite Parliament, is now the home of the United Kingdom Supreme Court. Photo: Ilona5555/ Shutterstock.

ALBERT HE[R]

sometimes angry. Scenes of this sort were regularly carved or moulded in bronze or stone, and used for the decoration of Victorian town halls. Instances of such decoration survive at Northampton and Rochdale, amongst many others. Burton-on-Trent favours an image of King John presenting Burton's market charter, but in similarly dramatic pose, today sadly defaced by local pigeons. Middlesex Guildhall, now the United Kingdom Supreme Court, opposite Parliament in Parliament Square, is decorated with a stone frieze showing John and the barons, carved by Henry Fehr *c.*1906. Across the Atlantic, in 1913, Frank Brangwyn painted a notably 'socialist' image of King John signing Magna Carta for the Cuyahoga county courthouse at Cleveland Ohio. Two years later, Albert Herter was paid $28,000 to paint four large murals for the Supreme Court Room of the State Capitol Building at Madison, Wisconsin, one of them showing a far more conservative and patriarchal King John at Runnymede. Another such was painted by Frederick Webb Ross for the the federal courthouse at Terre Haute, Indiana. Even grander images of the 'signing' of Magna Carta, amongst other great scenes of legal history, adorn the bronze doors of the Supreme Court Building in Washington, completed in 1935, 17 feet high and weighing 13 tons. More recently still, a stone 'baron' holding Magna Carta, flanked on the left by Moses with the laws of God, and on the right by a founding father with the American Declaration of Independence, was placed over the entrance to the Superior Court of Los Angeles, formally opened in 1959.

To the statesmen of Europe or America, Magna Carta seemed to embody stability and an age-old respect for legal process. Not so to radicals who demanded the clearing away of the dead wood of the past. For those in England who wanted parliamentary reform and an extension of the right to vote, Magna Carta remained, as it had been for Tom Paine, a totem of popular sovereignty. In the debates over the Great Reform Act of 1832, the historian, Thomas Babington Macaulay (1800–59), described the Reform Act, 'this Greater Charter of the Liberties of England', as a fit successor to the baronial charter of 1215. Thereafter, Magna Carta served as a model for the 'People's Charter' proposed by 'Chartists' calling for the extension of the parliamentary franchise. In the same spirit, from the 1860s onwards, suffragettes calling for 'Votes for Women' used the imagery of

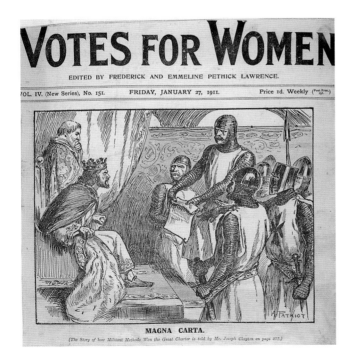

83 Edited by Frederick and Emmeline Pethick Lawrence, *Votes for Women* was the publication of the Women's Social and Political Union. An article in the issue of January 1911 describes how the militancy of the barons succeeded in securing Magna Carta. London, British Library, C.121.g.1 (Arncliffe Sennett Collection, vol. 13). © The British Library Board.

Magna Carta to appeal against what they regarded as the male 'tyranny' of the Westminster Parliament. With the spread of empire, Magna Carta and the English system of law were exported across the globe. The Privy Council in London now acted as court of last resort for many millions of imperial subjects. Even so, there was no clear agreement whether Magna Carta should serve as a universal or as a specifically 'Anglo-Saxon' guarantee of liberties. In 1914, for example, a group of Punjabi Sikhs seeking entry to Canada from the steamship *Komagatu Maru* were denied entry and imprisoned. They cited Magna Carta in their appeal against what they considered illegal detention. The Canadian courts and then the Court of Appeal in London denied their claims, confirming in the eyes of many that not all citizens of empire were considered equal under the law. This at a time when the late governor general of Canada, the 4th Earl Grey, was engaged in schemes to build a vast monument to British imperial race solidarity on the site of the former Crystal Palace at Sydenham Hill in south London, intended to commemorate the ties that bound England and America together through genetically-transmitted Anglo-Saxon 'freedom'.

Runnymede and Magna Carta remained integral to this tradition. As Rudyard Kipling, put it in 1905, in an inscription for Grahamstown, South Africa, intended to commemorate the English dead of the late Boer War:

84 When Punjabi Sikhs aboard the *Komagatu Maru* were denied entry to Canada, they cited Magna Carta in their appeal against what they considered illegal detention. 'Komagata Maru incident [Gurdit Singh with passengers]', 1 January 1914. Photo: Vancouver Public Library, 9 VPL photo 012.

They came of that same stubborn stock that stood
At Runnimede for Freedom without fear;
Wherefore they gave the treasure of their blood
To 'stablish Freedom here.

Plans for the celebration of Magna Carta's 700th anniversary in 1915 were entrusted to the chairmanship of Lord Bryce, himself a Liberal politician, professor of law and British ambassador to the United States from 1907 to 1913. In 1914, to commemorate the centenary of peace between Britain and America, it had been Bryce who had presided over the purchase and restoration of Sulgrave Manor in Northamptonshire, the Washington family home, as a monument to Anglo-American solidarity. Similar Anglo-American celebrations were planned for Magna Carta in 1915. They were necessarily suspended as a result of the outbreak of the First World War. The war itself, and the consequent great depression, dampened enthusiasm for Britain's imperial destiny, and with it tended to modulate the commemoration of Magna Carta to a rather more plangent, recessional key. Just such a transformation had already been apparent as early as 1911, in Kipling's verses on 'What say the Reeds at Runnymede?'. Here, the wind on Thameside whispers rather than trumpets England's ancient liberties. Only when threatened by tyranny does this whisper wake to a roar.

The very reeds of Runnymede were threatened with destruction after 1918, by potential building work in the meadow between Staines and Windsor. Rescue came only in 1929, thanks to the American-born Lady Fairhaven, widow of a successful British sewerage engineer who had brought modern sanitation to the town of Fairhaven, Massachusetts. Lady Fairhaven's gift of 188 acres of land at Runnymede to the National Trust was accompanied by the building of two lodges there as a memorial to her late husband. Their architect, Sir Edwin Lutyens, had himself achieved fame with his designs both for the imperial capital at New Delhi, and for the Cenotaph in Whitehall, intended to memorialize the dead of the First World War.

Thereafter, Runnymede has been endowed with further stone monuments, to the Air Force dead of the Second World War, and to President J.F. Kennedy, with only a domed rotunda, commissioned by the American Bar Association in 1957 to commemorate Magna Carta itself as a 'Symbol of Freedom Under Law'. The Kennedy memorial was

85 James Bryce, 1st Viscount Bryce, British ambassador to the United States from 1907 to 1913, chaired the committee overseeing the seven hundredth anniversary celebrations for Magna Carta. Photograph by Harris & Ewing. Washington D.C., Library of Congress, Prints and Photographs Division, (LC-H25-14059).

86 *previous page* The Magna Carta memorial at Runnymede, commissioned 1957 by the American Bar Association: 'Symbol of Freedom Under Law'. Photo: © Bill Reid.

87 *above* Cara Rogers Broughton, Lady Fairhaven, and her sons, who in 1929 gave to the National Trust 188 acres, including the area at Runnymede. Photo: Courtesy of The Millicent Library, Fairhaven, Massachusetts.

unveiled in May 1965, in theory during a year of celebrations for Magna Carta's 750th anniversary, in reality marked by rather uneasy efforts to balance the aspirations of the newly independent British Commonwealth nations against the tarnished glory of their mother country. This was the year of Winston Churchill's state funeral (24 January 1965). The great and good of Westminster, rather than focus on distant Runnymede, preferred to make Parliament itself the focus of their celebrations. The 14th meeting of the Commonwealth Heads of Nations was thus treated to a memorial service in St Paul's Cathedral on 10 June, in commemoration of Magna Carta, but with the climax of their celebrations reserved for

22 June, when a gathering to celebrate the 700th anniversary of Simon de Montfort's reforming Parliament of 1265 was staged in Westminster Hall, attended by the Queen, by both Houses of Parliament and by the speakers of more than forty other Commonwealth assemblies.

Britain was itself by this time entering a period of hedonism and social upheaval in the aftermath of post-war austerity. Even in 1965, however, Magna Carta remained a potent symbol not just of Englishness but of the wider Anglophone attachment to democratic process. Its heyday in this respect perhaps came twenty years earlier, during the Second World War and in particular during the dark days of 1940 and 1941 when Britain stood virtually alone against the assembled might of Nazi-occupied Europe. To Churchill and those keen to forge an alliance between a beleaguered Britain and the United States, Magna Carta symbolized all that was most threatened by totalitarianism. In 1941, as described in the next chapter, Churchill seriously entertained proposals that Lincoln Cathedral's Magna Carta be gifted to the American people. The scheme collapsed. But in its place, the 'Atlantic Charter' agreed between Churchill and Franklin D. Roosevelt at Placentia Bay, Newfoundland, in August 1941, served not only to define Anglo-American goals for the post-war world, but to maintain the idea of liberty as something that only a 'charter' could guarantee. Ironically, at more or less the same time that Churchill and Roosevelt

88 While Churchill's idea of permanently gifting the Lincoln Magna Carta to the US was quashed, the Atlantic charter agreed with Franklin Roosevelt in Placentia Bay, Newfoundland, in August 1941, perpetuated the idea of liberty as uniquely embodied in a 'charter'. Photo: *Franklin D. Roosevelt and Churchill in Quebec, Canada.* Washington D.C., U.S. National Archives and Records Administration, Franklin D. Roosevelt Library Public Domain Photographs, compiled 1882 – 1962 (195301).

were meeting, the supporters of Sir Oswald Mosley, interned since May 1940 as potential traitors, were using Magna Carta to argue their right to fair trial and release from imprisonment. Even at the height of war, and subsequently of Cold War, Magna Carta retained its power to serve all political causes, from the most radical to the ultra-conservative.

REFERENCES

In general, see the classic studies by Faith Thompson, *Magna Carta: Its Role in the Making of the English Constitution, 1300–1629* (Minneapolis 1948), and Anne Pallister, *Magna Carta: The Heritage of Liberty* (Oxford 1971). For America, see A.E. Dick Howard, *The Road from Runnymede: Magna Carta and Constitutionalism in America* (Charlottesville 1968); Gary L. McDowell, *The Language of Law and the Foundations of American Constitutionalism* (Cambridge 2010), and (to be used with caution) Peter Linebaugh, *The Magna Carta Manifesto: Liberties and Commons for All* (Berkeley 2008). I have benefited here from an as yet unpublished essay by Gordon Wood, and cf. G.S. Wood, *The Radicalism of the American Revolution* (New York 1992). More recently, see the contributions by Justin Champion, Miles Taylor, Joyce Lee Malcolm and Nicholas Vincent, in *Magna Carta: The Foundation of Freedom* (2015). For English exceptionalism, still classic is Alan Macfarlane, *The Origins of English Individualism* (Oxford 1978), and from a self-consciously radical perspective, see most recently Andy Wood, *The Memory of the People: Custom and Popular Senses of the Past in Early Modern England* (Cambridge 2013). For Magna Carta and the Lords Appellent, see the feature by Nigel Saul on the website http://magnacartaresearch.org. For Blackstone, Wilfrid Prest, *William Blackstone: Law and Letters in the Eighteenth Century* (Oxford 2008), esp. pp.138–41, 164–7, 209 (for the gout). For the clash between interpretations of 'liberty', J.C.D. Clark, *The Language of Liberty 1660-1832: Political Discourse and Social Dynamics in the Anglo-American World* (Cambridge 1994); David Armitage, *The Ideological Origins of the British Empire* (Cambridge 2000); Eran Shalev, *Rome Reborn on Western Shores: Historical Imagination and the Creation of the American Republic* (Charlottesville 2009), and the collection of essays edited by Jack P. Greene, *Exclusionary Empire: English Liberty Overseas, 1600–1900* (Cambridge 2009). For Lord Grey, and the site of Runnymede, Thomas Otte, '"The Shrine at Sulgrave": The Preservation of the Washington Ancestral Home as an "English Mount Vernon" and Transatlantic Relations', in *Towards World Heritage: International Origins of the Preservation Movement, 1870–1930*, ed. M. Hall (Farnham 2011), pp.109–135. For the abortive celebrations of 1915, see the introduction to *Magna Carta Commemoration Essays*, ed. H. E. Malden (London 1917), and for those of 1965, *The Seventh Centenary of Simon de Montfort's Parliament 1265–1965: An Account of the Commemorative Ceremonies and an Historical Narrative* (London 1965).

CHAPTER 5

The charter as artefact:
Winston Churchill and America's
Magna Carta

November 4, 1939.

Dear Archie:-

Your plan for taking care of the
Magna Carta during the war seems to me
excellent and I see no difficulties except
possibly one. There may be a good many
cartoons and some ribald remarks in and out
of the press about the surrender of the
great British Magna Carta to the young
stepchild that goes by the name of the
United States.

I think that in your remarks you
can make the happy suggestion that there
could properly be criticism if the Magna
Carta had been turned over to the executive
branch of the government, i.e., the King
John of modern days; but that as the library
is the Library of Congress the precious
document has been retained in the safe hands
of the barons and the commoners.

Very sincerely yours,

[signature: Franklin D. Roosevelt]

Honorable Archibald MacLeish,
Library of Congress,
Washington, D. C.

AC.9636

I N 1939, bowing to representations from the British government's Department of Overseas Trade, and ultimately to a personal request from the British Foreign Secretary, the Dean and Chapter of Lincoln agreed that their original of the 1215 Magna Carta, since the time of its first issue stored in the Lincoln Cathedral archives, should be allowed to travel out of England for public display at New York World's Fair. The British government insured the charter against loss or damage up to a value of £100,000, clearly in the hope that so remarkable an object, exhibited in the USA, might foster closer Anglo-American co-operation.

As it transpired, the Lincoln charter arrived in America just as political crisis in Europe reached its climax. Hitler's threatened invasion of Poland, the Nazi-Soviet pact, and the fact that no official alliance existed by which Britain and France could call upon American assistance in the event of war, raised Anglo-American relations to the very top of the agenda for many officials within the British Foreign Office. It was on the eve of this crisis, in June 1939, that a letter was received at 10 Downing Street, addressed to the British prime minister, Neville Chamberlain, by the prominent Conservative politician and former government minister for the Colonies, Leo Amery. Amery had himself received a letter from an American citizen, J. W. Hamilton, Secretary to the International Magna Carta Day Association, whose patrons included yet another prominent British Conservative politician: the former prime minister, Stanley Baldwin.

What Hamilton proposed, and what Amery now supported was that the Lincoln Magna Carta be permanently gifted by Great Britain to the United States of America. There, so Hamilton suggested, 'It might do more finally to obliterate all recollection of previous disagreements by reasserting the common origin of our liberties than anything that could be imagined'. To offset any loss to the Dean and Chapter of Lincoln, it was suggested that the British government pay sufficient financial

89 *left* Franklin Roosevelt was delighted with the suggestion that Lincoln Cathedral's Magna Carta should temporarily reside in the Library of Congress during the war. He even went so far as to anticipate adverse press reactions, offering advice to Archibald MacLeish, the Librarian of Congress. Franklin Delano Roosevelt (1882–1945) to Archibald MacLeish (1892–1982) regarding plans to bring Magna Carta to the Library of Congress, November 4, 1939. Washitngton, D.C., Library of Congress Archives, Manuscript Division, Library of Congress (001) mc0001.

compensation to enable the Dean and Chapter to shore up the fabric of their cathedral, considered to be in imminent danger of collapse.

Chamberlain's response, sent at the end of July 1939 and effectively dictated by British Foreign Office officials, was that 'Such a gift would merely be represented in malevolent quarters as a clumsy bribe to gain American goodwill'. The charter was too rare an object simply to be given away, and of the small number of originals, one at least had been burned during the Great Fire of London (clearly a case of confusion here between the Great Fire of 1666 and the Cotton Library fire of 1731). Amery was asked to advise Hamilton and his supporters that to release any of the original Magna Cartas from British custody 'would give rise to insuperable opposition'. So the matter was dropped, at least for the moment.

By the time that the World's Fair closed, in the autumn of 1939, Britain and Germany were at war. Rather than risk Magna Carta to the high seas now patrolled by German U-boats, the charter was deposited for safe-keeping in the Library of Congress. The occasion was marked by a suitably patriotic speech from the British Ambassador, Lord Lothian. Lothian reminded his listeners that:

> Inscribed on the musty parchment before us, we see the nucleus of most of our liberties, of trial by jury, of *habeas corpus*, of the principles of [no] taxation without representation, of the Bill of Rights and of the whole constitution of modern democracy … The principles which underlay Magna Carta are the ultimate foundations of your [American] liberties no less than ours. Samuel Adams appealed to the "rights of Magna Carta to which the colonists, as free citizens, have undoubted claim". It was in their name that your ancestors threw the tea into Boston harbor and rejected the claim of King George III to tax the colonies for defense. It was in their name that, after bitter sacrifices and frustration, they drew up that constitution which Mr Gladstone, one of the greatest champions of human freedom, described as "the most wonderful work ever struck off at a given time by the brain and purpose of man".

The press coverage of this event, and of Lord Lothian's speech, was for the most part enthusiastically pro-British. The *Chicago Daily News*, for example, reported that:

91 Archibald MacLeish, Librarian of Congress (left), receiving Magna Carta from the British Ambassador, Philip Kerr, 11th marquess of Lothian, for safekeeping during the War. Photograph: Harris & Ewing. Washington, D.C., Library of Congress, Prints and Photographs Division (20540).

Deposit of one of the four remaining originals of Magna Carta in the Library of Congress is somewhat like a visit of a venerable grandparent to the home of grandchildren. The forty-eight bills of rights in our States' constitutions, and the first ten amendments of the United States Constitution, are direct descendants of this medieval parchment.

The *Augusta Chronicle*, on the same day, suggested that:

> It is of deep significance that it should fall to the lot of the United States Government to protect this symbol of the rights, liberties and privileges of our Anglo-Saxon friends abroad, because with democracy under fire throughout the world, the United States stands as a bulwark of the democratic way of life and a strong defender of the right of freemen to enjoy the privileges set down in our Constitution and the Magna Carta.

Not everyone was so enthusiastic. Amongst the advocates of American isolation, General Hugh Johnson, whose vividly expressed opinions were syndicated across North America, was prepared to accept the dependence of the United States Constitution upon a legal tradition reaching back to Magna Carta, but remained deeply suspicious of British motives. 'Would it seem to be too much like mooching,' General Johnson wrote, 'to suggest

that, instead of just letting us hold this one, they give it to us outright?'

In April 1940, the charter itself once made the journey between Washington and New York, to be displayed in the British Pavilion of the 1940 New York World's Fair. There, on 4 July 1940, a bomb plot was only narrowly foiled through the quick thinking of two policemen, killed in the subsequent explosion. A reminder this that public opinion in America was by no means so universally pro-British in 1940 as it was to become by 1945. Magna Carta's return to New York coincided with a new escalation of hostilities in Europe. In May 1940, Germany invaded Belgium, Holland and France. Within a matter of weeks the British army, or what remained of it, had been evacuated from the beaches of Dunkirk. France itself capitulated in the face of overwhelming German military superiority. It was at this unprecedented moment of crisis, amidst the darkest of threats not merely to Britain but to the entire future of democracy, that J.W. Hamilton, Secretary to the International Magna Carta Day Association, once again wrote to England, this time to the King George VI, suggesting that 15 June be celebrated each year throughout the English-speaking world as Magna Carta Day, and that the Lincoln Magna Carta, still on exhibition in New York, be presented to the people of the United States once the World's Fair ended later that year.

This proposal met with a response only a little less lukewarm than Hamilton's earlier proposal of 1939. On 10 October 1940, John Colville, private secretary to the prime minister, wrote to the Foreign Office backing the idea of a gift of Magna Carta to the American people, and reporting that it had already excited the personal interest of Mrs Churchill. Once again, however, the Foreign Office prevaricated. The charter itself was due to return in December to safekeeping in the Library of Congress. But proposals were afoot in the United States for a coast-to-coast touring exhibition, taking in ten leading universities, with the city of Cleveland, Ohio offering to meet any additional insurance premium. Canada also expressed an interest in hosting such a tour. On 17 December, a reluctant approach was made from the Foreign Office to the Dean of Lincoln, but with the openly expressed hope that the Dean and Chapter would refuse permission for any nationwide tour. This is precisely what happened, with the Dean, R. A. Mitchell, writing on 3 January 1941 that no permission would be granted for the charter to tour America unless he could be assured that the tour was 'a matter of urgent national importance'.

Still, however, the idea persisted that the charter might be given to the American people. On 13 March 1941, in the immediate aftermath of the Lend-Lease Act intended to bring American aid to the British war effort, a private American citizen, T. North Whitehead, once again raised the idea of such a gift, suggesting that the Dean and Chapter of Lincoln be compensated for the loss of their charter by the grant either of £100,000 in war bonds and one of the British Museum originals of the 1215 Magna Carta, or of £250,000 in war bonds in full settlement of all claims, the gift to be announced by the king or prime minister, Winston Churchill, in a broadcast address to the American people. Now, for the first time, the British Foreign Office began to change tack from cautious disapproval to lukewarm support. Officials there noted that Churchill himself had referred to Magna Carta in his statement on the passage of the Lend-Lease Act in March and that, at this crucial stage in the war, anything likely to enhance Anglo-American friendship was heartily to be welcomed. Propelled by the active support of both Duff Cooper, Minister of Information, and R.A. ('Rab') Butler, junior minister in the Foreign Office, the idea was rapidly passed up the chain from departmental level to Downing Street and the British War Cabinet. As Sir Alexander Cadogan, Permanent Under Secretary at the Foreign Office, minuted in a form of words subsequently adopted as the official Foreign Office communiqué to the prime minister's office on 18 March 1941:

> I have always wanted to do this. I should like to say to the Americans, "You are giving us aid on a scale which makes it almost impossible for us materially to repay. Any material repayment we could offer can only look insignificant. We shall owe you a debt which can never be discharged. May we give you – at least as a token of our feeling – something of no intrinsic value whatsoever: a bit of parchment, more than 700 years old, rather the worse for wear. You know what it means to us. We believe it means as much to you. Will you accept it as a symbol and a seal of our compact to fight to the last against the forces of evil?

The War Cabinet discussed the affair, but opinion was now divided. Some members of Cabinet were in favour. Others were concerned as to how such a presentation might be viewed by the British Dominions. If an original Magna Carta were to be given to the United States, might not

92 Duff Cooper (opposite below), Minister of Information, and R.A Butler (opposite above), junior minister in the Foreign Office, who helped to advance the idea of gifting the Lincoln Magna Carta to the US. Alfred Duff Cooper, 1st Viscount Norwich. Photograph: Howard Coster, NPGx11434 © National Portrait Gallery, London. Richard Austen Butler, 1st Baron Butler of Saffron Walden. Photograph: Walter Stoneman, NPGx45740. © National Portrait Gallery, London.

giving it, we rise to the height of liberty and
bear all the fighting strength that is in us.
Without the aid which you have promised,
we might not conquer, but with it, we
certainly shall. All that we have we
shall give. When material strength on
either side has been added up, there may
not appear to be much disparity, but
the "hidden weapon" of moral force will
turn the Scales, and the truth will prevail."

　　　I have presumed to put the foregoing
in inverted commas, but I cannot aspire
to draft speeches or declarations. I only
hazard a line on which something
worthy could be drafted.

　　　　　　　A.B.
　　　　　　　　　March 13. 1941.

　I should like the Prime Minister
to read these minutes by the week-
end.
　I am very much in favour of
making this gift. I would repay
Lincoln Cathedral by giving them
one of the British Museum copies.
This would necessitate a Bill & thus
give an opportunity for airing demo-
-cratic principles here.
This psychological moment is probably as good as any other.

Mr. Butler

Bring before
Cabinet on
Monday.

WS
13.3

RCB 14/3

Australia, Canada, New Zealand and South Africa all expect similar gifts? The transfer to Lincoln Cathedral of one of the British Museum Magna Cartas would necessitate an act of Parliament. Some, including Leo Amery in a letter to Churchill of 18 March 1941, now demanded not only that the gift of Magna Carta to America be made but that it be made as soon as possible, suggesting 15 June 1941, Magna Carta Day, as a suitable date, and urging that preliminary discussions be held to ensure that President Roosevelt prepare a speech of welcome. Churchill himself has marked in red ink here, in a memorandum dated 21 March 1941, 'I prefer this, as it gives more time'. At this point, however, cold reality began to dawn upon the scheme's supporters.

So far, Cadogan, Butler and their allies had built many a castle in the air. They had discussed war bonds, and imagined Magna Cartas moving from the British Museum to Lincoln and from Lincoln to the United States. No-one, however, had considered the harsh reality that the Lincoln Magna Carta was not the British government's property to give away. In particular, no approach whatsoever had been made to the Dean and Chapter of Lincoln to establish how they might view such a gift. Bearing in mind the Dean of Lincoln's refusal to countenance the much less radical proposal of a touring exhibition of the charter, it must surely have been apparent that the Dean and Chapter would most likely view the gift of their charter to America not with approval but with outrage and dismay.

The extraordinarily close association of the Lincoln copy with Lincoln Cathedral, where it had always been stored apparently since the time of its first issue in 1215, and the fact that the British Museum only possessed two originals of the 1215 charter, one of which was burned and entirely illegible, the other of which was legible but without a seal, were facts likely to pose yet further problems. The Dean and Chapter would be unlikely to accept a gift of the burned and illegible 1215 charter, but giving them the unburned copy would be to leave no legible original of the 1215 charter still in the British Museum. Despite suggestions that the Dean and Chapter of Lincoln, or if that failed the Dean and Chapter of Salisbury be effectively bullied into giving away their 1215 Magna Cartas for the greater public good and as if of their own free will, by the second week of April 1941, Churchill had decided to back off. 'Better leave it alone', he minuted to Butler. By November 1941, although the idea of giving Magna Carta to the United States had by no means been dropped, the prevailing view was that such a gift were better left until the war itself was over. The entry of

93 *opposite* Alexander Cadogan's memo proposing that the Lincoln Magna Carta be gifted to the US. Note the hearty agreement by Rab Butler, and Winston Churchill's comments in red ink. London, National Archives, TNA FO371/26269. © National Archives, London.

94 *above* Sir Alexander Cadogan, Permanent Under Secretary at the British Foreign Office. From *Potsdam Album*, 1945. Independence, MO, Truman Library Photographs, 63-1457-74. © Harry S. Truman Library.

the United States into the war in December 1941, in the aftermath of the attacks on Pearl Harbour, merely confirmed this assessment.

After a period when, together with other national treasures, the Lincoln charter was sent from Washington to Fort Knox for safekeeping, the saga of how to give Magna Carta to the United States resumed in January 1945. By this time, the librarian of Congress had begun to wonder whether the loan of the Lincoln Magna Carta might be continued after the war, perhaps by the replacement of the Lincoln charter with one of the other originals still in the UK, perhaps on an indefinite basis. The return of the Lincoln charter to England was still being discussed a year later, by which time the Library of Congress was proclaiming that 15 million Americans had taken the opportunity to view it. Lord Halifax, British ambassador to Washington, proposed to return the charter to England in the safe-keeping of the captain of the *Queen Elizabeth* sailing from New York on 18 January 1946. Doubts as to whether the captain would be prepared to accept so heavy a responsibility were allayed only when the Foreign Office sent an official request to the captain for his assistance. The charter came back to England not by diplomatic bag but in the same bronze and armour-plated case, weighing 60 lbs, in which it had previously been displayed in Congress. This was now presented as a token of thanks to the Dean and Chapter of Lincoln. Far from Lincoln losing its charter to the USA, the US thus lost its showcase to Lincoln. The ship docked at Southampton on 23 January, and by the following day the British press was reporting Magna Carta's imminent return to Lincoln. There was, nonetheless, a postscript.

On 5 April 1946, a special service held in Lincoln cathedral to welcome back the charter was interrupted by an unknown woman who stood up at the back of the Cathedral shouting 'I denounce Magna Charta: it is a relic, and relics are denounced in the Bible'. Whether or not this denunciation was heeded by the Almighty, it was soon afterwards noticed that the Lincoln charter was showing signs of wear and tear, and in particular of fading to various of its letters. By December 1950, it was judged necessary to break into the armour-plated case and to send the charter to the Public Record Office for conservation. There, a minor disaster occurred. The Deputy

95 *opposite* Public viewing of Magna Carta on 28 November 1939, after its deposit in the Congressional Library. Washington D.C., Library of Congress, Prints and Photographs Division (LC-DIG-hec-27725).

96 *below* Magna Carta is placed into the vault of the RMS *Queen Elizabeth* by William Peters, Master-at-Arms (left), Sir Francis Evans, British Consul General in New York (centre), and Commodore Sir G.P. Bisset, Commander of the vessel. Washington, D.C., Library of Congress, Prints and Photographs Division (LC-DIG-ppmsca-38459).

Keeper of the Record Office, Sir Hilary Jenkinson, was forced to admit by March 1951 that the charter had suffered 'indubitable and regrettable' damage. This he blamed upon 'internal deterioration from some organic cause, for example a fungoid affection which might have developed in the long period during which it was, as I understand, immured between sheets of glass.' – words which have all the false authority of someone attempting rather to conceal than to reveal the truth. In reality, blame is to be attached here not to some imaginary fungus, but almost certainly to the fact that the charter was deliberately and perhaps carelessly dampened in the Record Office in order that it might be rebacked with modern parchment.

Meanwhile, no sooner did one Magna Carta return to England, than another prepared to cross the Atlantic in the opposite direction. Following discussions with the British Museum, it was now proposed that the Lacock Abbey original of the 1225 Magna Carta be sent to Washington in place of the Lincoln charter, on loan for a fixed period of two years. The Lacock charter had spent the war buried in the grounds of Lacock Abbey and had only recently been gifted to the Museum by Miss Talbot, Lacock's owner. The proposal was accompanied by further suggestions, backed by the newly promoted Lieutenant-Commander Douglas Fairbanks Jr. that 15 June be set aside as a public holiday throughout the English-speaking world.

The Lacock charter did indeeed cross to America, even though its loan necessitated a special act of Parliament, introduced to the House of Lords in May 1946 in a debate chiefly memorable for their lordships' inability to agree whether Magna Carta should be spelt with or without an 'h'. In December the charter and Miss Talbot were both transported across the Atlantic at the British taxpayer's expense, although in those days of post-war austerity, it was determined that Miss Talbot should be maintained whilst in America on an allowance to cover subsistence set at the hardly princely figure of three dollars a day, rising to eight dollars should she have to stay in a hotel, 'the allowance to cease on the day of sailing of the first homeward-bound ship that can accomodate her after the ceremony'. This despite the fact that in 1945 Miss Talbot had gifted Lacock Abbey and its entire estate village to the National Trust, at the same time giving the British Museum her Magna Carta, which she had carefully buried under one of the Abbey floors during the war wrapped in a box inside flannel and the whole enclosed in a metal container. Only she and the estate coachman were privy to its exact whereabouts. Even in the 1940s, Miss Talbot's Magna Carta would have fetched a king's ransom had she chosen to sell it rather than give it away. But as James Lees-Milne, secretary of the National Trust, recorded in his celebrated *Diary*, on first visiting Lacock in December 1943:

> (Miss Talbot) is a dear, selfless woman, and extremely high-minded. She has the most unbending sense of duty towards her tenants and the estate, to the extent that she allows herself only a few hundreds (of pounds) a year on which to live. She spends hardly a farthing on herself, and lives like an anchorite … (The abbey) was warm and smelled sweet and cosy. Miss Talbot said "I hate fresh air. It is the cause of most of our ills in England."

In December 1948, two years after its arrival in the United States, and despite attempts to prolong its stay including yet further suggestions that it be gifted to the American nation, the Lacock Magna Carta returned to England in the custody of A. J. Collins of the British Museum, arriving on New Year's Day. For the moment, the USA was once again without a document which the Librarian of Congress, writing to the British Foreign Secretary, had only recently described as possessing:

Fully as much significance for citizens of the United States as it does for the citizens of the United Kingdom. While there exist in public institutions in England several copies of the document as originally issued ... there is not in the United States any such copy.

As for the idea that 15 June should be celebrated throughout the English-speaking world as Magna Carta Day, this too became buried under a dead weight of petty objections. It had been hoped in some quarters that such a celebration might serve as a valuable weapon in the nascent Cold War. In January 1947, an anonymous official in the British Dominions Office had pointed out the advantages that such celebrations might have, not only for Anglophone democracy but for the furtherance of British colonial interests:

> The forces of law and order in the modern world are deficient in slogans, rallying-points and ceremonial. The disruptive elements of modern societies on the contrary, with their Communist Manifesto, Red Flag and the 1st May celebrations, are well provided. How important these assets are to the Communist crusaders is rarely as fully appreciated as it should be by the critics of Marxism. The difficulty has always been for the constructive forces in society to achieve some rational symbolism which can at the same time harness and inspire some genuine enthusiasm and emotional support ... Magna Carta offers more promise in this respect. Hopes should naturally not be pitched too high, but success may well exceed them, reversing perhaps the experience over Empire Day.

Set against this, however, were the objections of the Ministry of Education, which pointed out that most American schools were on vacation by 15 June, so that the proposed day of celebrations could have little or no effect in the indoctrination of American youth. Moreover, far from combatting communism, the proposal might actively encourage communist propaganda. As the British Foreign Office official, E.J. Perowne, pointed out, the charter itself had been issued not to the common people but to the much more restricted class of 'free men': a fact which might well incline the communists against it. Worse still, a senior civil servant, K.W. Blaxter of the Colonial Office, minuted in February 1947, that there was even the risk that Magna Carta might be interpreted by ignorant or ungrateful 'Colonial peoples' not as a symbol of British authority, but as in some way a guarantor of popular rights. As Blaxter pointed out:

> In some colonies where ill-disposed politicians are ever on the lookout for opportunities to misinterpret our good intentions, its celebration might well cause embarrassment, and in general there is a danger that the Colonial peoples might be led into an uncritical enthusiasm for a document which they had not read but which they presumed to contain guarantees of every so-called "right" they might be interested at the moment in claiming.

There can have been few more honest, yet few more extraordinary statements ever penned by a British writer on Magna Carta.

In the world of post-colonial politics, not all was gloom. In particular, thanks to a fortuitous rediscovery, the people of Australia were destined to become proud owners of an original Magna Carta. The story here is a complicated one, which I have told elsewhere, and of which a summary must suffice. In 1951, the headmaster and governors of the King's School at Bruton in Somerset found themselves in possession of a Magna Carta from the 1297 issue. Local legend suggested that the school had acquired this document by accident, perhaps discovered in a boy's desk in the late 1930s. In reality, it had come to them by rather more devious means. In origin, theirs was the version of the 1297 charter sent originally into the county of Surrey. From there, the document found its way to Easebourne Priory on the Surrey Sussex border, perhaps because the nuns of Easebourne had a connection to the then sheriff, an office whose holders administered Surrey and Sussex as a joint concern. After the Reformation of the sixteenth century, the muniments of Easebourne were dispersed. Many of the more important of the priory's early documents found their way, means unknown, into the possession of a west country solicitor, John Louch. At Louch's death in 1905, his son, Francis Quekett Louch, presented the majority of his early deeds to the British Museum, now the British Library. These included an original of the 1297 Forest Charter, also sent to Surrey, also previously preserved at Easebourne, today British Library Additional Charter 53712 (below no.39). This is undoubtedly 'twin' to

the Bruton School Magna Carta, which meanwhile seems to have escaped from Louch family possession to Bruton School, where it was rediscovered c.1936. One possibility is that it was accidentally transferred, within the Louch family solicitor's office from a deed box concerning the Easebourne estate to a deed box concerning Bruton School.

Offered for sale in 1951, the charter was valued at £12,500, including seller's commission. Originally, the British Museum intended to bid, but could not meet the asking price. There was a heated dispute in the government committee charged with controlling the export of items of historic significance. By this time, however, the Australian government had become involved, with a press campaign launched to bring Magna Carta to the southern hemisphere, in time for the state visit to Britain by the Australian prime minister, Robert Menzies. The money was not easily found, but in part out of fear that the document would otherwise be sold to America, in late October 1952, Magna Carta was dispatched from London, arriving in Sydney Harbour a month later. Displayed in the King's Hall of the Australian Parliament House in Canberra, at the Melbourne Olympics of 1956, and briefly in the Australian National Library to which there was a foiled attempt to remove it in 1968, Australia's Magna Carta continues to remind its many visitors of the ties that bind Great Britain to the constitutional democracies of the British Commonwealth. The fact that its rediscovery and removal to the Pacific rim was attended by so complicated a series of accidents and institutional rivalries should serve as a reminder of the birth pangs of the post-imperial world.

Meanwhile, the Magna Cartas remaining in British institutional collections slumbered on, more or less unmolested. There were Commonwealth celebrations in London, in June 1965, to mark the charter's 750th anniversary, but these events were muted, not least for

99 Permanent display of 1297 Magna Carta at Parliament House in Canberra, Australia. © Parliament House, Canberra, A.C.T.

fear of exciting controversy in lands that now considered themselves
fully independent and with a less than perfect memory of the 'liberties'
supposedly guaranteed to them under previous British rule. Ironically, it
was the approach of another anniversary, dear to the very first of Britain's
colonies to achieve independence, that stirred up the next great row over
Magna Carta.

In the two hundred years since the American Revolution, a large part
of the American public had come to regard Magna Carta as a guarantee
not only of their own rights and liberties, but as a peculiarly significant
part of the American heritage. The abortive Magna Carta celebrations of
1915 had been sponsored by a former British ambassador to Washington,
himself closely involved in Anglo-American friendship networks. As early
as 1929, it had been with American support, and to a large extent with
American money, that the site of Runnymede had been saved for public
ownership, donated to the National Trust by Cara Leland Broughton,
Lady Fairhaven, the daughter of one of the founders of Rockefeller's
Standard Oil Company. Throughout the 1950s and 60s, Runnymede

100 Gerald Ford, President of
the United States, and Queen
Elizabeth II at the state dinner on
17 July 1976 in the White House
to celebrate the US bicentennial.
Photo, Ricardo Thomas.
Washington D.C., White House
Photograph, Courtesy Gerald R.
Ford Library (B0570-24).

had continued to serve as a shrine to Anglo-American friendship, with its domed rotunda paid for by the American Bar Association, and after 1965, its John F. Kennedy Memorial, approached by fifty irregular granite steps and carved with words from President Kennedy's inaugural address, promising 'to ensure the survival and success of liberty'.

Hence the very particular concern that the British government began to express for the proper celebration of the events of 1776. The bicentennial of 1976, it was argued, must on no account become an occasion for anti-American or anti-British sentiment. As early as 1971, it was apparent to those to whom such things mattered that Great Britain would need to plan carefully ahead, to ensure that the bicentennial was marked with sufficient pomp and circumstance. In particular, influential figures in British government were concerned that the celebrations should have as their 'centre-piece' some appropriately magnificent gift. Only by such means could Britain remind America that she was still a nation to be reckoned with, prepared, after two hundred years, to remain magnanimous in the celebration of ancient defeat.

It was to this end that a bicentennial Liaison Committee was established, under the chairmanship of Lord Lothian, cousin and successor to the peer who, as British Ambassador in 1939, had deposited the Lincoln Magna Carta in the Library of Congress for safekeeping. Lord Lothian's committee was supplied with a budget, of £500,000, and was basically told to get on with it: above all to ensure that the bicentennial went 'with a bang'. By what precise means the worm entered the bud remains unclear, but by the end of 1974 the Liaison Committee, having beaten around many a bush, arrived at a rather startling proposition.

In 1974, as in 1939, an undertaking had been made by a British institutional archive that itself possessed an original Magna Carta, in this instance the British Library, that it would be prepared to loan its charter to America, subject to guarantees over safe transport and handling. The charter in question was the unburned but unsealed original of the 1215 Magna Carta, Cotton Augustus ii.106 (below no.2). As on an earlier occasion, what had begun as a proposed loan was very swiftly transformed by the politicians into the possibility of a permanent gift.

An original of Magna Carta, so Lord Lothian's Liaison Committee now decided, should be presented to Washington by Her Majesty the Queen, as a suitably memorable gift from the British Parliament to the Congress and people of the USA. This was best done by persuading the

101 Winston Churchill MP (grandson of the wartime prime minister), who, as part of the Bicentennial Liaison Committee, favoured the gift of the British Library's Magna Carta to the US. Photo: David Fowler/ Shutterstock.

British Library (recently released from its dependence upon the British Museum) that its own Magna Carta, due to be loaned to Washington for the year of the bicentennial celebrations, be instead transformed either into an outright gift or a loan in perpetuity. Meeting on 12 February 1975, less than a year away from the rapidly approaching day of reckoning, the Liaison Committee recommended that such a gift be made. Those members who were in favour included Sir John Foster, Sir John Catlin, Lady Harlech and Winston Churchill MP, grandson of the wartime prime minister, who at this time was still a force to be reckoned with, and who played a prominent role in the bullying and bluster that ensued.

As another committee member, Sir Edward Ford, formerly of the Queen's private office, pointed out, even were an outright gift to prove impossible, the advantage of a permanent loan, say of no less than 99 years, was that no payment would be required and that the question of ownership would not arise. By contrast, were one of the English cathedrals to be persuaded to give up its Magna Carta, or even were the British Library to give one of its, there would have to be financial compensation. Since the British Library Magna Carta was valued, at

the most conservative estimate, at over £1 million, necessitating an insurance premium of £75,000, and since the Liaison Committee was supposed to be working to a budget of no more than £500,000, the mathematics here made sound sense.

As in 1939, or 1941, or again after 1947, the reaction from the British Library was both swift and unambiguous. No such gift or loan should be allowed or even contemplated. To give away any of the Library's

102 When the idea of making a gift of the British Library's Magna Carta to the US was ruled out, Harold Wilson suggested a 'centre-piece' gift from the archives of Windsor Castle. © Allen Warren.

Magna Cartas would be openly to flout the terms of the bequests by which both Sir Robert Cotton in the seventeenth century, and Miss Talbot in the twentieth, had gifted their manuscripts to the nation. Moreover, to give away any part of the national heritage was surely to invite demands from other parties even better entitled than the USA to claim the return not just of books and manuscripts but of objects and antiquities whose proper display in British collections was virtually the sole justification for their remaining in British custody. Were Magna Carta to go to Washington, then what else might the London museums be forced to disgorge: the Lindisfarne Gospels, the bronzes of Benin, even, God forbid, the Elgin Marbles?

Not only in the British Library but in its old rival, the Public Record Office, there were clearly concerns that the British Government's search for a 'centre-piece' to the 1976 celebrations might result in the giving away of documentary treasures. Such fears were well founded. Not only was an unofficial search instituted in the Public Record Office to find such a potential 'centre-piece', but when that failed, according to a conversation with the prime minister, Harold Wilson, reported in February 1975, Mr Wilson himself suggested that a search be made of the Round Tower at Windsor Castle where, he claimed, there was 'a great deal of absolutely fascinating original stuff going back to a very early stage in British history'. The fact that any of this 'stuff' which could conceivably belong to government had long ago been transferred to the Public Record Office, and that the Windsor Castle archives were themselves the private property and hence the personal possession of Her Majesty the Queen seems not unduly to have troubled the prime minister.

Whilst the prime minister failed to stand guard over the national heritage, the Americans themselves came to the rescue. On 14 February 1975, Elizabeth Hamer Kegan, Assistant Librarian of Congress wrote to Jeffrey Ede, Keeper of the Public Record Office, to express alarm at the very idea of the British government presenting Magna Carta to America as a gift. 'Removal of an important document from archival custody', she wrote, 'Even by an order in Council, act of Parliament, of whatever is necessary – would set an unfortunate precedent for archival and public establishments everywhere, including the United States.'

James B. Rhoads, Archivist of the United States himself wrote to Ede: 'I am in complete agreement with your position on not alienating official

103 Armed with the support of librarians and curators, Viscount Eccles, chairman of the British Library Board, wrote to the Liaison committee rejecting the idea of gifting the British Library's Magna Carta to the US. David McAdam Eccles, 1st Viscount Eccles. Photo: Bassano Ltd. NPG x77266. © National Portrait Gallery, London.

government documents … Once begun, the precedent could become an embarrassment to us all.'

If a presentation were to be made, all concerned suggested, then it should be made from a private rather than a public collection. Armed with such support from America and no doubt emboldened by discussions of his own conducted with various of his fellow archivists and keepers of public collections, on 6 March 1975, Lord Eccles, Chairman of the British Library Board, wrote to Lord Lothian and his committee in no uncertain terms:

> For us to make a permanent loan or gift of the one good copy [of Magna Carta] we possess and propose to lend for one year would be considered an irresponsible act on the part of a national institution such as the British Library. Far from generating goodwill, it would cause a storm of protest in this country. Moreover, you will know that in 1966 the Trustees of the British Museum turned down a request from Canada for a loan of Magna Carta in connection with the Canadian Centennial

104 A replica of Magna Carta in gold leaf within a gold enamel case, created by the goldsmith Louis Osman, displayed in the Crypt of the US Capital. © U.S. Capital, Washington D.C.

Celebrations held in 1967. If it became known that having turned down a loan request from the North American member of the Commonwealth it was now intended to house the manuscript permanently in the United States, the protests would spread from this country to Canada and beyond.

So far, so good. The suggestion that a liaison committee that itself enjoyed only semi-official status could somehow determine the fate of manuscripts that had been in public ownership for hundreds of years, scattering the public records to the winds like so much celebratory confetti, was soundly and satisfactorily squashed. The committee was forced to think again. Its eventual solution, whose fruits are still to be seen in the Rotunda of Congress in Washington, was to commission a well-respected goldsmith, Mr Louis Osman, to make a gold and enamel case and, within it, a replica of Magna Carta on gold leaf. It was in this case that the British Library charter was displayed during its time in Washington in 1976. On the charter's return to England, both the case and the gold facsimile were gifted to Congress by the British Houses of Parliament.

The story of the display case is not without its diversions. Proposals, for example, that the case be mounted on a 300 million year-old, three ton granite rock hewn from the sea shore of South Uist in the Outer Hebrides encountered all manner of problems, not least the cost of hiring the Royal Air Force to pluck this boulder from the waves, and the resistance of the security officers in Washington to the idea of anything so massive being placed within so sensitive a place as the Rotunda of Congress. Mr Osman's likening of his display cabinet to an illuminated medieval manuscript inspired a magnificently pedantic exchange with the British Library, whose Keeper of Manuscripts, D. H. Turner, objected to the term 'illuminated manuscript' as a very loose phrase to describe the art of what were in reality several centuries, and who suggested instead that the display case be thought of as a 'casket' or 'reliquary', enshrining something of no aesthetic value, like a piece of bone, or in this instance parchment, but of 'untold thaumaturgical importance'. The Foreign Office official who compiled the file has placed a marginal exclamation mark next to this last phrase, and a letter of 12 December 1975 from the Information Counsellor in the British Embassy at Washington gently points out that Mr Turner's 'analogy of the "reliquary" with a "casket" is most unhappy, (since) over here casket means coffin'.

Some surprise was expressed at the British end of things that the chief American authority who it was proposed should write the guidebook to the British Library Magna Carta displayed in Washington should be a Mr William ('Bill') Swindler. At the American end there was disquiet at the superciliousness and pedantry of the British. In short, a very typical story of Anglo-American understanding. The case itself, and its gold-leaf facsimile, being products of the 1970s, are unlikely to appeal to the tastes of any later period in human history.

More promisingly, in 1975, and at the height of the British Library's fears that their Magna Carta might still be plucked from them, we receive perhaps the clearest and most honest appraisal of the charter's importance to the English-speaking world. In a letter to Lord Lothian, dated 19 December 1975, Lord Eccles drew attention to the fact that with Magna Carta, they were dealing with 'the most sensitive document in Britain'. It was at much this same time, in June 1975, that we first read of the efforts being made by the Chief Justice of the United States, Warren Earl Burger (Chief Justice 1969–86), acting in concert with the Director of the Folger Shakespeare Library in Washington, to obtain the purchase of an original Magna Carta, of the 1297 issue.

There can be no doubt that the charter referred to here was the 1297 Magna Carta at that time still in the possession of the Brudenell family of Deene Park in Northamptonshire. The Brudenells were a distinguished lot, perhaps most famous for producing the 7th earl of Cardigan (1797–1868), the 'Homicidal Earl', widely blamed for the military disaster of 1854 known as the 'Charge of the Light Brigade'. In the more distant past, they owed their fortunes to marriage, in the fourteenth century, to a Buckinghamshire heiress, which perhaps explains how they had come into possession of the exemplar of the 1297 Magna Carta addressed to Buckinghamshire. Alternatively, it may have come to them via later service, as MPs for Buckinghamshire in the 1400s, as Chief Justice in the 1520s, or from later members of the family who were keen antiquaries and manuscript collectors. By whatever means it arrived in their possession, by 1975, theirs was the only original Magna Carta still in private, as opposed to institutional, hands.

105 Ross Perot, who purchased a 1297 Magna Carta in 1983. It was sold by the Perot Foundation in 2007 for $21.3m. © Allan Warren.

...I am
prepared
to die

This is virtually the complete text of
the now famous speech in his defence
by Nelson Mandela at the Rivonia Trial
which ended in June 1964.
Certain brief passages relating to the
technical details of the defence
have been omitted

A Christian Action Pamphlet   Price one shilling and sixpence

106 In his famous speech at
the Rivonia Trial in 1963, Nelson
Mandela declared, 'The Magna
Carta, the Petition of Rights and
the Bill of Rights are documents
which are held in veneration by
democrats throughout the world.'
Nelson Mandela, *I am prepared to die*
(London, 1964).

The attempt to negotiate its purchase for America
in 1975 was swiftly quashed, in part at least to avoid
embarrassment to the British Parliamentary committee
that had laboured so long and so hard to bring the British
Library's Magna Carta to Washington as a 'centre-piece'
for the bicentennial celebrations. Nonetheless, we have
here the first seeds of an idea – the permanent purchase
by an American institution of an original Magna Carta,
and in particular of the Brudenell Magna Carta – that
was to bear fruit a few years later. In 1983, Ross Perot (b.
1930), the Texan billionaire who had made his fortune from
the early computing revolution, negotiated its purchase
for a price rumoured to have been in excess of $1 million.
An export licence was granted, despite the document's
historic significance. In part this reflected prevailing Cold
War political realities. A keen free market conservative,
outraged by the treatment of American war veterans,
Perot twice stood as independent candidate for the US
presidency. In 1992, on his most successful outing, he
achieved nearly 20 per cent of the popular vote, the highest such vote
cast for any independent since Theodore Roosevelt in 1912. His Magna
Carta, meanwhile, was deposited for safe keeping and public display in
the National Archives in Washington. In 2007, to raise money for good
causes including assistance for wounded soldiers and their families, the
charter was sold at auction by the Perot Foundation for $21.3 million. Its
purchaser, the private equities billionaire, David Rubenstein, returned
the document to public custody in Washington in 2011 gifting a further
$13.5 million to the National Archives to fund a new gallery and visitors'
centre.

Both as a totemic symbol of freedom under law, and as a guarantor
of the rights of the private citizen, not least to the possession of property,
Magna Carta remains an object of veneration in America, fêted by those
of all political persuasions (and of none). As a link to distant antiquity,
and as a reminder of the role of the United States within the wider free
world, it has no real peer.

Today, as for much of the twentieth century, the idea and hence the
very words 'Magna Carta' embody notions of freedom, liberty and
justice. During the Rivonia Trial in 1964, for example, Nelson Mandela

made a powerful speech, citing Magna Carta, the Petition of Right and the Bill of Rights as documents held in veneration throughout the democratic world. In communist-ruled Czechoslovakia, and drawing directly upon the tradition of Magna Carta, the document entitled Charter 77 (published in 1977 by Václav Havel and his fellow intellectuals) called on the Czechoslovak government to uphold human rights, many of them already outlined in the Helsinki Accords of 1975. Several of the charter's signatories, including Havel, were jailed. In 1994, in southern Mexico, the revolutionary Zapatista Army of National Liberation declared war on the Mexican state. A spokesman for this movement, Subcomandante Marcos, invoked Magna Carta as a defence against the powers of the state, underscoring the right of ordinary people to share common resources.

As this suggests, Magna Carta is often invoked today to conjure up a spirit of democracy or freedom. As recently as 2014, the inventor of the World Wide Web, Sir Tim Berners-Lee , called for 'A Magna Carta for the internet' as protection against multinational corporations and intrusion by the security services. Similar demands have been raised for a Magna Carta, by the disabled, by coal miners, and by various other constituencies that consider their liberties or rights to be threatened. Magna Carta has

107 Václav Havel, co-author of *Charter 77*, a demand for human rights, which drew directly on the tradition of Magna Carta. Photo: Drahotín Šulla/TASR.

thus become a notion embodying a wide set of individual and collective freedoms: liberty, democracy, equality and justice are all sheltered beneath its broadest of broad umbrellas.

It is precisely because of its ability to appeal to all political persuasions, to radicals and conservatives, royalists and republicans, Catholics and Protestants, believers and atheists, slave-owners and abolitionists, the advocates of equality and the defenders of inequality, that Magna Carta remains so fascinating. As a totem of all that the English-speaking world holds dear, it has travelled far from its starting point as a treaty of peace between king and barons. None of this could have been predicted in 1215. Very little of it emerges from the text, as opposed to the legacy and myth of the Runnymede charter. Even so, as long as liberty, democracy and the rule of law remain topics of public debate, Magna Carta will continue to be popularly venerated. Much of its story may be shrouded in make-believe. But the myths that people tell about themselves are revealing of underlying aspirations. To this extent, Magna Carta and its role in the curbing of tyranny remains a worthy object of pride.

REFERENCES

For the story of 1940–8, see the relevant British Foreign Office, Dominions Office and Cabinet Office files: London, The National Archives FO 371/22834; FO 371/24245; FO 371/38735; FO 371/51657; FO 371/51658; FO 371/61073; FO 371/68065; FO 371/91013; DO 35/1130. For the attempted bomb plot in New York, James Mauro, *Twilight at the World of Tomorrow: Genius, Madness, Murder, and the 1939 World's Fair on the Brink of War* (New York 2010). For the botched repairs to the Lincoln charter, see London, The National Archives PRO 1/1159; PRO 1/1176. Miss Talbot's touching memories of the Lacock Magna Carta are recorded in her autobiography, *My Life and Lacock Abbey* (London 1956) pp.188–90, 214–16, 255, pp 259–60, with a fine photograph of the author dressed as Ela countess of Salisbury facing p.224. Other information was supplied by Ted and Di Hayward, descendents of the Lacock coachman. For reminiscences of Miss Talbot by James Lees-Milne, see the first three volumes of his diaries: *Ancestral Voices* (London 1974) entry for 15 December 1943; *Prophesying Peace* (London 1977), entry for 15 August 1944, and *Caves of Ice* (London 1983), entry for 16 March 1946. For the exchanges of 1975–6, see London, The National Archives FCO 13/774-9; FCO 26/1729; FCO 81/72-3; PREM 16/1153. The story of the Bruton charter is told in greater detail in my booklet, *Australia's Magna Carta* (Canberra, Senate of Australia, 2011, 2nd ed. 2015). For the Brudenells, see Joan Wake, *The Brudenells of Deene* (London 1953, 2nd ed. 1954).

PART TWO

❖

The Archival and Documentary Evidences for Magna Carta

INTRODUCTION

The many faces of
Magna Carta

Visitors to several of England's cathedral cities (Durham, Hereford, Lincoln, Oxford, Salisbury), and even those who find themselves in more distant locations (Washington or Canberra) often express surprise that a document supposedly the most important in legal history, can be viewed in all manner of places not just as a 'copy' but as an 'original' Magna Carta. Surely, they ask, the 'original' Magna Carta must be housed in the British Library in London, in The National Archives at Kew, or perhaps still lurks somewhere in the keeping of King John's successors as kings and queens of England? It is to answer this and other such questions that the second part of this book has been written.

At Runnymede, on or around 15 June 1215, King John allowed his seal to be applied to a document that, had it survived would rank as the absolute first and original form of Magna Carta. As we have seen, the Victorians and their successors delighted in portraying these events in paint or stone. In reality, the document that King John allowed to be sealed has long ago vanished. We perhaps come closest to the field of Runnymede with an early draft of the details subsequently incorporated within Magna Carta, known as 'The Articles of the Barons' (below no.27). This represents a list of clauses that the barons demanded and the king conceded, originally sealed with the king's seal. It was probably carried away from Runnymede by Archbishop Langton. Certainly it was in the archive of the archbishops of Canterbury at Lambeth Palace by the time of Archbishop Laud, from whose papers it was looted following Laud's impeachment in 1640. Passing through various hands thereafter, it eventually came to rest in the British Museum, now the British Library.

The 'Articles' include virtually everything that subsequently went in to Magna Carta, but arranged in a different order and with slightly different emphasis and wording, clause by clause. As this suggests, the charter itself was the outcome of heated negotiation, in which numerous

Ne cadat in obſcurum
P.
RADVLFVS SHELDON
Arm:

verbal formulae were hammered out. As a result, and given that a large
number of parties convened at Runnymede, it was easy for unofficial or
premature terms of agreement to escape from the field of negotiation
and subsequently to become incorporated in local, unofficial copies of
the settlement. There were perhaps as many as a thousand individuals at
Runnymede in June 1215: the king and his court, the bishops and abbots,
the barons in large number, each with a large party of knights, squires and
other attendants.

As a result, it is hardly surprising that Magna Carta 1215 circulated in
several versions. Beyond the official chancery versions (sometimes known
as 'engrossments', below described as 'exemplars' or 'originals') issued
on single sheets of parchment and sealed with the king's seal, other less

108 Hereford Cathedral holds
one of the four surviving
exemplars of the 1217 Magna
Carta. Wenceslaus Hollar, *Hereford
Cathedral, etching, published
1673* (Pennington 981; Turner,
New Hollstein German, 2248).
The Thomas Fisher Rare Book
Library, University of Toronto,
Hollar_k_0955. © University of
Toronto.

official versions survived unsealed, sometimes supplied with clauses that had subsequently been altered in final negotiation, sometimes with clauses that suited particular constituencies but that were never officially incorporated within the charter (e.g. below no.32). At the great abbey of St Albans, for example, whose chroniclers early got to work on dissecting the text agreed at Runnymede, access to the charter seems to have been obtained not from the official chancery version sealed by the king, but from an unofficial copy carried away from the negotiations of June 1215. This seems to have included an entire clause, otherwise lost, insisting that the constables of the castles of Northampton, Kenilworth, Nottingham and Scarborough swear oaths to obey any decision taken by a majority of the twenty-five barons appointed to oversee the charter's enforcement. Furthermore, since the St Albans chroniclers were not above doctoring or altering charters when this could be done in their own interest, it was they, rather than the negotiators at Runnymede, who added the name of Fawkes de Breauté, one of the king's more unpopular mercenary captains, to the list of foreigners whose removal from office was a condition of Magna Carta clause 50. In due course, it was the St Albans chroniclers, and their miscopying of later versions of the charter, who helped put into circulation a series of hybrid texts, incorporating elements of both the 1217 and the 1225 Magna Cartas, never officially issued as such, but passed down as one of the chroniclers' legacies (e.g. below no.38).

109 The monks of St Albans Abbey, including Matthew Paris (shown above), produced versions of Magna Carta in their chronicles that drew from various official and unofficial texts. BL, Royal MS. 14 C VII, f. 6r. ©The British Library Board.

We should remember here that 'Magna' Carta was indeed a very 'large' document, and that each of its 3,600 Latin words had to be copied out laboriously by hand. To protect against the possibility that there might be unofficial amendments, and to supply an authentic text, on or shortly after 15 June 1215, 'letters testimonial' were issued by Archbishop Langton, the archbishop of Dublin, seven other English bishops and the pope's representative, Master Pandulf. Known sometimes as the bishops' '*inspeximus*' (from its opening words, declaring that bishops had 'inspected' the text that they then went on to recite) this seems to have passed into the archives of the king. According to its authors, it was intended to ensure 'that no-one may add to the aforesaid form or subtract from it or reduce it'. This was done without the bishops or the pope's representative in any way granting their own formal authority to the document that was here merely recited rather than officially confirmed. The bishops' sealed letters were still in the king's archive as late as the 1320s, when they were copied into a book intended to preserve a wide array of the king's archival treasures, known from this book's binding and place of storage as *The Red Book of the Exchequer* (today TNA E 164/2 fos.234r-6r, below no.46). Thereafter, they have long since vanished, leaving only the *Red Book* copy as proof of their existence. They bring us closer, perhaps, than any other text to the precise words of the charter as agreed at Runnymede.

For the rest, for the Runnymede charter as for all subsequent reissues, we depend either upon copies made into books (as with the *Red Book* copy of the 1215 charter) or upon single sheets of parchment, sealed and delivered to the various localities of England as a means of broadcasting the charter's terms. Of these, all told, at least twenty-four survive: four from 1215 (below nos.1–4), only one from 1216 (no.5), four from 1217 (nos.6–9), four from 1225 (nos.10–13), four from 1297 (nos.14–17), and six from 1300 (seven if we count a peculiar unofficial version from Oxfordshire; nos.18–24).

110 The bishops played a critical role in the events of 1215, guaranteeing the authentic text of the Charter and overseeing its publication. BL, Royal MS. 2 A XXII, f. 221r. © The British Library Board.

Ne messe ne baptesme ni auert
Vi anz & iii quartiers & vn mois
Durast lentredit a Estrois
Ij mirent la pape out amoniz
Q le pestrent de mte boin
En temps le roi ont gite guerre
entre les barons Denglerre
Qui esteit dit Laluis arme
Le sir Roi Phelipp de france nee
Il fist pais en la terre
E nuls vers altres ni monist guerre
Onsij regna · xvi · anz & demy
Le sei pleignent si amy
Wimestre esteit porte
E gnt honur ensepelee

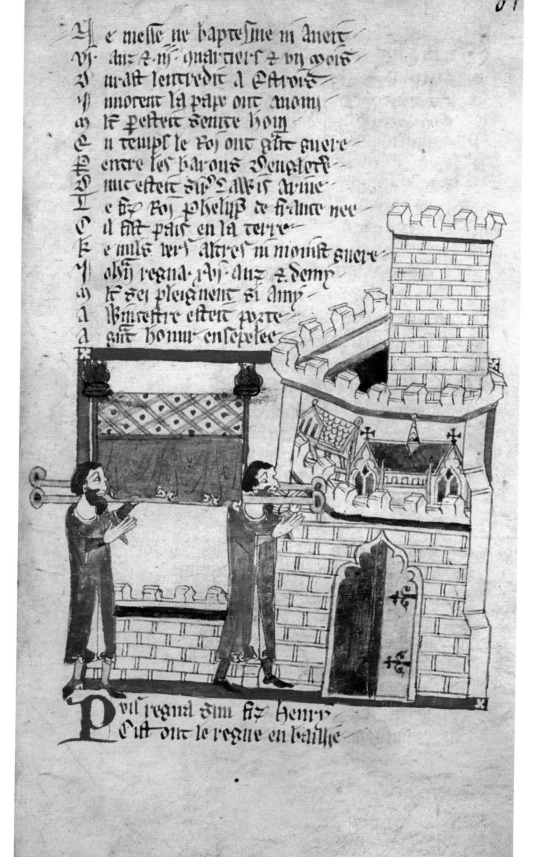

Puis regna son fiz Henri
Cist out le regne en baillie

This should remind us that the 1215 charter is in many ways rivalled and outnumbered by its subsequent reissues. The Runnymede charter is perhaps the most famous document in world history. Yet as a legal instrument it was never enforced. The king refused to dismiss his alien constables and mercenaries. The barons held on to the city of London and then seized control of Rochester Castle, supposedly in the neutral keeping of Archbishop Langton. By the end of the first week in September, only twelve weeks after the charter's initial award, both sides were once again moving towards war. The king's clerical supporters published letters declaring the baronial leaders excommunicate rebels. Archbishop Langton was suspended from office (below no.30). In Rome, having been alerted to the contents of the Runnymede charter, the pope declared it annulled (below no.31).

There things might have rested. Magna Carta would be remembered today, like other constitutional experiments of the twelfth and thirteenth centuries, as a settlement that failed. Instead, events ensured its survival. King John died in October 1216, in the midst of civil war fought against the barons and their allies summoned from France. His body was carried from Newark-on-Trent to Worcester for burial. He left a nine-year-old boy as his son and heir. There could be no question of this boy king, Henry III, devising policy or leading armies in battle. Instead a regency emerged, headed by the seventy-year-old William Marshal, earl of Pembroke, with the French-born bishop of Winchester and the Italian-born papal legate, Guala Bicchieri, as the king's co-guardians.

On 12 November 1216, in a council meeting at Bristol, the regency government reissued Magna Carta, both as an apology for past misrule and as a promise of future good government. In the process, nearly half of the original text was cut away (below no.5). Out went the clauses regulating Jewish debt, communal consent for taxation, the farms paid by sheriffs for their counties, the insistence that sheriffs and other officers know the laws of England, that the king expel his alien constables, that all hostages be released, and that settlements be devised with both the Welsh and the Scots. Above all, out went all mention of the baronial committee of twenty-five set above the king to judge his actions and to impose justice whenever the king acted beyond the law. Even the

111 With the eastern half of England held by the allied French and rebel forces, John was buried at Worcester, in the western reaches of the kingdom (not, as this fourteenth-century text suggests, at Winchester). BL, Egerton MS. 3028, f. 61r. © The British Library Board.

112 This cast shows how the tomb effigy of William Marshal appeared before the original, at Temple Church, was damaged in an air raid in the Second World War. V&A REPRO.A.1938-7. © Victoria and Albert Museum, London.

opening clause of the charter was altered, so that instead of guaranteeing a specific right of free election to English bishoprics and abbeys, the charter now merely promised respect for the unspecified liberties and rights of the Church.

Four originals of the charter issued at Runnymede survive, so far as we can tell distributed for the most part via the bishops and cathedral churches. Two of them are today in the British Library (below nos.1–2), the other two in the cathedral libraries of Lincoln and Salisbury (nos.3–4). Of the issue of November 1216, only one original survives, in the archives of Durham Cathedral, to which it almost certainly addressed (no.5). Two early copies found their way into the archives of the kings of France, perhaps carried there by an adherent of Prince Louis, at that time pursuing his own claim to the English throne (below no.33 i–ii). By January 1217, the reissued charter had also been sent into Ireland, duly modified so as to apply to the Church both of England and of Ireland (below no.49).

Thus far, the charter of 1216 divulged nothing but aspirations. No enforcement of it would be possible until the king and his councillors recovered power. This they did a year later, in November 1217, following the defeat of the rebels in battle. As part of the resettlement of England, in November 1217, the regency government reissued Magna Carta (below nos.6–9). This was done very much in the same form as in 1216, without the obnoxious clauses relating to the twenty-five barons, with minor modifications, intended to clarify procedure in county and sheriffs' courts, to ensure the destruction of 'adulterine' castles constructed during the recent war, and for the first time, with a series of clauses intended to frustrate the devices of lawyers. Thus the 1217 charter demanded that no land be alienated so that it could not support the services due from it, and that no land be granted to the Church simply to evade secular service. This is significant, both as an indication that baronial interests remained dominant in the rephrasing of the charter, and also as evidence of the way in which Magna Carta was developing as a legal instrument, not just as a political device.

Even more significantly, the 1217 reissue was accompanied by an entirely new, rather briefer charter, dealing with administration of the king's forests (below no.34 i–ii). In as much as a third of the land mass of England lying under forest jurisdiction (the whole of the counties of Essex and Hampshire, for example), landlords had previously struggled to clear or cultivate land in theory set aside as habitat for the king's deer and other game. It was the contrast between the longer charter of liberties and the Forest Charter that as early as 1217 led the king's chancery to refer to them as respectively the 'great' and the 'small' charter, coining the phrase 'Magna Carta' to describe the longer text. As yet, there was no clear decision as to whether it should be called 'Magna Carta' ('the big charter') or 'Maior Carta' ('the bigger charter'). Ambiguity here persisted into the 1220s. Thereafter, the form 'Magna Carta' won out.

The charter was once again reissued in 1225 (below nos.10–13), again with minor modifications to the text of 1217, again in company with a revised Forest Charter (below no.35 i–iv). These 1225 charters were issued with the support of Archbishop Langton as a means of guaranteeing

114 The seal (shown here) of the papal legate, cardinal Guala Bicchieri, together with that of William Marshal, authenticated the 1216 and 1217 issues of Magna Carta. Oxford, Bodleian Library, MS. Ch. Oxon. Oseney 142c*.

English liberties in return for a grant of taxation intended to assist the king's armies in France. The charters of 1216 and 1217 had both been issued under the seals of the king's guardians, William Marshal and the legate Guala. Guala's seal in effect gave papal approval to the text. The 1225 issue, by contrast, was made under the new seal of Henry III. Partly because of this, partly because of the particularly solemn circumstances in which Langton gave ecclesiastical support to the charter of 1225, it was this 1225 text that hereafter became the definitive version, renewed in turn in 1265, 1297, 1300, and perhaps on other occasions for which our evidence is lacking.

Given Magna Carta's significance to political, legal and constitutional history, it might be supposed that historians had long ago collected every detail that there is to be known about the charter and, in particular, about each of the surviving 'original' versions issued in the charter's first hundred years. In fact, between 1810 and 2007, virtually no such work was attempted. A provisional list of originals was included in the catalogue that I wrote in 2007 to accompany the New York sale of the 1297 Magna Carta now in the National Archives in Washington. The census that follows has nonetheless been both revised and significantly augmented.

REFERENCES

For the originals of the 1215 charter, see the two classic articles, by Fox, 'Originals', and Collins, 'Documents', and below nos.1–4.

CHAPTER 6

Statute making
and the publication of law to 1300

Ego Stephanus dei gratia assensu cleri et populi in rege Anglorum electus, et a Willelmo Cantuariensi archiepiscopo et sancte romane
ecclesie legato consecratus, et ab Innocentio sancte romane sedis pontifice postmodum confirmatus, respectu et amore
dei sanctam ecclesiam liberam esse concedo, et debitam reverentiam illi confirmo. Nichil in ecclesia vel reb[us]
et personis ecclesiasticis simoniace actum ut innisum esse promitto. Ecclesiasticarum personarum et omnium clericorum et rerum eorum iusticiam et potestatem et distributionem honorum ecclesiasticorum in manu episcoporum esse confirmo. Dignitates ecclesiarum privilegiis earum confirmatas, et consuetudines earum antiquo tenore
habitas, inviolate manere statuo et concedo. Omnes ecclesiarum possessiones et tenuras quas die illa
habuerunt qua Willelmus avus meus rex Anglorum fuit vivus et mortuus, sine omni calumpniantium reclamatio-
ne eis liberas et absolutas esse concedo. Si quid autem de habitis vel possessis ante mortem eiusdem reg[is]
quibus nunc caret ecclesia deinceps repetierit, indulgentie et dispensationi mee vel restitu[en]
dum vel discutiendum reservo. Quecumque vero post mortem ipsius regis liberalitate regum largitione
principum oblatione comparatione vel quolibet inmutatione fidelium ecclesiis collata sunt confirmo. Pacem et
iusticiam me in omnibus facturum et pro posse meo conservaturum eis promitto. Forestas quas Willelmus avus meus et Willelmus secundus avunculus meus instituerunt et tenuerunt mihi reservo. Ceteras vero
omnes quas Henricus rex superaddidit ecclesiis et regno quietas reddo et concedo. Si quis episco-
pus vel abbas vel alia ecclesiastica persona ante mortem suam rationabiliter sua distribuerit, vel distribuen-
da statuerit firmum manere concedo. Si vero morte preoccupatus fuerit pro salute anime eius ecclesie
consilio eadem fiat distributio. Dum vero sedes propriis pastoribus vacue fuerint, ipse et omnes earum
possessiones in manu et custodia clericorum vel proborum hominum eiusdem ecclesie committantur donec
pastor canonice substituatur. Omnes exactiones et iniusticias et meschenningas sive per vicecomites
vel per alios quoslibet male inductas funditus exstirpo. Bonas leges et antiquas et iustas consuetudines in
murdris et placitis et aliis causis observabo, et observari precipio et constituo. Hec vero omnia conce-
do et confirmo. Salva regia et iusta dignitate mea. Testibus Willelmo archiepiscopo Cantuariensi et Henrico archiepiscopo Rothomagensi
et Henrico episcopo Wintoniensi et Rogero episcopo Salesberiensi et Alexandro episcopo Lincolniensi et Nigello episcopo Eliensi et Simone episcopo Wigornensi et Bernardo episcopo
sancti David et Audoeno episcopo Ebroicensi et Roberto episcopo Abrincensi et Roberto episcopo Herefordensi et Johanne episcopo Rovecestrensi et Adelulfo episcopo Carleolensi
et Roberto cancellario et Henrico nepote regis et Roberto de Sigillo et Roberto comite Gloucestrie et Willelmo comite Warennie et Roberto comite
Legrecestrie et Roberto comite Warwicensi et Roberto de Ver et Milone Gloucestrie et Briano filio comitis et Roberto de Oilli constabulario
et Willelmo Martel et Hugone Bigot et Humfrido de Buhun et Simone de Bello campo dapifero et Willelmo de Albineio et Eudone dapifero et Roberto de Ferrariis et Willelmo de Aubeni et Simone de Sancto Licio et Willelmo de Albeniaco et Pagano filio Johannis et Hamone de Sancto
Claro et Johanne de Baiocis. Apud Oxineford. Anno ab incarnatione domini M.C.XXXVI. in communi consilio.

LAW TODAY is a matter of the word processor and the printing press. Legislation drafted by government officials is presented to Parliament for approval, and if passed, is granted royal assent. Statute making in the Middle Ages was a far less well regulated affair. Law was in theory made by kings who derived their authority from God. Not only was God the ultimate law maker, but custom and tradition were to be respected in law, so that kings did not so much make 'new' laws as ensure that justice was done by using or improving laws that in many cases were either ancient or unwritten. Moreover, since few kings were literate (King John being in all likelihood a significant exception in this respect), and

115 *left* One of the chief duties of kingship was the provision of law and justice and so kings, from the earliest times, issued law codes. BL, Royal MS. 10 D VIII, f. 1r. © The British Library Board.

116 *opposite* Before Magna Carta, the coronation charters of Henry I and King Stephen (an exemplar of the latter shown here) promised good government and guaranteed the freedom of the Church. Oxford, Bodleian Library, MS. Rawl. Q. a. 1.

since the counsel of the bishops and other great men had to be heeded if law were to be effectively observed, law was best made in counsel, often in great public assemblies.

In England, from long before Magna Carta, kings had issued law codes. In doing so, they presented themselves as both just and powerful. Such codes were to a large extent intended to maintain peace and to avoid violent feuding between rival kinship groups. However, although they were issued and preserved, it is far harder to find them enforced. A great deal of justice was done not according to written law but by custom. Even when the kings of England began to divide their realm into a series of shires, each with its own royal officials and local courts, only a relatively small proportion of what we would today consider legal business found its way to these courts, either at the level of the county (the shire court) or the more local 'hundred' ('wapentakes' in northern England). Much more was decided by local lords or within the kin. Change here came only slowly after 1066.

To govern their new lands, the Norman kings made relatively few new laws. Much more significant was the way in which the old law codes of the Anglo-Saxon past were collected and preserved. An extraordinary amount of what we know of Anglo-Saxon law comes to us from collections compiled after 1100, and in particular from such great books as the *Textus Roffensis* (a Rochester Cathedral manuscript of the 1120s) or the various manuscripts of the so-called 'Quadripartitus' tradition, from much the same date. Here, English or Latin versions of Old English law codes were combined with attempts to define the laws and procedures of the present day. No matter that several of these collections relied upon the invention of laws that were not really 'Anglo-Saxon'. The so-called *Leges Edwardi Confessoris*, for example, purporting to be the laws of Edward the Confessor, or the *Instituta Cnuti* (attributed to King Cnut) were mid-twelfth-century confections rather than genuine records of pre-Conquest law making. Even so, they testified to the desire to restore a tradition of legality and peace that the Norman Conquest was supposed violently to have disrupted.

As for entirely new laws, what we know of them suggests that they continued to be made by the king with the assistance of his councillors, claiming not so much to invent new laws but to ensure a return to the good old laws of the past. This was the claim of Henry I's Coronation Charter, issued in 1100, promising to undo the evil practices of his late

117 A rare copy of the Assize of Clarendon, issued by John's father, Henry II, is preserved in a legal compilation held at the Bodleian Library. Oxford, Bodleian Library, MS. Rawl. C 641 ff. 18v-19r.

A ui a partyz escoute de sey sosche.

De meysmes sa manche li essue len le nes.

A ui en prumte e soyt de suen se tyt.

Mielz uaut torn de molin que pez de mastin.

K i loign mauit a sez a.

De tigier ploze qui la lippe pert.

Seignor e ore sunt tost mue.

A char de lou sause de chien.

Tant gwe chael od li uiel chiens ueuie.

Qui crieue moysson ne fait mystere.

Perecos est de uin.

Plus tyre cul que corde.

L egiere est chose a destoxbier ainz quel seit omeiee.

Ki ne creit son pere crei e son parastre.

Vel estalon fait tost poutre peire.

De petit aguillon chasce lon graint asnesse.

Ptie de cul tient lettre de chief.

Poure home na ley.

Richesce paist folie.

A ui siet seche qui uait leche.

Peche ne dort.

Ki enchinge fait a creindre.

Tute rien a uient reuert fors sol tant od lon deu sert.

Amor uentre cure rien.

Qui riens na riens ne pert ne ses amis nel plaignent

Fol marchant solement barguigne.

Incipit Assisa de Clarenduna facta a rege Henrico secundo de assensu Archiepiscoporum, Episcoporum, Abbatum, Comitum, Baronum totius Anglie.

In primis statuit predictus rex Henricus de consilio omnium baronum suorum pro pace servanda et iusticia tenenda, quod per singulos comitatus inquiratur et per singulos hundredos per duodecim legaliores homines de hundredo et per quatuor legaliores homines de qualibet villata per sacramentum, quod illi verum dicent, si in hundredo suo vel in villata sua sit aliquis homo qui sit rettatus vel publicatus quod ipse sit robator vel murdrator vel latro, vel aliquis qui sit receptor robatorum vel murdratorum vel latronum, postquam dominus rex fuit rex. Et hoc inquirant iusticie coram se et vicecomites coram se. Et qui inventi fuerint per sacramentum predictorum rettati vel publicati quod fuerint robatores vel murdratores vel latrones vel receptores eorum postquam dominus rex fuit rex, capiantur et eant ad iudicium aque, et iurent quod ipsi non fuerunt robatores vel murdratores vel latrones si receptores eorum postquam dominus rex fuit rex de valentia quinque solidorum quod sciant. Et si dominus eius vel capitalis eius vel homines eius recalcitraverint ei per plegium infra tercium diem postquam captus fuerit, replegietur ipse et catalla eius donec ipse faciat legem suam. Et qui robatores vel murdratores vel latrones vel receptores eorum capti fuerint per predictum sacramentum, si iusticie non fuerint tam cito venture in illum comitatum ubi capti fuerint, vicecomites mandent per aliquem prudentiorem iusticie per aliquem intelligentem hominem quod tales homines ceperunt, et iusticie remandabunt vicecomiti ubi voluerint quod illi adducantur ante illos, et vicecomites illos adducant ante iusticias; et cum illis ducentur de hundredo et de villata ubi capti fuerint, duos legales homines ad portandum recordationem comitatus et hundredi quare capti fuerint, et ibi ante iusticiam facient legem suam. Et de illis qui capti fuerint per predictum sacramentum huius assise, nullus habeat curiam vel iusticiam vel catalla nisi dominus rex in curia sua coram iusticiis eius, et dominus rex habebit omnia catalla eorum. De illis vero qui capti fuerint aliter quam per hoc sacramentum, sit sicut esse solet et debet. Et vicecomites qui eos ceperint ducant eos ante iusticiam sine alio summonicione quam inde habent. Et cum robatores vel murdratores vel latrones et receptores eorum qui capti fuerint per sacramentum vel aliter adducti fuerint coram eis, vicecomites et ipsi recipiant eos statim sine dilatione. Et in singulis...

brother, William Rufus, and to return relations between king and barons to the halcyon state of King Edward the Confessor. Henry I (1100–1135), like his successors King Stephen (1135–54) and Henry II (1154–89), seems to have used the county courts as the best means of broadcasting and preserving his Coronation Charter. Since bishops and abbots continued to play an important role in such courts, and since it was they rather than the earls or sheriffs who maintained the best-kept archives, it was in ecclesiastical hands rather than the shire hall that such charters were best preserved.

We have no surviving original of Henry I's Coronation Charter, but evidence for its preservation in the cathedrals of Canterbury, Rochester, York and half a dozen English Benedictine monasteries. King Stephen granted two great charters of liberties directed to the realm as a whole. The first, apparently issued shortly after his coronation in December 1135, like the similar coronation charter issued by King Henry II in 1154, is known only because it was copied into a collection of laws closely associated with the city of London. The second of Stephen's charters of liberties, issued at Oxford early in April 1136, was intended to buy support from the Church, and opens (in imitation of Henry I's Coronation Charter, subsequently adapted for Magna Carta) with a promise that the Church itself is to be 'free' (*libera*). Besides copies preserved in the cathedral archives of Canterbury and York, three originals of this charter survive, one at Salisbury Cathedral, one at Exeter Cathedral (with facsimile in *Statutes* (1810), 3 no.3) and the third, deriving ultimately from Hereford Cathedral, in a manuscript now in the Bodleian Library at Oxford (Rawlinson Q.a.1 fo.26 above fig.116). A lost Canterbury original was perhaps purloined by Sir Edward Dering (1598–1644) at much the same time that Dering made off with Canterbury's 1215 Magna Carta (below no.1). Clearly, the Church was centrally involved in the distribution of Stephen's charter.

For the next great leap forwards in law and legislation we must turn to the reign of King John's father, Henry II. It was under Henry, beginning in the 1160s and with even great impetus after 1174, that the royal law courts began to claim jurisdiction over an ever growing number of pleas. This was in part the result of financial imperatives, since the doing of justice was a lucrative affair. It was facilitated by a series of new and speedy procedures that the king made available to litigants, for example to those seeking the recovery of land that had recently and unjustly been seized from them ('*novel disseisin*'), or land that should have been theirs by

inherited right ('*mort d'ancestor*'). Such procedures were initiated by letters ('writs') obtainable from the king or his justiciar, enforced according to written rules known as 'assizes' that Henry II began to issue from the 1150s onwards. The texts of very few of these assizes have been preserved. Most can be traced only from their impact upon legal or administrative procedures or through the survival of a treatise on English law composed late in Henry's reign and popularly (though almost certainly wrongly) attributed to Ranulf de Glanville, the king's chief justiciar.

Those of the assizes of Henry II that survive do so exclusively as copies rather than original single-sheets. Most are known only because they were copied out by the chronicler Roger of Howden, himself a clerk loosely attached to Henry's court as justice and diplomat. Were it not for Howden, even such fundamental rulings on crime and property as the Assize of Clarendon (1166) or the Assize of Northampton (1176) would have vanished more or less without trace. Apart from Howden's copy, the Assize of Clarendon, in many ways the most significant law code of its period, is known from only one other independent source, in an Oxford manuscript of laws copied together with King John's Magna Carta, shortly after 1215 (Oxford, Bodleian Library MS. Rawl. C. 641 above fig.117).

This same Oxford manuscript preserves Henry II's Inquest of Sheriffs (1170), itself also to be found in another Oxford collection (Bodleian Library MS. e Mus. 222 fo.155r–v, in a late twelfth-century manuscript once in the library of Darley Abbey in Derbyshire). The articles of enquiry for this inquest, in some ways the most important investigation of official malpractice before Magna Carta, are preserved only because they were copied into the collection of letters kept for Gilbert Foliot, bishop of London, itself known from two copies preserved in Oxford (Bodleian Library MS. e Mus. 249 fo.89r–v, above fig.118, and MS. Douce 287 fos.87v–88r, the first from Belvoir Priory, the second from the Priory of Lesnes in Kent). A similar serendipity attaches to the assizes of Richard I (again known almost exclusively from Roger of Howden) and to the earliest legislation issued by King John. In May 1199, for example, John issued an important decree on the fees to be paid in his chancery for the issue or reissue of charters. This is known only from a copy preserved by the chancellor, Archbishop Hubert Walter, still today in the archbishop's archive at Lambeth Palace (MS. 1212 fos.21r-v, 115v-116r).

It is worth noticing here that, before Magna Carta, and save where a document, such as Stephen's charter of 1136, directly concerned

119 Royal charters intended for general publication were distributed and preserved by the Church. This exemplar of the 1217 Magna Carta was probably housed at St Peter's Abbey, Gloucester, where it was carefully folded for storage. Here showing the archival marks on the back (or 'dorse') of the document. Oxford, Bodleian Library, MS. Ch. Glouc. 8 (below no.8).

Magna Charta
Anno 2 Reg. Johñ. III

Regis Johis

Carta Libertatum

the liberties of the Church, it was almost unheard of for the king's legislation or more general rulings to survive in their original single-sheet form. A rare exception is a newsletter dispatched by Henry II in the late autumn of 1174, reporting the peace agreed between himself and his rebellious sons Henry, Richard and Geoffrey. This too was copied by Howden and survives elsewhere in monastic copies from Peterborough. However, at least two single-sheet originals also survive, one in the archives of Durham Cathedral (Durham, University Library Special Collections MS. D. & C. Durham 2.1.Reg.13), the other in London, from the library of the omniverous manuscript collector Sir Robert Cotton (BL MS. Cotton Charter VII.12, formerly Cotton Charter Augustus A loc. numm.1). Both, it might be surmised, survived originally in ecclesiastical archives, one at Durham, the other in a still unidentified location. Neither is written in the hand of any scribe otherwise known to have been attached to the royal chancery, reminding us of the exceptional nature of documents like this, produced *en masse* for distribution at very short notice. Whatever role the sheriffs and shire courts may have played in the process of publication, the network of distribution and preservation for such documents seems to have been closely associated with, or even controlled by, the Church.

Law remained king-made. A letter sent by King John in May 1207, for example, complained that various of the leading men of Ireland had written to him in a commanding tone, almost as if they wished to make 'a new assize' (*nouam assisam*) in the king's land. It would be unheard of, the king warned, for any such new law to be made without the assent of the prince of that land. On his next crossing to Ireland, in 1210, the king is said 'to have decreed and commanded that the laws of England be obeyed in Ireland, depositing these laws, reduced to writing, in the Exchequer at Dublin' (*Patent Rolls 1225–32*, 96). Meanwhile, even for such highly significant legal instruments as those governing the relations between king and Church following the king's surrender to the Pope in 1213–14, we depend just as much upon documentary evidences surviving in cathedral or other ecclesiastical archives as we do upon the central records of royal government. The royal chancery's records were themselves at this time treated not as 'public records' but as the king's private archive, intended for the king's use and, in so far as they assisted with the collection of revenue, for the king's financial profit.

And so we come to Magna Carta. Four originals of the 1215 Magna Carta survive (below nos.1–4). It has long been recognized that peculiar circumstances governed their issue. Since the settlement at Runnymede was intended to lead to a major overhaul of local government, and since the king's sheriffs and local officers were implicated in many of the evil customs that Magna Carta was intended to remedy, enforcement of the charter could not be entrusted to the sheriffs alone. On 19 or 20 June, a

120 In the late fourteenth century the 'security clause' of Magna Carta 1215 was investigated as a precedent for the restraints placed upon Richard II. BL, Harley MS. 4380, f. 181v. © The British Library Board.

121 Exemplars of the 1215 Charter might have been entrusted to monasteries, as distant from Runnymede as Byland Abbey, Yorkshire. Photo: AC Ridder/ Shutterstock.

few days after the text of the charter itself was finally agreed, letters were composed, addressed to the sheriffs of England, informing them of the firm peace that had now been made between king and rebels and demanding not only that they have Magna Carta publicly read but generally enforced. Only a single original exemplar of these letters survives, today in the archives of Hereford Cathedral (below no.28), addressed to the sheriff of Gloucestershire.

Besides this, we have two lists, copied into the chancery rolls, recording the dispatch both of the letters patent for enforcement of the peace and of what seem to be original Magna Cartas, on a county by county basis, but distributed initially not to the sheriffs but via a series of a middlemen. In so far as we can read the king's mind in the summer of 1215, John had no real intention that Magna Carta either be publicized or implemented. Having restored peace, he intended merely to bide his time until the Runnymede settlement, like so many earlier settlements between kings and barons, was overtaken by events. It was the success of the barons in achieving the charter's publication that sets the crisis of 1215 apart from all such crises in the past. And in this, the barons relied first and foremost upon the active co-operation of the English bishops. Not only were copies of the charter assigned to the bishops of Worcester and Lincoln, both of them former officials in the king's chancery, but no less than ten Magna Cartas were given to Master Elias of Dereham, steward of Archbishop Langton, for distribution in at least twelve counties and amongst the Cinque Ports.

As a result, it is perhaps not surprising that one of the four surviving Magna Cartas of 1215 is that which was sent to the bishop of Lincoln (below no.3), and that two of the three others came to rest in cathedral archives with which Master Elias had close connections, at Canterbury (no.1), and Salisbury (no.4). The fourth 1215 Magna Carta (no.2), unreported before 1628 when it was given to Sir Robert Cotton by a London barrister, may well have come from yet another Cathedral library as yet unidentified. The total of thirteen charters recorded as having been issued in June and July 1215 corresponds neatly with the number of English dioceses that at this time had a bishop in office. Set against this, however, we have the fact that Gloucester Abbey, as late as the 1390s, seems not only to have possessed originals, all still extant, of the 1217 Magna Carta (below no.8), the 1237 Parva Carta (no.36 iii), and the letters patent of Edward I issued in 1301 concerning the confirmation of the charters (no.42), but also a 1215 Magna Carta (whence the copy in Gloucester Cathedral Library Register A fos.35v–40v no.83) and both the Magna Carta and Forest Charter of 1297 (Ibid. fos.27v–32v nos.80–1). Gloucester's 1215 charter was described in the 1390s (Ibid. fo.35v) as 'King John's charter of the liberties of England concerning the twenty-five barons', an interesting proof that memory of the twenty-five was preserved into the reign of Richard II (himself the object of reforms by a committee of 'Lords Appellant'). A similar interest in the twenty-five barons of 1215 occurs in another manuscript from the vicinity of Gloucester, again from the 1390s, here reciting selective passages of the 1215 Magna Carta, particularly those related to the twenty-five barons, embedded within a larger dossier of materials associated with the Lords Appellant and their leader, Thomas Duke of Gloucester (TNA C 115/78 (Lanthony Priory, Register of Prior William de Chiriton, 1377–1401) fo.123r–v).

Gloucester Abbey became a cathedral church only in the sixteenth century. Its access to (or possession) long before this of a 1215 Magna Carta might suggest that the greater abbeys as well as the cathedrals had a significant role to play in the publication not only of the Runnymede charter, but of Magna Carta's later reissues. Certainly copies of the 1215 charter, in no case clearly derived from any of the surviving originals, were inserted into the cartularies or copy books of several other great monasteries, including St Augustine's at Canterbury (Lambeth Palace Library MS. 1213 fos.189r–94r), Reading Abbey (Ibid. MS. 371 fos.57v–59v, where it is preceded by a list of the baronial twenty-five, below no.44), Montacute Priory in Somerset (Oxford, Trinity College MS. 85 fos. xiiii–xix, part only), St Nicholas's Priory at Exeter (BL MS. Cotton Vitellius D ix fos.94r–96r), and in a list of titles belonging to Byland Abbey in Yorkshire (BL MS. Egerton 2823 fo.56v), where it is described as the 'Charter committed to us, of King John on the common laws of England, called Runnymede'. The Byland rubric may even suggest that the Cistercians of Byland were entrusted with the original 1215 charter sent into Yorkshire, just as the knights of Wiltshire are later recorded as depositing their 1225 charter with the nuns of Lacock (below no.11). Various of the other monastic copies of 1215, by contrast, including potentially those at Gloucester, could have been made from exemplars that only came late into monastic possession. At Peterborough, for example (whose monks possessed an unauthorized copy of the 1215 charter, with textual variants from the 'official' version) or at St Albans (whose monks set to work to 'improve' the text of 1215, itself known to them only late and by indirect means), it is clear that the copying of 'Runnymede' charters in no way implies that such charters were originally in monastic custody.

If we are correct to suppose that only a dozen or so Magna Cartas were drawn up and issued from the chancery after Runnymede then it is surely a remarkable testimony to the respect in which they were held in the country at large that no less than four of them, nearly a third of the original issue, have survived to the present day. Alongside these, the

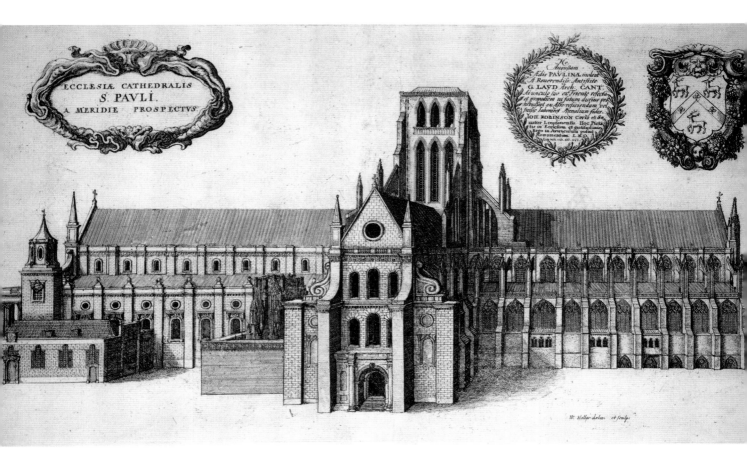

survival of the originals of so many other texts crucial to the negotiations of 1215, including earlier drafts of the Runnymede settlement, French translations carried onto the field of Runnymede and the original sealed 'Articles of the Barons' (below nos.25–7) supplies further evidence that such documents were treated almost as holy relics to be preserved and venerated from the moment of their issue. By contrast, the only such original Magna Carta document preserved in the king's archives to the present day is the papal bull of August 1215, declaring Magna Carta null and void (below no.31).

Magna Carta, as we have seen above, should have died in September 1215, unmourned by the king and, as a peace treaty, repudiated by the barons. Its survival was the result of accident, and above all of the death of King John. For the Magna Carta reissued by the councillors of the

122 It was at Old St Paul's Cathedral, destroyed in the Great Fire of 1666, that the 1217 Magna Carta and Forest Charter were issued. Wenceslaus Hollar, *St Paul's. South side, etching, 1658* (Pennington 1018; Turner, New Hollstein German, 1696). The Thomas Fisher Rare Book Library, University of Toronto, Hollar_k_0973. © University of Toronto.

nine-year-old Henry III in November 1216, we have the official copy on the chancery rolls of an elaborate letter, of which only the version sent to Ireland still survives, announcing the death of John, the new king's coronation and the decision, made at Bristol, with the counsel of bishops, abbots, earls and barons to abolish bad customs and by the restoration of liberties to restore the realm to the condition it had enjoyed in the time of 'our noble ancestors'. Here the oaths sworn to the king by his subjects and the king's grant of 'liberties and free customs' are paired as contingencies. As to the true state of affairs, the closing sentences of this letter, promising a response to the suggestion that the king's mother and brother be sent for safety into Ireland, supply a more realistic picture of the desperate straits in which the royalists then found themselves (*Foedera*, 145; Stubbs, *Select Charters*, 333–5).

On 6 February 1217, the king sent further letters to Ireland, commending the loyalty of the Irish barons and, in reward, promising them inclusion in the same liberties that were set out in the charter (clearly Magna Carta) sealed with the seals of the king's guardians, that itself was now to be sent into Ireland (*Foedera*, 146; *Patent Rolls 1216–25*, 31). It was this 1216 charter, slightly altered so as to apply to the Irish as well as the English, that henceforth seems to have been the form of the charter observed in Ireland. In England, the 1216 charter seems to have been publicly proclaimed at least once again, in June 1217, when orders were issued for it be read in the county courts and for its terms to be enforced (*RLC*, i, 336). Thereafter, it too faded into obscurity. Only one original of the 1216 charter survives, in the archives of Durham Cathedral (below no.5). The bishop of Durham in 1216 was the king's chancellor, Richard Marsh, and we can well imagine why Marsh might have preserved the 1216 charter but disposed of all memory of the far more noxious charter of 1215. Elsewhere, copies of the 1216 charter are virtually unknown, save for two early versions that reached the French royal archives, probably via Louis of France who at this time was in occupation of large parts of southern England (below no.33 i/ii).

After Louis' defeat and surrender, Magna Carta was reissued again, late in 1217. This version survives in at least four originals (below nos.6–9) and in almost as many cartulary copies as the charter of 1215. In diplomatic

123 In 1225 the bishops enforced Magna Carta, solemnly pronouncing a sentence of excommunication against all who would break the Charter's terms. BL, Royal MS. 6 E VI, f. 216v. © The British Library Board.

terms it is a most peculiar document. The king himself, being a mere boy, had no seal of his own. Like the 1216 charter, the 1217 Magna Carta was therefore sealed with the seals of the papal legate, Guala, and the king's guardian, William Marshal earl of Pembroke. Unlike the 1216 charter, however, none of the originals of the 1217 charter has a dating clause. This has led to speculation as to the circumstances of its award, perhaps as early as September 1217, immediately after the making of peace, more likely in November, following a great council that also decreed the issue of the so-called Charter of the Forests. Such a charter, regulating the rights of king and barons to the exploitation of land placed under forest law, had itself been anticipated throughout the negotiations of 1214–15, from the time of the Unknown Charter onwards.

The 1217 Forest Charter, which survives in two originals, preserved in the cathedral archives of Durham and Lincoln cathedrals (below no.34 i–ii), is dated at St Paul's London on 6 November. An identical clause, with date 6 November, occurs in some but not all surviving copies of the 1217 Magna Carta. Why the 1217 Magna Carta was not originally supplied with a date remains uncertain. One explanation might lie with the need for all originals of the charter to be sealed both by the legate and William Marshal. For this to be achieved, it was perhaps considered better to draw up a large number of single sheets, all to be sealed on the same occasion, left undated in case they should be required for distribution subsequently.

Precisely such an eventuality seems to have come to pass in March 1218, when letters to the sheriff of York and more than twenty other counties announce the distribution of Magna Carta and the Forest Charter, with provision for them to be publicly and solemnly read in the county court. Here oaths were to be taken to observe the charter's terms, with sheriffs ensuring the enforcement of 'every point' (*singula puncta*) of the charters, paying particular attention to the final clause of the 1217 Magna Carta, demanding the destruction of all castles constructed since the start of the civil war in 1215 (*RLC*, 1, 377–7b). Enforcement of this same clause on castles was also commanded in letters from Pope Honorius III of 29 March 1219. Thus far, and despite the papal legate's support for the charters of 1216 and 1217, the pope himself had issued no explicit approval for a document, in theory condemned in August 1215 by his predecessor, Innocent III. The papal letters of 1219 suggest not only that the pope by now had his own copy of the 1217 Magna Carta, but tacitly approved of the charter as redrafted since 1216 (*Guala Letters*, 29–31 no.38n.).

As this suggests, having loomed large in the publication and distribution of the 1215 Magna Carta, the Church continued to play a role in its enforcement thereafter. In March 1218, for example, we find exemplars of the charter intended for publication in Somerset and in Rutland being sent to the local diocesans, Jocelin bishop of Bath and his brother, Hugh bishop of Lincoln (*RLC*, i, 377b–8). We have already encountered Archbishop Langton acting as midwife to the Runnymede charter. After his return from exile, the archbishop continued to press for the charter's enforcement. In 1225, it was Langton and his fellow bishops who took the lead in negotiating consent for taxation in return for the latest and definitive reissue of Magna Carta. On this occasion, the charter was accompanied by a solemn sentence of excommunication pronounced by Langton and the bishops against all who should infringe its terms (*Councils and Synods*, i, 137–8). Similar sentences may have been delivered by the papal legate in 1216 and 1217. If so, they go unrecorded. They were undoubtedly repeated thereafter, most notably in 1237 (below no.36 i–iii), and in 1253, when Langton's successor as archbishop, the king's uncle Boniface of Savoy, drew up a solemn document pronouncing anathema against all who infringed the charters (below no.37 i–ii). This in turn was communicated to the pope, who in 1254 confirmed the bishops' sentences. A further papal confirmation was obtained in 1257. Orders for the publication of the pope's letters of 1254 required that they be read in churches and in county and hundred courts not just in French but in English, being distributed together with further copies of Magna Carta itself now officially endorsed by the Church (below no.37).

By this time, Magna Carta had undoubtedly begun not only to be read, but on occasion to be written in French. A French translation of the 1215 charter, apparently made very soon after the events at Runnymede from the version of the charter sent into Hampshire, survives copied into a Norman manuscript of the 1220s or 30s (below no.47). French translations of the 1225 charter are occasionally met within books of statutes. The orders for publication of the pope's letters of 1254 suggest that vernacular publication, perhaps in English as well as in French, was already a common expectation (below no.37). Certainly, for the reforming Provisions of Oxford forced upon King Henry III in 1258, letters were dispatched to the counties in both French and English commanding publication and enforcement of what otherwise survives merely as a Latin text (Poole, 'Publication', 450). Meanwhile, the county court remained the chief venue

124 It was under Edward I that the Chancery began keeping Statute Rolls, onto which the 1297 reissue of Magna Carta was entered. BL, Cotton Vitellius MS. A. XIII, f. 6v. © The British Library Board.

for publication of Magna Carta as of other royal decrees.

In 1234, for example, at the end of a period of nearly two years during which Henry III and his chief minister, King John's friend, the bishop of Winchester, had attempted to govern arbitrarily and against the terms of Magna Carta, we find the republication of the charter marking the end of the bishop's regime. Not only were the sheriffs commanded to enforce and proclaim the Magna Cartas and Forest Charters that since 1225 had been kept in safe custody in each county, but the king himself had the charter read to him, in order to decide on the proper and lawful interpretation of its clauses relating to the holding of local courts and the treatment of those accused of felonies pending proper trial (*Close Rolls 1231–4*, 587–9, 592–3). This was to deal specifically with clauses 29 and 35 of the 1225 Magna Carta, not least by reiterating the principle that those accused were to be considered innocent until proven guilty. The safe keeping of the 1225 charter is further suggested by the original exemplar preserved in Lacock Abbey, marked on the back with a memorandum that it had been deposited at Lacock by the knights of the county of Wiltshire (below no.11). In 1234, as on many other occasions, both during the thirteenth century and thereafter, we have evidence for the public reading or proclamation of Magna Carta without proof that there was any official reissue of the document itself.

This in turn raises the question of numbers. We must allow for at least thirteen originals of the Runnymede charter distributed in 1215, and for more than twenty exemplars dispatched shire by shire for the reissues of 1217, 1225, 1265 and 1297. In 1216, amidst civil war, there were perhaps rather fewer. In 1300, for the final and definitive reissue there were perhaps a great many more. Certainly, it is the 1300 issue that survives in the greatest number today, in at least two cases (below nos.21, 23, at Faversham and for the borough of Sandwich) in exemplars that suggest a distribution extending beyond the county courts to other constituencies including towns and perhaps the greater churches. Even so, the total numbers seem never to have been very great. On a liberal estimate (in fact more of a guess) of sixty copies for the 1300 charter, and assuming that the issues of 1215, 1216, 1217, 1225, 1265, 1297 and 1300 were the only issues that involved the distribution of single-sheet exemplars under the king's seal, we would still only be dealing with a document issued in between 180 and 200 original exemplars.

Once again, it is remarkable that as many as one in ten of these (all told twenty-three authenticated originals) still survive. Given the taste that rats and mice have for parchment, given the archival chaos brought about by Reformation and civil war in the sixteenth and seventeenth centuries, given the fact that many of the greater cathedral archives of England have been looted and that the archives of the medieval sheriffs were never well kept, it is some proof of the veneration in which Magna Carta was held, both in the Middle Ages and thereafter, that so many original thirteenth-century exemplars have survived.

As for the legislation of later thirteenth-century kings, this too was only haphazardly preserved. It was only under Edward I that the chancery began to maintain a specific roll of statutes (TNA C 74/1), preserving Magna Carta as reissued in 1297. Before this, even Magna Carta was not enrolled in chancery. As for original single sheets of legislation, and with the notable exception of Magna Carta and the Forest Charter, these remain extremely rare. A draft writ of 'liberate' (ordering the release of funds from the treasury), issued in the name of Henry III, orders the payment of thirty shillings to Master Thomas of Wymondham, and four shillings and seven pence for parchment, expended in 'thirty pairs of our statutes to be sent to the itinerant justices perambulating our realm and to all our sheriffs' (TNA C 47/34/1/22), perhaps for the 1267 Statute of Marlborough (*Statutes* (1810), 19–25). Of the originals for which payment is here recorded, not a single one survives.

Both Henry III and Edward I issued a large body of legislation, but of this there are only two manuscripts that can be identified as 'official' originals, sent out under the king's seal, both now preserved in The National Archives at Kew: TNA E 175/11/5 (an official copy of the Statute of Wales 1284, apparently sent to the Exchequer), and TNA MS. PRO E 30/26/210 (an official copy of the Statute of Westminster II 1285, with remnants of a seal). The copies entered on the Statute Roll were assumed, into the 1930s, to be official and authoratative texts. It was as such that they were published by the editors of *Statutes of the Realm*, from 1810 onwards. However, more recent research suggests that the earliest legislation entered in the Statute Roll was drawn not from chancery originals but from unofficial copies or memoranda. Moreover, it was compiled some years after the issue of each statute, the first entries on the roll being made *c.*1299. Only later, in the fourteenth century, did the Statute Roll develop as a true master copy.

125 Copies of Magna Carta can be found in statute books, such as this of *c*.1300, which includes a copy of the 1225 Charter from its confirmation of 1265. Oxford, Bodleian Library, MS. Add. C. 1, ff. 3v-4r.

In the meantime, privately-produced copies of early statutes circulated at first on single sheets, in scroll format. Virtually all such early scrolls have perished, no doubt recycled as so much waste parchment once their contents had been copied into the books of statutes that from the late thirteenth century onwards became the chief unofficial means by which legislation was preserved, taught and memorialized. Of the few such scrolls that survive, we have a single-sheet copy from the mid-thirteenth century, recording slightly garbled texts of the 1225 Magna Carta and Forest Charter (London, Society of Antiquaries MS.544). William Blackstone, in the 1750s, fought a successful battle to prove that this was an early copy, not, as the Antiquaries themselves believed, an unrecognized original. From some years before this, and perhaps the very earliest such record, we also have a thirteenth-century copy in scroll format of the 1215 Magna Carta (Oxford, Bodleian Library MS. Lat. hist. a. 1 (P)), apparently made for public display, subsequently acquired by an unknown Italian collector or institution (below no.32).

A collection of charters and statutes in roll form, made for the disgraced Exchequer official, Adam of Stratton, including copies of Magna Carta 1225, the Statute of Merton 1236 and the Provisions of Westminster 1259, is today in The National Archives (TNA E 175/11/3). Several late thirteenth-century statutes, together with the 1300 reissues of Magna Carta and the Forest Charter, are to be found both in BL MS. Landsdowne Roll 11 (nicely decorated, apparently for the family that served as hereditary foresters of Savernake) and in a roll now at Chippenham (Wiltshire Record Office 9/32/1, thirteen membranes, stitched together Exchequer style, head to head). Like many other copies in early statute books, this last assigns a numbering system to the various clauses of Magna Carta (in 35 clauses), demonstrating that the charter was already being cited clause by clause, long before William Blackstone, and then William Stubbs, devised a definitive clause numbering from the 1750s onwards.

Even for Edward I's statutes of the 1270s and 80s, and here omitting documents that appear to represent official or semi-official drafts

126 England's bishops, responsible for Magna Carta's enforcement, ensured that the Charter was widely copied and distributed. BL, Royal 6 E VI, f. 145r. © The British Library Board.

preserved in the royal chancery or Exchequer, such as TNA E175/11/4 (Statute of Acton Burnell 1283) or E 175/11/6 (Statute of Wales 1284), we rely upon near-contemporary copies. One such, of the Second Statute of Westminster 1285 in scroll form (BL MSS. Additional 19559, acquired by the British Museum in 1853), is three metres long with blue and red line dividers, endorsed with Anglo-Norman lawyers' doggerel and with a series of interpretations in Latin and Anglo-Norman French. Two other copies of this same statute, both more or less contemporary, are to be found as Bedford, Bedfordshire Record Office MS. WW1 (from the muniments of the Trevor family, just possibly a damaged official version of the statute), and as BL MS. Additional 31891 (acquired in 1881, twelve feet long). Another, perhaps slightly earlier, takes the form of a copy of Edward I's Statute of Gloucester (1278), apparently made from the original statute as delivered to the sheriff of Sussex (Philadelphia, University of Pennsylvania MS. Schoenberg 144114, purchased by the dealers Les Eluminures from Bloomsbury Book Auctions, London 10 December 2008 for £7,200, subsequently sold to Philadelphia for a price reported as $94,250). A scroll of three membranes, perhaps originally from Guisborough Priory in Yorkshire, later owned by Lord Gisborough (Northallerton, North Yorkshire Record Office MS. ZFM 350), preserves copies and Anglo-Norman translations from shortly after 1300 of both the so-called 'Confirmatio Cartarum' of 10 October 1297, by which Edward I agreed to the renewal of Magna Carta and the Forest Charter, and of the text of the latest substantive reissue of Magna Carta, dated 28 March 1300.

In the specialist literature, two other such scrolls are recorded: one in Nova Scotia (King's College MS. MM2, the so-called 'Brevia Placitata' and 'Casus Placitorum', before 1275), the other in California (San Marino, Huntington Library HM27186, six membranes sewn chancery style, with a text of Westminster II on the front, Winchester and 'Casus Placitorum' on the dorse together with a more recently added copy of a statute of 14 Edward III). Not previously noticed, but from the early to mid-fourteenth century, a roll reciting the 1300 Magna Carta and Forest Charter, stitched together with a lawyer's copy of the assize of bread and ale, has recently come to light in St John's College Cambridge (Archives D98.46, in 38 clauses), perhaps preserved for the use of the Cambridge Hospital of St John.

As this should suggest, beyond the twenty-four surviving single-sheet Magna Cartas, the text was chiefly preserved not in enrolled copies, of which there are precious few, but in lawyers' books of statutes and registers of writs. Of these, many hundreds survive from the mid-thirteenth century onwards. They represent the continuation, albeit now in mass-produced quantities, of the twelfth-century tradition of unofficial collections of law and legislation. As we have seen, such lawyers' copies played their own role in the later history of Magna Carta, not least because it was from just such a copy that the 1265 Magna Carta seems to have been drafted. In the process, the framers of this document reintroduced a distinction to the text, first discussed at Runnymede in 1215 but thereafter omitted from all official issues of Magna Carta, by which earls were required to pay £100 to inherit their lands, mere barons only 100 marks (£66).

By this time, so ubiquitous were the charters of liberties that it is hard to imagine any royal official or any member of political society remaining ignorant of their terms. Even so, it was precisely to guard against such ignorance that Simon de Montfort and the barons, for their reissue of the charter in 1265, demanded that henceforth it be read twice a year in the county courts. Even more strenuous efforts were required in 1300, when the so-called 'Articles upon the Charters', intended to deal with the enforcement of the 1300 reissue, demanded that the charters henceforth be publicly read not once or twice but at least four times a year.

The Church itself pursued a similar, totemic insistence on the charters' frequent and public recital. In 1279, for example, a church council at Reading presided over by the archbishop of Canterbury, John Peckham, demanded that Magna Carta be publicly displayed in every cathedral and collegiate church in England, all of these copies being annually renewed each Easter. In the ensuing Parliament, the archbishop was forced to back down. The demand that Magna Carta be displayed in church porches was rescinded (*Councils and Synods*, ii, 851, 856–7, 887). Even so, in due course the text of the charter was to be found not only copied into the books of statutes kept by lawyers and those interested in the common law, but enshrined within the standard treatises on canon law by which the Church was governed. The Church's chief concern here lay in part with clause 1 of the charter and its protection of specifically ecclesiastical liberty, in part with the need to save souls and hence to ensure that nobody, through ignorance, incur the automatic sentences of excommunication imposed, since 1225, on any infringements of the charter. In all of this, Magna Carta was already far on the road from statute to icon.

REFERENCES

Reginald Lane Poole, 'The Publication of Great Charters by the English Kings', *EHR*, xxviii (1913), pp.444–53, remains extremely useful. For the laws of the Anglo-Saxons, Patrick Wormald, *The Making of English Law: King Alfred to the Twelfth Century*, i, (Oxford 1999); Bruce O'Brien, *God's Peace and King's Peace: The Laws of Edward the Confessor* (Philadelphia 1999); Paul Hyams, *Rancor and Reconciliation in Medieval England* (Ithaca 2003); John Hudson, *The Oxford History of the Laws of England. Volume II: 871–1216* (Oxford 2012), and most recently Bruce O'Brien, 'Pre-Conquest Laws and Legislators in the Twelfth Century', *The Long Twelfth-Century View of the Anglo-Saxon Past*, ed. Martin Brett and David A. Woodman (Farnham 2015). See also J.C. Holt, 'The Assizes of Henry II: the texts', in *The Study of Medieval Records: Essays in honour of Kathleen Major* (Oxford 1971), pp.85–106; Paul Brand, 'Henry II and the Creation of the English Common Law', *Henry II: New Interpretations*, ed. C. Harper-Bill and N. Vincent (Woodbridge 2007), pp.215–41. For the Irish letters of 1207, *RLP*, 92. For publication in 1215, see Collins, 'Documents', pp.275–9; Ifor Rowlands, 'The Text and Distribution of the Writ for the Publication of Magna Carta, 1215', *EHR*, cxxiv (2009), pp.1422–31; Carpenter, *Magna Carta* (2015), pp.9–17, 373–403. For the circumstances of publication in 1225, 1253–4, and for the Council of Reading 1279, *Councils and Synods with Other Documents Relating to the English Church: II (A.D. 1205–1313)*, ed. F. M. Powicke and C. R. Cheney, 2 vols (Oxford 1964); David Carpenter, 'Magna Carta 1253: The Ambitions of the Church and the Divisions within the Realm', *Historical Research*, lxxxvi (2013), pp.179-90; Felicity Hill, 'Magna Carta and Pastoral Care' (forthcoming). For publication after 1215, including in the vernacular, J.C. Holt, 'The St Albans Chroniclers and Magna Carta', *Transactions of the Royal Historical Society*, 5th series xiv (1964), pp.67–88, below nos.45, 47–8. For the transmission of the Irish text of 1216/17, below no.49. For the publication of later legislation, and for manuscript transmission, see H.G. Richardson, 'The Early Statutes', *Law Quarterly Review*, l (1934), pp.201–23, 540–71; T.F.T. Plucknett, *Legislation of Edward I* (Oxford 1949); Paul Brand, 'English Thirteenth Century Legislation', *Colendi iustitiam et iura condendo. Federico II legislatore del Regno di Sicilia nell'Europa del Ducento*, ed. A. Romano (Rome 1997), pp.325–44; ibid., *Kings, Barons and Justices: the Making and Enforcement of Legislation in Thirteenth-Century England* (Cambridge 2004), and the three indispensable catalogues by Sir John Baker, *English Legal Manuscripts*, 2 vols (Zug 1975–8); *English Legal Manuscripts in the United States of America*, 2 vols (London, Selden Society, 1985–90), and *A Catalogue of English Legal Manuscripts in Cambridge University Library* (Woodbridge 1996).

CHAPTER 7
Scribes and sealing

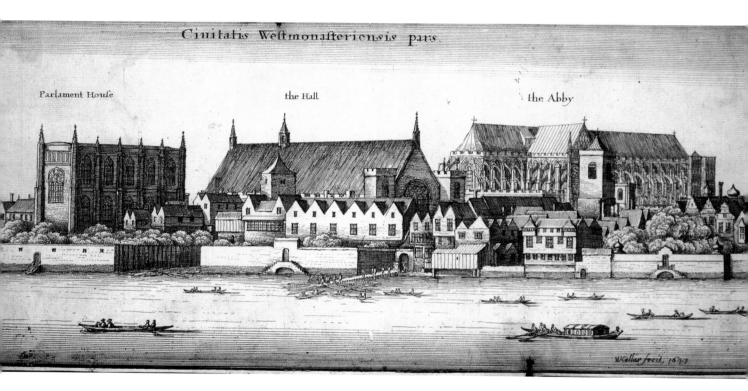

Cuitatis Westmonasteriensis pars.

Parlament House   the Hall   the Abby

W. Hollar fecit, 1647

127 In the course of the thirteenth century, Westminster became home to growing numbers of clerks employed in royal service. Wenceslaus Hollar, *Westminster from the River, etching, 1647* (Pennington 1037; Turner, New Hollstein German, 950). The Thomas Fisher Rare Book Library, University of Toronto, Hollar_k_0989. © University of Toronto.

S o far, we have dealt with the issue and survival of the document known as Magna Carta. It remains to deal briefly with the document's physical appearance. For a document of such iconic significance, it is peculiar that the twenty-three surviving Magna Cartas (twenty-four if we include a locally produced single sheet from Oseney Abbey, below no.24) are presented in at least three distinct formats. Sixteen of the twenty-four charters are longer than they are wide, in 'portrait' format (nos.1, 4, 6, 8–14, 16–20, 23). Four (or five, if we include the peculiar version from Oseney Abbey) are wider than they are long, in 'landscape' format (nos.2, 7, 15, 21, and cf. no.24), and three are more or less square (nos.3, 5, 22). All three of these basic formats were used for the very first issue of the charter, in 1215. The royal chancery, it seems, had no fixed preconception of what Magna Carta should look like, save that its sheer size was likely to be one of its more impressive features.

Although increasingly known as 'Magna' Carta ('the great' charter, a term first applied to it in 1217), it should be noted that Magna Carta is, in purely physical terms, by no means the largest, widest or longest instrument issued from the thirteenth-century chancery. Henry II and Richard I had sealed much larger single sheets, and even the general run of King John or Henry III's monastic confirmation charters frequently approach or exceed Magna Carta in their physical scale. The size of such documents was limited by one factor above all others. To be issued as an officially sealed original, a royal charter had to fit on to a single sheet of sheepskin parchment. Since medieval sheep were much smaller than modern breeds, and since only parts of their skin were suitable for parchment, charters were limited in size and had to be written in deliberately abbreviated characters. In the case of a large text such as Magna Carta, the script had to be made smaller, rather as modern word-processing allows for use of a footnote rather than a plain text

128 Highly skilled scribes were sometimes called upon to produce large-scale charters, which would have taken several hours to write out. Royal MS. 6 E VII, f. 514r. © The British Library Board

'font size'. All of the surviving Magna Cartas display an expert ability to write to scale. Only in the fourteenth century did the chancery begin to accommodate much longer texts by allowing charters to spread from a single parchment membrane to two or more sheets joined together at the foot and jointly sealed

A great deal of the detail in the work of the royal chancery was left to the discrimination of individual clerks and scribes. The chancery itself was an increasingly bureaucratized operation. Even by John's reign, the skeleton staff that had written royal letters in the early twelfth century had begun to expand. More and more clerks were drafted in to write the many thousands of writs now controlling procedures in the king's courts. King John's chancery ordinance of 1199 assumes the existence of a staff of half a dozen officials, responsible for the approval, dictation, writing and sealing of royal letters. By the mid-thirteenth century this establishment had at least doubled in size. By the reign of Edward I, it was issuing several hundred letters a day and employed many dozens of clerks, all of whom had to be found lodgings in the vicinity of the increasingly cramped Palace of Westminster. John's chancery, by contrast, remained an itinerant affair, travelling the length and breadth of the king's dominions as the king himself dispensed royal lordship and justice. It was only during the reign of Henry III, in part as a result of the king's own long minority, that Westminster became the fixed centre of government activity. A start here, nonetheless, had been made as early as the twelfth century with the removal to Westminster from Winchester, the ancient capital of the West Saxon state, of the Exchequer (the king's financial office) and the records of the king's government.

These records themselves became more sophisticated and more numerous as time went by. England was already a heavily taxed and therefore a partially bureaucratized realm by 1066. Domesday Book, compiled twenty years after the Conquest but based to a large extent upon memories and written records stretching back half a century or more, is itself testimony not so much to Norman as to Anglo-Saxon traditions of record keeping. Over the course of the next century, written records remained essential to the cross-Channel empire that the Normans pioneered. Only by the dispatch of written instructions could the Norman and Plantagenet kings govern their far-flung lands in England or France. Only by reading the written reports and accounts prepared by their officials, could kings maintain control over public finances, strained to the limits by the costs of warfare in France, Wales and Ireland. In the process, the kings of England, with their administrative centres at Winchester and Westminster, came not only to issue but to preserve a rich documentary archive, in many cases still surviving to the present day. Domesday Book, as early as the twelfth century, was being referred to, from its place of keeping, as the 'Roll of Winchester'. By the reign of King John, we have our first references to an official specifically appointed to supervize the king's archive at Westminster. His name, William 'Cuckoo Well', is perhaps a reflection of his obligation to preserve echoes of the administrative past. King John is also the first post-Conquest king of England known to have maintained his own private library, extending from books that might be regarded as entirely predictable (an Old Testament, a Pliny, a Valerius Maximus) via the theological (Origen, Augustine, Peter the Lombard's *Sentences*, Hugh of St-Victor's *De sacramentis*) to the downright esoteric (Candidus Arianus, *De Generatione divina*).

Meanwhile to maintain control over the increasing volume of administrative business, the English royal Exchequer began to maintain rolls of its financial accounts. Known as the 'Pipe Rolls' (apparently from their resemblance to lengths of piping), these survive in broken sequence from 1130 onwards. By the reign of Henry II they had been joined by rolls recording judicial business conducted in the king's courts (today surviving from the 1190s onwards). From King John's accession in 1199, this documentary tide was massively swelled by the survival of the rolls of the royal chancery, preserving copies of tens of thousands of charters and letters issued in the king's name. These chancery rolls, although they first survive from John's reign, were in some instances merely the continuation of more ancient series, now lost. The majority, however, seem to have been first maintained by John, whose own paranoia and determination to control the processes of government perhaps explain their making.

Their bulk is impressive. Beginning in 1199 with a roll of the king's outgoing charters, within the next few years they extend to rolls of royal letters close (sealed so that the seal had to be broken were the letter to be read) and patent (sealed so as to be read without breaking the seal). This in turn implies an exponential growth in the size of the chancery establishment, as more clerks were needed not only to write the king's letters but to copy them into the rolls. Some today question the capacity of modern historians to write in such detail of the events of so distant

Carta Domini Iocelini Bathon̄ = Wiltoniens̄ Ep̄i.

Carta Domini Hugon̄ Lincol̄ niens̄ Ep̄i.

a past. A glance at the chancery rolls of John's reign should convince such doubters of the the sheer wealth of information at our disposal: tens of thousands of charters and writs copied out year by year in roughly chronological sequence.

The rolls also serve as introduction to those members of the chancery staff most crucial to the publication of Magna Carta. For the Runnymede settlement to be distributed it had first to be written out, with goose quill pens on sheepskin. To transform sheepskin into parchment, the materials had to be laboriously prepared, with the 'hair' side rubbed smooth and the whole polished and ruled so as to receive the strokes of the pen. The Runnymede settlement, like all royal charters, was negotiated in the French language of the Plantagenet court (itself mocked by the French as a regionalized version of the French of Paris). It was written, however, in Latin, the language of government and the Church. Although many people could read Latin, relatively few could write it, not only because of its grammatical pitfalls but because the skills of the scribe were themselves laborious to acquire. In part to save on parchment and ink, in part to advertise their own particular expertise, scribes adopted a heavily abbreviated form of writing, half way between modern handwriting and shorthand. In this, very few words were written out in full. A word like 'omnibus', for example, could be contracted to merely one or two marks, with further pen strokes above or below to indicate the omission of letters such as 'm' or the standard Latin 'case' endings to words. The word for 'and' could be written as a single pen stroke (the origins of the modern ampersand '&'). Place names and personal names, turned into Latin, could appear in a bewildering variety of forms. We find this in the 1215 Magna Carta, with disagreement amongst the scribes of the four surviving charters as to whether Runnymede should be spelled as *Runningmed* (below nos.1, 4), *Ronimed* (no.2) or *Runimed* (no.3). A contemporary French translation of the charter offers the entirely unintelligible form *Roueninkmede* (no.47).

The work of a scribe was dull and laborious. It was nonetheless significant. For a scribe to lose concentration was potentially disastrous. A single missed stroke of the pen, or a single error in Latin grammar, could entirely transform a document's meaning. Hence the insistence, reported in English government from the 1170s onwards (itself merely repeating demands voiced earlier by the Roman emperor Justinian) that no royal letters should contain corrections. If a mistake were detected,

129 John oversaw a prodigious increase in royal record keeping, including the production of rolls recording the king's charters. TNA C 53/12 m.5, Charter Roll 16 John (1214-15). © National Archives, London.

the faulty document must be discarded and written again from scratch. Our modern phrase 'from scratch' is itself a legacy of the medieval past, since the only way for parchment to be corrected, once ink had been applied to it, was for the offending passage to be scratched clean with a sharp piece of bone or metal. In practice, with a document as long and as complex as Magna Carta, errors inevitably crept in, so that we have signs of correction even to this most important of texts. The most obvious of these are the amendments and corrections to various clauses inserted in the bottom margins of the two original 1215 Magna Cartas preserved in the British Library (below nos.1–2). Even later, however, we can find occasional instances in the reissues of the charter where scribes have made corrections, sometimes by erasure and rewriting, sometimes by inserting words or letters immediately above the offending line. Only when these corrections reach extreme proportions, as they do with one of the exemplars of the 1300 Magna Carta (below no.24, apparently an 'unofficial' exemplar produced at Oseney Abbey in Oxfordshire), can we be fairly confident that we are dealing with documents produced unofficially, outside the royal chancery.

Scribes were human beings. On cold winter's mornings when the ink froze, or late at night when their eyes grew tired, they gave vent to their frustrations. The records of medieval English government are themselves littered with such *cris de coeur*. In the 1160s, for example, one of the scribes writing the Exchequer's Pipe Roll grew tired of his work. Copying out a long and laborious list of Exchequer receipts, he ended with a remark, perhaps aimed at one of his colleagues: 'Richard de Neville is a black, bad man'. Like those attending dull meetings even today, scribes were given to doodling. The most famous outcome of this appears at the end of one of the Exchequer rolls of the 1230s dealing with Jewish debts. The scribe here used the end of the roll to make a large and elaborate drawing of Isaac of Norwich, Jewish money lender, portrayed in Satanic guise surrounded by demons and devils (fig.130). Other such drawings come to us from the scribes of King John. In the summer of 1216, for example, the court was approached by a woman named Philippa of Paulton. This relatively humble petitioner was satirized in a cartoon, drawn in the margin of one of the chancery rolls, showing her as a 'mad crane', half woman, half bird (TNA C 54/14 m.5, whence *RLC*, i, 281b).

Thanks to detailed work on the twelfth-century royal chancery, we can be confident that King John's father, Henry II, had his charters written by upwards of a dozen professional scribes, of whom only four or five were in service together at any one time. Two scribes in particular took responsibility for a disproportionate quantity of this work, between them writing no less than 170, or more than a third, of the king's surviving 500 original charters. When occasion demanded, the king continued to put his seal to documents that had been drafted outside the chancery by scribes attached to the beneficiaries of his charters. Thus, under Henry II the monks of Canterbury or Caen, and the canons of Lincoln Cathedral continued to draw up their own charters, written according to the rules of the royal chancery, but composed locally and then merely presented to the king and his writing office for authentication under the royal seal. The same seems to have remained true of King John's chancery, where we occasionally encounter not only Latin formulae but handwriting that suggests beneficiary rather than chancery production.

The scribes of the twelfth century often wrote in idiosyncratic hands, relatively easy to tell apart from one another. This remained true of the scribes working at court during the early years of King John. By 1215, however, there was already a tendency towards uniformity, perhaps

131 Most of King John's charters, like those of his father Henry II, were produced by scribes employed by the Crown. Oxford, Bodleian Library, MS. Rawl. Q. b. 6, f. 360r.

as a result of the now far more onerous routine required to maintain the chancery's many enrolments. This in turn encouraged an already established trend towards routine and mass production, away from the laborious traditions of monastic writing practice (forming letters with two or more individual pen strokes) to what we today call 'cursive' handwriting (where letters, and sometimes groups of letters, are all formed from a single pen line). As a result of growing uniformity and of the sheer number of scribes employed in chancery, it becomes increasingly difficult to identify particular charters as the work of particular chancery scribes. Even so, two of the surviving originals of the 1215 Magna Carta (below nos.1–2), together with the Articles of the Barons (no.27) could well have been written within the king's writing office. The other two Magna Cartas, today surviving at Lincoln and Salisbury, were written in hands more reminiscent of scribes working in episcopal households. Indeed, they may well have been written not by royal but by episcopal scribes, the Lincoln charter by a scribe of the Bishop of Lincoln, the Salisbury charter by a scribe of Salisbury's Dean and Chapter.

From our knowledge of the subsequent reissues of the charter, in 1216, 1217 and 1225, it is apparent that later Magna Cartas continued to be produced within the chancery, perhaps without the imperatives of speed that had determined production in 1215, and therefore without the need to employ scribes from outside the usual ranks of chancery professionals. Through to the 1230s, the writing of Henry III's charters remains sufficiently flamboyant to allow us to trace the work of individual scribes. Thereafter, the deadening hand of uniformity descends. By the reign of Edward I (1272–1307), estimates of the number of clerks in and around the royal court range as high as 1500 individuals. By this time, the writing of Edward's letters and charters was so routine as to defy all attempts at the identification of particular scribes. This is ironic, since it is from this same period that we first begin to find the names of individual chancery officers inserted in the bottom right hand corner of royal letters, following on from the final dating clause.

In Magna Carta, such 'signatures' first appear in the reissue of 1297, two of whose exemplars (below nos.14, 16) have the names of chancery officers, John of Stowe and Hugh of Yarmouth, inserted in the bottom right hand corner of the text block. As I have argued elsewhere (*Sotheby's MC*, 41–5), it is more likely that the names inserted here are those of the chancery officials responsible for the charters' warranty and issue, rather

132 A charter confirming the foundation of the Grandmontine Priory at Rouen, produced by a royal scribe in the first year of John's reign, written in a characteristic chancery hand. BL, Add. MS. Ch. 11314. © The British Library Board.

26 Septr 1199

Johannes Dei gra Rex Angl Dns Hybnie Dux Norm. Aquit. 7 Com Andeg Archiepis.

Epis Abbib3 Comit Baron Justic Viceom 7 Omib3 Balluis 7 fidelib3 suis Norm. 7 Domsacim Maiori

Vic 7 Omib3 Balluis suis Rothomag Salt. Sciatis nos concessisse 7 hac presenti Carta nostra confirmasse

Bonis hoib3 Grandi montis fundatione domus qm Pat noster H bone memorie in dnico suo iuxta Roth

mag fecit 7 donatione qm idem Pr noster eis fecit ad victualia sua Scilt. Ducentas libs Andeg reci-

piendas Annuatim de Vicecomitatu Rothomagen. videlicet Centum libras ad Pascha. Et Centum ad fest Sci

Michael O nare volum 7 firmiter precipim quod & eas habeant in libam 7 perpetuam elemosinam 7 singul

annis ad predcos tinios eas in predco Vicecomitatu recipiant Sicut in Carta Dm H Pris nri gomet.

His Test R Epo Sci Andree Willo Lunge Espee Com Sarisb Willo Com Arundell Hug

de Gornaco Rog Constabtario Cestr Willo de Cantilupo Petro de Stoke Dat per man

Symon Archid Wellen 7 Johis de Gr apud Chynon XXVI die Septembr is anno

Regni nostri tri Et iro

than those of the scribe. The appearance of the name of Hugh of Yarmouth in this position in the Canberra Magna Carta (below no.16) helps confirm that this charter was originally stored as a part of a pair, in the same archive as the sole surviving exemplar of the 1297 Forest Charter now in the British Library (below no.39). Both of these documents were expedited for issue to the county of Surrey, as is revealed by the writing that appears on the face of each, either side of the seal impression. Similar marks on the fold appear in other examples of the 1297 and 1300 Magna Cartas, identifying particular charters as the exemplars sent into Buckinghamshire (no.14), to the city of London (nos.15, 18) or to the men ('the barons') of the Cinque Ports town of Faversham (no.21). On occasion further notes here supply details of the chancery's operations: the examination of particular charters by the chancellor (no.19) or by men named Master Edmund of London (no.21) and 'R. de Stard' (no.15), and in one unique instance the name of the officer (Roger Hodelyn of Newport Pagnell, no.14) assigned to proclaim a particular exemplar of the charter to the men of Buckinghamshire. To some extent, these addresses and notes of warranty merely continue the tradition of the 1215 Lincoln charter. This (below no.3) is endorsed with what may well have been a contemporary address: *Lincolnia*, apparently written in the same hand that wrote the text itself.

There is one further consequence to the work of the scribes of Magna Carta, often overlooked although highly significant. Because each exemplar was written out by hand, and because no one exemplar of any particular issue of the charter can be claimed as the 'master', not even the unique exemplar of the 1216 charter surviving at Durham (below no.5), each single sheet may contain minor verbal differences that materially alter both the transmitted text and our understanding of its meaning. Sometimes, these distinctions are fairly major, as they are between three of 1217 charters that end with a particular form of words that is not repeated in the fourth surviving original (below no.9). By a slip of the pen, the scribe of the Washington original of the 1297 charter has altered the meaning of clause 33 of the charter by employing the feminine Latin pronoun *que* as opposed to the masculine *qui* (*Sotheby's MC*, 24). Many other such variants still await discovery. It is worth stressing here that despite more than four hundred years of scholarly enquiry, there has never yet

133 Richard I, like his predecessors since the Norman Conquest, was shown on the reverse of his seal as a warrior riding into battle. Equestrian seal (1195) of Richard I of England, Museum of Vendée. Photo © Selbymay.

been a word-by-word edition of Magna Carta and its reissues in which the variations between each of the originals have been noted. This is perhaps not surprising given that the present book includes the first full census of such originals, several of which have previously gone unnoticed or ignored. Even now, therefore, Magna Carta has still to yield up at least some of its secrets.

Having been written, royal charters had then to be authenticated. We have already encountered some of the later signs of authentication in the notes written on the face of various of the exemplars of 1297 and 1300, recording warranty or examination by particular officials within chancery. Even then, however, the charter could not be considered authentic without its bearing an impression of the king's seal. Dating back to ancient Mesopotamia and beyond, the practice of sealing was a method by which those of high status, regardless of their own ability to write, could leave a 'sign' upon their documents, often a sign that combined letters impressed in wax or metal with a memorable image by which the grantor could hope to be recognized.

Seals were already in use for English royal charters before the Norman Conquest. Edward the Confessor, indeed, was the first English king to adopt what previously had been a continental practice, pioneered by the Holy Roman emperors, of using a double sided seal, impressed in coloured wax. Where previously seals could be carried by their owners, in the form of a ring or die that could be impressed in a single piece of wax, double sided seals demanded more elaborate equipment, including a 'seal press' (to ensure the alignment of the two sides of the metal seal die) and the

134 Seal matrices, like this example made in the second half of the thirteenth century for Inchaffray Abbey in Perthshire, produced double-sided seals with detailed imagery. British Museum, M&ME 1917,11-10,1. © Trustees of the British Museum.

135 a. *top* John's seal was executed with an impressive degree of precision, allowing the king's face and the three lions passant on his shield to be seen in detail. Eton College, ECR 27 2 reverse. © Eton College.

b. *above* The obverse of John's seal, like those of his forebears, showed the king enthroned and crowned, holding a sword and sceptre as symbols of his power. Eton College, ECR 27 3. © Eton College.

cutting or folding of the bottom of documents, to allow a parchment tag or silk threads to carry the weight of the wax seal. To begin with, natural or brown beeswax was the only material used in the sealing of English royal documents. By the mid-twelfth century this had come to be supplemented by a variety of pigments, allowing for green or reddish brown seal impressions, with green, in due course, winning out as the standard colour for the seals of documents that granted rights or property in perpetuity.

The Norman Conquest also ushered in another change to the appearance of the English royal seal. Where Edward the Confessor had shown himself on both sides of his seal seated in majesty carrying rods or sceptres as symbols of his peace and justice, William the Conqueror intruded a new, more martial symbolism. The king was now shown on one side of his seal enthroned in majesty. On the other, he appeared as a mounted warrior riding into battle, brandishing a spear or a sword.

It was a seal descended from this tradition that King John used to seal both the Articles of the Barons (below no.27) and all surviving originals of the Magna Carta issued at Runnymede. Most readers will know that John did not 'sign' Magna Carta, in the sense that he himself made no pen marks on the document and used no 'signature' to declare his assent. Even to suggest that the king 'sealed' Magna Carta is itself an anachronism, since it is most unlikely that kings either wished to, or knew how to manipulate the equipment, including the seal press, used for the impression of their double sided seals. At best, perhaps, the king passed his hand over the document or held it in some ritual way, to signal his assent. We read of just such a practice in the 1160s, when John's father, Henry II, signalled his approval for a charter of St Albans Abbey by taking threads from his silk cloak and placing them on the document, perhaps to be used as cords from which the seal itself could in due course hang.

The Articles of the Barons (no.27) retain a fragment of King John's seal, attached using a parchment tag, now stored apart from the document itself. Another seal fragment, reduced in the Cotton fire of 1731 to a shapeless lump, hangs from one of the two Runnymede Magna Cartas preserved in the British Library (below no.1). The other three surviving originals are without seals, in two cases with traces suggesting that they were originally sealed on silk cords, rather than on parchment tags.

136 a. *left* A smaller seal was used by the regency council to issue Magna Carta in 1297, identical to this example preserved with another royal charter. BL, Add. Ch. MS. 34949. © The British Library Board.

b. *below* Edward I's great seal was attached to exemplars of his 1300 Magna Carta as well as to letters patent, of 1301, ordering the Charter's enforcement. Oxford, Bodleian Library, MS. Ch. Glouc. 26, reverse.

Sealing on parchment tags remained the standard method for subsequent issues of the charter (nos.5–9, 14, 18, 19, 21–4), although cords continued to be used in a minority of instances (nos.10–12, 15, 16, ?17, 20), especially for the issue of 1225. What is perhaps most surprising here is that, of the surviving Magna Cartas that still carry seals, the great seal of England appears only (in melted form) on the burned Cotton charter (no.1), on the issue of 1225 (nos.10–12), and on three of the exemplars of the 1300 issue (nos.19–21). A higher number of the surviving exemplars carry the seals not of the king himself but of those acting on his behalf: the papal legate Guala (no.7), William Marshal, earl of Pembroke (nos.6, 8), and the vice-regents of Edward I acting during the king's absence overseas in 1297 (nos.14–16). This latter seal, smaller than the great seal, with the king on the majesty side shown carrying wands or sceptres in each hand (rather than the orb and sword shown on the majesty side of the great seal), was only properly identified in 2007, at the time of the sale of the Washington exemplar of the 1297 Magna Carta. It carries us back to a more ancient tradition of royal seals, directly transmitted from the more 'peaceful' image of Edward the Confessor used to seal documents before 1066 (*Sotheby's MC*, 46–8). The appearance of the seal of Abbot John of Oseney on one of the seven surviving exemplars of the 1300 Magna Carta is amongst the many indications that this most peculiar exemplar is a local, rather than a chancery-manufactured instrument.

Most of the surviving Magna Carta seals, including that of the abbot

of Oseney, were made in green or green-coloured wax. Even so, we find natural wax used for two of the three sealed 1297 charters (nos.14, 16) and for all sealed examples of the 1300 charter (nos.19–21). There is no easy explanation for this, other than the fact that uncoloured wax was considered appropriate for routine or duplicate instruments, whereas green wax was reserved for the more solemn privileges granted in perpetuity. To seal Magna Carta in natural wax was thus to declare it, by 1297, not so much a new and solemn convenant, but a mere confirmation of routine. To this extent, even the document's sealing confirms Magna Carta's wider trajectory, from controversial new measure to universally respected totem.

REFERENCES

For scribes at the Plantagenet court, the classic study remains that by T.A.M. Bishop, *Scriptores Regis* (Oxford 1961). For the growth of bureaucracy and the royal chancery, Michael T. Clanchy, *From Memory to Written Record* (London 1979, 3rd ed. Chichester 2013); Nicholas Vincent, 'Why 1199? Bureaucracy and Enrolment under John and his Contemporaries', *English Government in the Thirteenth Century*, ed. Adrian Jobson (Woodbridge 2004), pp.17–48; David Carpenter, '"In Testimonium Factorum Brevium": The Beginnings of the English Chancery Rolls', *Records, Administration and Aristocratic Society in the Anglo-Norman Realm: Papers Commemorating the 800th Anniversary of King John's Loss of Normandy*, ed. Nicholas Vincent (Woodbridge 2009), pp.1–28. For reading, writing and book keeping at the Plantagenet court, Nicholas Vincent 'The Great Lost Library of England's Medieval Kings? Royal Use and Ownership of Books, 1066–1272', *1000 Years of Royal Books and Manuscripts*, ed. K. Doyle and S. McKendrick (London 2013), pp.73–112; Vincent, 'Scribes in the Chancery of Henry II, King of England 1154–1189', *Le scribe d'archive dans l'Occident médiéval : formations, carrières, réseaux. Actes du colloque international de Namur, 2–4 mai 2012*, ed. X. Hermand, J.-F. Nieus and É. Renard (Turnhout 2015). For sealing practice, Vincent, 'The Seals of King Henry II and his Court', *Seals and their Context in the Middle Ages*, ed. Phillipp R. Schofield (Oxford 2015). For unofficial annotation of government records, Andrew H. Hershey, *Drawings and Sketches in the Plea Rolls of the English Royal Courts, c.1200–1300*, List and Index Society Special Series 31 (2002). For prohibitions against the correction of slips of the pen, Collins, 'Documents', pp.262–4.

137 One of the surviving exemplars of the 1300 Magna Carta was produced not by the royal chancery but by the Abbey of Oseney, whose abbot is depicted on the document's seal. Oxford, Bodleian Library, MS. Ch. Oxon. Oseney 143b*.

CHAPTER 8

A census of Magna Carta manuscripts

WHAT FOLLOWS represents the fullest census of Magna Carta manuscripts published since the unreliable and outdated list in the first volume of the official *Statutes of the Realm* (1810). Including the issue of 1300, there are today twenty-three (or, depending upon how one counts them, twenty-four) surviving originals of Magna Carta issued by the royal chancery as single sheets of parchment. Their provenance is in some cases known. Thus, in alphabetical order, the following cathedral or monastic archives preserved the following Magna Cartas: Canterbury Cathedral (no.1), Durham Cathedral (nos.5, 10, 19), Easebourne Priory (no.16), Gloucester Abbey (no.8), Hereford Cathedral (no.9), Lacock Abbey (no.11), Lincoln Cathedral (no.3), Oseney Abbey (nos.6, 7, 24), Salisbury Cathedral (no.4) and Westminster Abbey (no.22). Of these archives, some certainly (Easebourne no.16, and Lacock no.11), and others almost certainly (Oseney nos.6, 7, 24, and Westminster no.22) served merely as repositories for charters deposited at the suggestion of sheriffs or county communities. The paired 1300 Magna Carta and Forest Charter today at Oriel College, Oxford (nos.20, 41 iv) seem originally to have been intended for preservation in the archives of St Mary's, the Oxford University church. Other such paired Magna Carta and Forest Charter sets survive at Durham (from both 1225, nos.10, 35 i, and 1300, nos.19, 41 i), amongst the scattered remains of the archive of Easebourne Priory (used as repository for the Surrey exemplars of 1297, nos.16, 39), in the archives of the borough of Sandwich (from 1300, nos.23, 41 v), and just possibly for Lincoln (1225, no.35 ii, and cf. no.13).

In all cases, including Durham, charters were preserved in cathedrals or monasteries even though they were intended first and foremost for publication in the county or borough courts. Only where the county or borough had a very firm tradition of preserving its own instruments (as was the case with the London Guildhall, nos.15, 18, or the Cinque Port towns of Faversham and Sandwich nos.21, 23) did the county or town itself serve successfully as custodian. In one instance, a charter addressed to the county court (no.14, for Buckinghamshire) has been preserved by means unknown, ending up in a private family estate archive. In others, we have at least four Magna Cartas of unknown provenance (nos.2, 12, 13, 17), including one unprovenanced exemplar of the original settlement made at Runnymede (no.2).

Of the miscellaneous evidences associated with Magna Carta between 1215 and 1305, a list is supplied below of a further 25 instruments (nos.25–49, covering thirty-seven individual manuscripts, in most cases original single sheets). Once again, the majority of these survived in ecclesiastical custody, especially in cathedral or episcopal archives (nos.27–8, 30, 34 i–ii, 35 i–ii, iv, 36 iii, 37 ii, 38, 39, 41 i, 42), or in at least four cases in the archives of the king (nos.29, 31, 43, 46). Unprovenanced single sheets here include nos.35 iii, 36 ii–ii, 37 ii, 40, 41 ii–iii, vi. For these, as for the unprovenanced Magna Cartas, it is to be hoped that their endorsements may eventually help resolve their presently orphaned state.

Divided into their various issues, the twenty-four surviving original Magna Carta single sheets are as follows:

FIRST ISSUE OF 15 JUNE 1215

There are four surviving single-sheet originals. Many editions, including Blackstone (1759), pp.10–24 (from the Pine engraving of no.1, with variants from no.46 below); William Blackstone, *Law Tracts* (Oxford 1762), ii (as in Blackstone (1759), but here with variants added from no.2 by the British Museum librarian, Charles Morton); *Statutes* (1810), pp.9–13 no.7 (from no.3 with facsimile, and with readings from nos.1–2, 46); *Foedera*, 131–2 (from no.3); Bémont, *Chartes*, pp.24–39 no.5; Stubbs, *Select Charters*, pp.291–303; Holt, *Magna Carta* (1992), pp.441–73. There is a detailed typescript collation of the four originals by J.C. Fox (*c.*1924) (BL MS. Additional 41178 fos.10r–18r), and a more selective comparison by Carpenter, *Magna Carta* (2015), pp.36–69, and cf. Collins, 'Documents', pp.267–8; Carpenter, *Magna Carta* (2015), pp.10–15, noting that the texts of nos.1 and 2 more often agree with one another, and that no.4 is the least canonical of the four.

1. London, British Library MS. Cotton Charter xiii.31b. Burned and now almost entirely illegible. Known by earlier writers as Ci. Approx. 310 x 505 + 49mm, mounted on a (modern) sheet of parchment approx. 363 x 554mm. On permanent public display. Written in a neat chancery-style hand, 86 lines. Revisions to, or words omitted from clauses 48, 53, 56, 61 written at the foot of the document, with *sigla* to indicate their correct positioning within the text, cf. Carpenter, *Magna Carta* (2015), pp.56, 58, 60, 62; Collins, 'Documents', pp.261–2. In both the Lincoln and Salisbury originals (below nos.3–4) these are incorporated within the main body of the text. Originally sealed *sur double queue*, single slit and tag, seal impression melted by fire to a shapeless blob of wax. Generally supposed to have been acquired by Sir Edward Dering from records at Dover castle, and hence presumed to be the original directed either to the county of Kent or more likely to the Cinque Ports (Collins, 'Documents', pp.260–1). In reality, as proved by the identity between the text of this original and the text copied into the chief cartulary of Canterbury Cathedral Priory (Canterbury Cathedral Archives MS. Register E fos.47r–48v (15r–16v) no.61, and cf. Carpenter, *Magna Carta* (2015), pp.15–16, 477–80), the charter sent to Canterbury. Presumably removed by Dering with other Canterbury charters from the cathedral archives, in the 1620s. As a *Carta Magna … de Ronemed*, listed as charter C61, in Maidstone, Kent Archives U350/Z16, a list in Dering's possession *c.*1630, following the numbering system and rubrics of Canterbury Register E but perhaps to record originals then in Dering's possession. As C59, the Maidstone manuscript transcribes what could be an otherwise lost Canterbury Cathedral original of King Stephen's 1136 charter of liberties. Sent by Dering to Sir Robert Cotton in May 1630. Despite damage during the Cotton fire of 23 October 1731, still legible thereafter, as evidenced by a fine facsimile engraving made in 1733 by John Pine showing most of the writing intact, with a copy made by David Casley 18 December 1731 (BL MS. Cotton Roll xiii.31b; Collins, 'Documents', 268–70). Probably rendered illegible by shrinkage following the decision to dampen and then remount the charter already damaged by fire, during restoration carried out in 1834, cf. Andrew Prescott, '"Their Present Miserable State of Cremation": The Restoration of the Cotton Library', *Sir Robert Cotton as Collector: Essays on an Early Stuart Courtier and his Legacy*, ed. C.J. Wright (London 1997), pp.391–454. Entered the British Museum together with the remainder of the Cotton library in 1753. Cf. Fox, 'Originals', pp.321–7; Collins, 'Documents', pp.260–1, 266, 268–70. © The British Library Board

2. London, British Library MS. Cotton Augustus ii.106.

On permanent public display and therefore inaccessible for measurement. Known by previous writers as Cii. Good condition. Approx. 514 x 343mm. Neat chancery-style hand, 52 lines. Revisions or mistakenly omitted words written at the foot, slightly fewer in number than in no.1 above, here affecting only clause 48, cf. Carpenter, *Magna Carta* (2015), 56; Collins, 'Documents', pp.261–2. Perhaps originally sealed *sur double queue*, on a parchment tag through a single slit. Fold now cut away, tag and seal impression missing, with two further slits to the right of the central slit which originally carried the tag and seal, the two additional slits interpreted in 1924 as indications that the charter had suffered 'stabs with a knife or a dagger – the visible evidence of [King John's] fury' (Fox, 'Originals', pp.334). More plausibly interpreted as marks left by Cotton's bookbinder when the charter was cropped for binding (Collins, 'Documents', pp.271–3). Dorse inaccessible, but said to carry the following endorsements: *magna carta Anglie per regem Iohannem* (s.xiv/xv); … *cista xx* (?s. xv); *venerabili et digno viro Roberto Cotton militi hoc antiquum presentat scriptum Humphredus Wyems primo Ianuarii 1628* (s.xvii). Marginal annotations in both the left and right hand margins, supplying brief abstract to individual clauses (s.xiv/xv, perhaps in the same hand that wrote the descriptive endorsement of this date). Provenance unknown, although the endorsement *cista*, implies archival arrangement (Collins, 'Documents', pp.261–2). Humphrey Wymes, the donor, was a London barrister, admitted to the Inner Temple 1607 (as Humphrey Wymes, son-in-law of Edward Stapleton, a Bencher of the Inn, d.1636). Recorded in 1616, called to the Bar (1620), in 1623 complaining of misbehaviours by the butler of Inner Temple in a context that implies he was still a relatively junior barrister (*A Calendar of the Inner Temple Records*, ed. F.A. Inderwick and R.A. Roberts, 5 vols (London 1896–1936), ii, pp.30, 96, 121, 136). An unsubstantiated account reports his finding the present charter in a London tailor's shop. Apparently the Magna Carta, distinct from the sealed version (above no.1), seen in the library of Sir John Cotton by Thomas Gale, then Dean of York, who informed Dr John Smith of Durham of its existence 'pasted into a very large church book of songs', apparently distinct from the sealed original above no.1: Smith to the antiquary William Nicolson (1655–1727), 23 January 1701/2, in *Letters on Various Subjects, Literary, Political and Ecclesiastical to and from William Nicolson*, 2 vols (London 1809), i, pp.227–8. First collated with no.1 above in the second (1762) edition of Blackstone (1759). Cf. Fox, 'Originals', pp.327–8; Collins, 'Documents', pp.261–2, pp.271–3. © The British Library Board

3. Lincoln Cathedral Archives A1/1/45. On permanent public display, most recently in Lincoln Castle. Good condition, though the text itself somewhat faded. Approx. 451 x 454 + 55mm, with margins of approx. 11 (left), 18 (top) and 11mm (right). The *I* of *Iohannes* in a fairly flamboyant majuscule, occupying one line, but with decorative descender stretching down four lines in the margin, restrained majuscule lettering in the first line, the five words on the final line (*quintodecimo die Iunii regni nostri septimodecimo*) widely spaced so that the final stroke reaches the right hand margin. Slight damp damage along the horizontal and vertical folds of the document. Sections of the text are very faded, but mostly legible. Extensively repaired, with the addition of parchment to the fourth horizontal fold (from the top) on the back of the document. A neat chancery-style hand, 54 lines. Sealed *sur double queue* on cords through three holes placed in a triangular formation on the fold, cords and seal impression missing. Endorsed: *LINCOLNIA* (s.xiii in, both in the bottom left and bottom right hand corners, apparently in the hand of the text itself); *Concordia int(er) regem Ioh(ann)em et barones* (s.xiii ex); *per concessionem lib(er) tat(um) ecclesie et regni Angl(ie)* (s.xiii med); *I. j. XXX visa* (s.xiv). Marked on the fold: *Transcribed October 1806 T. E. Tomlins W. Illingworth Subcommissioners …* (s. xix, recording the inspection which resulted in a facsimile being printed in *Statutes* (1810), by the engraver James Basire). Apparently the exemplar of the charter delivered to Lincolnshire and ever since preserved in the cathedral archives, cf. Fox, 'Originals', pp.329–30; Collins, 'Documents', pp.264–6, 271. A text and engraved facsimile appears in *Statutes* (1810), pp.9–13 no.7. The scribe has recently been identified as the same who wrote charters of King John for Lincoln in January and again in July 1215, i.e. as a specifically Lincoln scribe rather than as an officer of the royal chancery. Cf. Lincoln, Lincolnshire Archives MSS. D. & C. Lincoln A1/1B/43-44. There is a strong possibility that the scribe who wrote this charter also wrote the exemplar of the 1217 Magna Carta, below no.7. © Dean and Chapter of Lincoln Cathedral.

4. Salisbury Cathedral Archives Press IV, C2: Royal Charters no.39. Good condition, save for the foot. On permanent public display, most recently in the Chapter House of Salisbury Cathedral, the dimensions here taken from photographs of the front and back in TNA MS. PRO 22/25, made in 1946 when the charter was repaired in London (cf. TNA MS. PRO 1/708). Approx. 354 x 405 + 30mm, with margins of approx. 10 (left), 4 (top) and 7mm (right hand side). Written in a neat business hand, closer in some ways to a book hand than to the business hand of the royal chancery. Small capital *I* for the king's name *Iohannes*, restrained majuscule lettering to the opening line, not infilled in the final line, 76 lines. Apparently sealed *sur double queue* on cords through two holes, cords torn away leaving considerable damage to the foot, the fold then trimmed away, seal impression missing. Endorsed: … *<divers>orio primi inclusorii ascendendo* (s.xiv, apparently an indication of its archival location); (*magna*, s.xvii) *Carta reg(is) Ioh(an)nis de libertat(ibus)* (s.xiv/xv) *ecclesie Anglicane et omnium legiorum regis* (s.xiv/xv) *dupplicatur* (s.xiv/xv); various post medieval endorsements, including *anno domini 1215* (s.xvi/xvii, a hand very similar to that of the antiquary and herald Robert Glover). Collins ('Documents', pp.276–7) reads the endorsement *dupplicatur* to imply Salisbury's possession of at least one other original or early copy, now lost. Perhaps, alteratively a record of its copying into the Cathedral cartulary, now Salisbury Cathedral Archives MS. Liber Evidentiarum C pp.51–9 no.58. Assumed to be the exemplar of the charter delivered to Wiltshire and thence stored in the cathedral archives, cf. Fox, 'Originals', pp.328–9; Collins, 'Documents', pp.265–6, 271, 276–7; J.C. Holt, 'The Salisbury Magna Carta', in Holt, *Magna Carta and Medieval Government* (London 1985), pp.259–64. The hand recently and still tentatively identified as close to that of a charter of Adam dean of Salisbury (1215–20), i.e. as a Salisbury rather than as a royal chancery scribe. Cf. Salisbury Cathedral Archives Press IV, E5: Warminster 1, with further suggestions, from Elaine Treharne and Andrew Prescott, that the hand resembles that of sections of the Salisbury Cathedral cartulary known as 'The Register of St Osmund'. © Dean and Chapter of Salisbury Cathedral.

ISSUE OF NOVEMBER 1216

There is a unique original. Editions in Blackstone (1759), pp.27–36 (with facsimile of seals); *Statutes* (1810), pp.14–16 no.8, and cf. below no.33 i–ii (*Layettes*, i, pp.434–7 no.1194); Stubbs, *Select Charters*, pp.335–9; *Guala Letters*, p.29 no.37.

5. Durham, University Library Special Collections, Durham Cathedral Muniments 1.2.Reg.3. In near perfect condition. Approx. 420 x 404 + 41mm, with margins of approx. 11 (left), 21 (top) and 7mm (right). The *H* of *Henricus* capitalized with further decorative work in the marginal extending from the ascender of the *H* to the level of the fifth line. Restrained majuscule lettering in the first line; infilling of the final line, so that the final pen stroke extends from the *o* of the final word *primo* to the end of the text on the right hand margin with fairly flamboyant majuscule lettering for *primo* and restrained majuscule lettering for *regni* and *nostri*. Three damp patches in the lower half of the document leading to fading but not the loss of lettering; one small hole in the middle of the sixteenth line, with loss of letters. A neat chancery-style hand, 49 lines. Sealed *sur double queue*, with two thin parchment tags (left tag: 12mm wide; right tag: 13mm wide) through two single slits; seal impressions missing, but presumably the seals of William Marshal and the legate Guala. Endorsed *Magna Carta Henr(ici) regis III* (s. xiv in); *Carta regis Henrici regis de libertatibus concessis hominibus regni sui* (s. xv); *Transcribed Sept. 1806 T. E. Tomlins. W. Illingworth* (s. xix), recording the inspection which resulted in a facsimile being printed in *Statutes* (1810). Presumably the exemplar sent to Durham. © Dean and Chapter of Durham Cathedral.

Henricus dei gratia Rex Angl(ie) Dominus Hyb(ernie) Dux Norm(annie) Aquit(annie) & Comes And(egavie) Archiepiscopis Episcopis Abbatibus Comitibus Baronibus Justiciariis Forestariis Vicecomitibus Prepositis Ministris Ballivis & omnibus fidelibus suis Salutem.
Sciatis nos intuitu dei & pro salute anime nostre & omnium antecessorum & successorum nostrorum ad honorem dei & exaltationem sancte ecclesie & emendationem Regni nostri per consilium venerabilium patrum nostrorum Domini Gualonis tituli sancti Martini presbiteri Cardinalis Apostolice sedis legati
Petri Wintoniensis. R. de sancto Asapho. J. Bathoniensis & Glastoniensis. S. Exoniensis. R. Cicestrensis. W. Coventrensis. B. Roffensis. H. Landavensis. Meneuensis. Bangorensis & S. Wigorniensis episcoporum & Nobilium virorum Willelmi Marescalli Comitis Penbroc. Ranulfi Comitis Cestrie. Willelmi de Ferrariis Comitis
Derby. Willelmi Comitis Albemarl. Huberti de Burgo Justiciarii nostri. Savarici de Malo leone. Willelmi Brigwer' patris. Willelmi Brigwer' filii. Roberti de Curtenay. Falkesii de Breaute. Reginaldi de Vautort. Walteri de Lasey. Hugonis de Mortuo mari. Johannis de Monemut. Walteri de Bello Campo
Walteri de Clifford. Rogeri de Clifford. Roberti de Mortuo mari. Willelmi de Cantilup'. Mathei filii Herberti. Johannis Marescalli. Alani Basset. Philippi de Albiniaco. Johannis Extranei & aliorum fidelium nostrorum. In primis concessisse deo & hac presenti carta nostra confirmasse pro nobis & heredibus nostris in perpetuum
quod Anglicana ecclesia libera sit & habeat iura sua integra & libertates suas illesas. Concessimus etiam omnibus liberis hominibus Regni nostri pro nobis & heredibus nostris in perpetuum omnes libertates subscriptas habendas & tenendas eis & heredibus suis de nobis & heredibus nostris. Si quis Comitum vel Baronum nostrorum sive aliorum tenentium de nobis in capite per servitium militare mortuus fuerit & cum decesserit heres suus plene etatis fuerit & relevium debeat habeat hereditatem suam per antiquum relevium. Scilicet heres vel heredes Comitis de Baronia Comitis
integra per centum libras. Heres vel heredes Baronis de Baronia integra per centum libras. Heres vel heredes militis de feodo militis integro per centum solidos ad plus. & qui minus debuerit minus det secundum antiquam consuetudinem feodorum. Si autem heres alicuius talium
fuerit infra etatem. dominus eius non habeat custodiam eius nec terre sue antequam homagium eius ceperit. & postquam talis heres fuerit in custodia cum ad etatem pervenerit. scilicet viginti unius anni habeat hereditatem suam sine relevio & sine fine. Ita tamen quod si ipse dum infra etatem fuerit fiat miles. nichilominus terra remaneat in custodia dominorum suorum usque ad terminum predictum. Custos terre huiusmodi heredis qui infra etatem fuerit non capiat de terra heredis nisi rationabiles exitus & rationabiles consuetudines & rationabilia servitia. & hoc sine destructione
& vasto hominum vel rerum. Et si nos commiserimus custodiam alicuius talis terre vicecomiti vel alicui alii qui de exitibus terre illius nobis respondere debeat. & ille destructionem de custodia fecerit vel vastum. nos ab illo capiemus emendam. & terra committatur duobus legalibus & discretis hominibus de feodo illo qui de exitibus nobis respondeant vel ei cui illos assignaverimus. & si dederimus vel vendiderimus alicui custodiam alicuius talis terre. & ille destructionem inde fecerit vel vastum. amittat ipsam custodiam & tradatur duobus legalibus & discretis hominibus
de feodo illo qui similiter nobis respondeant sicut predictum est. Custos autem quamdiu custodiam terre habuerit. sustentet domos parcos vivaria stagna molendina & cetera ad terram illam pertinentia de exitibus terre eiusdem & reddat heredi cum ad plenam etatem pervenerit terram
suam totam instauratam de carrucis & omnibus aliis rebus ad minus secundum quod illam recepit. Hec omnia observentur de custodiis Archiepiscopatuum. Episcopatuum. Abbatiarum. Prioratuum. ecclesiarum & dignitatum vacantium excepto quod custodie huiusmodi vendi non debent. Heredes maritentur absque disparagatione. Vidua post mortem mariti sui statim & sine difficultate aliqua habeat maritagium suum & hereditatem suam. nec aliquid det pro dote sua vel pro maritagio vel hereditate sua quam hereditatem maritus suus & ipsa tenuerint die obitus ipsius mariti. & maneat in
domo mariti sui per quadraginta dies post mortem ipsius mariti sui infra quos ei assignetur dos sua nisi prius ei fuerit assignata. vel nisi domus illa sit castrum. & si de castro recesserit statim provideatur ei domus competens in qua possit honeste morari quousque dos sua ei assignetur
secundum quod predictum est. Nulla vidua distringatur ad se maritandum dum voluerit vivere sine marito. Ita tamen quod securitatem faciat quod se non maritabit sine assensu nostro si de nobis tenuerit vel sine assensu domini sui si de alio tenuerit. Nos vero vel Ballivi nostri non seisiemus terram aliquam nec
redditum pro debito aliquo quamdiu catalla debitoris presentia sufficiunt ad debitum reddendum & ipse debitor paratus sit inde satisfacere. Nec plegii ipsius debitoris distringantur quamdiu ipse capitalis debitor sufficiat ad solutionem debiti. Et si capitalis debitor defecerit in solutione debiti non habens unde
reddat aut reddere nolit cum possit. plegii respondeant de debito. & si voluerint habeant terras & redditus debitoris quousque sit eis satisfactum de debito quod ante pro eo solverint. nisi capitalis debitor monstraverit se inde esse quietum versus eosdem plegios. Civitas London habeat omnes antiquas libertates & liberas consuetudines suas. Preterea volumus & concedimus quod omnes alie Civitates. & Burgi. & Ville. & Barones de Quinque Portubus & omnes portus habeant omnes libertates & liberas consuetudines suas. Nullus distringatur ad faciendum maius servitium de feodo militis nec de alio libero tenemento quam inde debetur. Communia placita non sequantur curiam nostram. sed teneantur in aliquo certo loco. Recognitiones de nova dissaisina. de morte antecessoris. de ultima presentatione non capiantur nisi in suis comitatibus & hoc modo. Nos vel si extra Regnum fuerimus capitalis
Justiciarius noster mittemus duos Justiciarios per unumquemque Comitatum per quatuor vices in anno. qui cum quatuor militibus cuiuslibet Comitatus electis per Comitatum capiant in Comitatu & in die & loco Comitatus assisas predictas. Et si in die Comitatus assise predicte capi
non possint. tot milites & liberi tenentes remaneant de illis qui interfuerint Comitatui die illo. per quos possint sufficienter iudicia fieri secundum quod negotium fuerit maius vel minus. Liber homo non amercietur pro parvo delicto nisi secundum modum ipsius delicti. & pro magno delicto. secundum magnitudinem delicti. salvo contenemento suo. & mercator eodem modo salva mercandisa sua. & villanus eodem modo amercietur salvo Wainnagio suo si inciderit in misericordiam nostram. Et nulla predictarum misericordiarum ponatur nisi per sacramentum proborum & legalium hominum de visneto. Comites
& Barones non amercientur nisi per pares suos. & non nisi secundum modum delicti. Nullus clericus amercietur nisi secundum formam predictorum. & non secundum quantitatem beneficii sui ecclesiastici. Nec villa nec homo distringatur facere pontes ad riparias nisi qui ab antiquo & de iure facere debent. Nullus vicecomes
Constabularius. Coronatores. vel alii Ballivi nostri teneant placita corone nostre. Si aliquis tenens de nobis laicum feodum moriatur & vicecomes vel Ballivus noster ostendat litteras nostras patentes de summonitione nostra de debito quod defunctus nobis debuit. liceat vicecomiti vel Ballivo nostro attachiare
& inbreviare catalla defuncti inventa in laico feodo ad valentiam illius debiti per visum legalium hominum. Ita tamen quod nichil inde amoveatur donec persolvatur nobis debitum quod clarum fuerit. & residuum relinquatur executoribus ad faciendum testamentum defuncti. Et si nichil nobis debeatur ab ipso
omnia catalla cedant defuncto. salvis uxori ipsius & pueris suis rationabilibus partibus suis. Nullus Constabularius vel eius Ballivus capiat blada vel alia catalla alicuius qui non sit de villa ubi castrum situm est nisi statim inde reddat denarios aut respectum inde habere possit de voluntate
venditoris. Si autem de villa fuerit teneatur infra tres septimanas precium reddere. Nullus Constabularius distringat aliquem militem ad dandum denarios pro custodia castri si ipse eam facere voluerit in propria persona sua vel per alium probum hominem si ipse eam facere non possit propter rationabi-
lem causam. Et si nos duxerimus vel miserimus eum in exercitum erit quietus de custodia secundum quantitatem temporis quo per nos fuerit in exercitu. Nullus vicecomes vel Ballivus noster vel alius capiat equos vel carettas alicuius pro cariagio faciendo nisi reddat liberationem antiquitus statutam
scilicet pro caretta ad duos equos decem denarios per diem. & pro caretta ad tres equos quatuordecim denarios per diem. Nec nos nec Ballivi nostri capiemus alienum boscum ad castra vel alia agenda nostra nisi per voluntatem ipsius cuius boscus ille fuerit. Nos non tenebimus terras eorum
qui convicti fuerint de felonia nisi per unum annum & unum diem. & tunc reddantur terre dominis feodorum. Omnes kidelli de cetero deponantur penitus per Tamisiam & Medeweiam & per totam Angliam nisi per costeram maris. Breve quod vocatur Precipe de cetero non fiat alicui de aliquo
tenemento unde liber homo amittere possit curiam suam. Una mensura vini sit per totum Regnum nostrum & una mensura cervisie & una mensura bladi scilicet quarterium London. & una latitudo pannorum tinctorum & russettorum & haubergettorum scilicet due ulne infra listas.
De ponderibus autem sit ut de mensuris. Nichil detur de cetero pro brevi inquisitionis de vita vel membris. sed gratis concedatur et non negetur. Si aliquis teneat de nobis per feodifirmam vel soccagium vel per burgagium & de alio terram teneat per servitium militare nos non habebimus
custodiam heredis nec terre sue que est de feodo alterius occasione illius feodifirme vel soccagii vel burgagii. Nec habebimus custodiam illius feodifirme vel soccagii vel burgagii nisi ipsa feodifirma debeat servitium militare. Nos non habebimus custodiam heredis vel terre alicuius quam tenet de
alio per servitium militare occasione alicuius parve serianterie quam tenet de nobis per servitium reddendi nobis cultellos vel sagittas vel huiusmodi. Nullus Ballivus ponat de cetero aliquem ad legem simplici loquela sua sine testibus fidelibus ad hoc inductis. Nullus liber homo capiatur vel imprisonetur aut dissaisiatur aut utlagetur aut exuletur aut aliquo alio modo destruatur. nec super eum ibimus nec super eum mittemus nisi per legale iudicium parium suorum. vel per legem terre. Nulli vendemus nulli negabimus aut differemus rectum aut iustitiam. Omnes mercatores nisi
publice antea prohibiti fuerint habeant salvum & securum exire de Anglia & venire in Angliam. & morari & ire per Angliam tam per terram quam per aquas ad emendum & vendendum sine omnibus malis toltis per antiquas & rectas consuetudines preterquam in tempore gwerre & si sint de terra contra nos gwerrina. Et si tales inveniantur in terra nostra in principio gwerre. attachientur sine dampno corporum vel rerum donec sciatur a nobis vel a capitali Justiciario nostro quomodo mercatores terre nostre tractentur qui tunc invenientur in terra contra nos gwerrina. & si nostri salvi sint ibi. alii salvi sint in terra nostra. Si quis tenuerit de aliqua escaeta sicut de honore Walingeford. Notingeham. Bolon. Lancastr. vel de aliis escaetis que sunt in manu nostra & sunt Baronie & obierit. heres eius non det aliud relevium nec faciat nobis aliud servitium quam faceret Baroni si terra illa esset in manu Baronis. & nos eodem modo eam tenebimus
quo Baro eam tenuit. Homines qui manent extra forestam non veniant de cetero coram Justiciariis nostris de foresta per communes summonitiones nisi sint in placito vel plegii alicuius vel aliquorum qui attachiati sunt pro foresta. Omnes Barones qui fundaverint Abbatias unde habent cartas Regum Angl'
vel antiquam tenuram habeant earum custodiam cum vacaverint sicut habere debent & sicut supra declaratum est. Omnes foreste que afforestate sunt tempore Regis Johannis patris nostri statim deafforestentur. & ita fiat de ripariis que per eundem J. tempore suo posite sunt in defenso. Nullus capiatur
vel imprisonetur propter appellum femine de morte alterius quam viri sui. Et si Rex J. pater noster dissaisivit vel elongavit Walenses de terris vel libertatibus vel aliis rebus sine legali iudicio parium suorum in Anglia vel in Wallia. eis statim reddantur. & si contentio super hoc orta fuerit. tunc inde fiat in mar-
chia per iudicium parium suorum de tenementis Angl' secundum legem Angl'. De tenementis Wallie secundum legem Wallie. De tenementis Marchie secundum legem Marchie. Idem facient Walenses nobis & nostris. Omnes autem istas consuetudines predictas & libertates quas nos concessimus in Regno nostro
tenendas quantum ad nos pertinet erga nostros. omnes de Regno nostro tam clerici quam laici observent quantum ad se pertinet erga suos. Quia vero quedam capitula in priore carta continebantur que gravia & dubitabilia videbantur scilicet de scutagiis & auxiliis assidendis. de debitis
Judeorum & aliorum & de libertate exeundi de Regno nostro vel redeundi in Regnum. & de forestis & forestariis. Warennis & Warennariis & de consuetudinibus Comitatuum. & de ripariis & earum custodibus. placuit supradictis prelatis & magnatibus ea esse in respectu quousque plenius
consilium habuerimus. & tunc faciemus plenissime tam de hiis quam de aliis que occurrerint emendanda. que ad communem omnium utilitatem pertinuerint & pacem & statum nostrum & Regni nostri. Quia vero sigillum nondum habuimus presentem cartam sigillis venerabilis patris
nostri Domini Gualonis tituli sancti Martini presbiteri Cardinalis Apostolice sedis Legati & Willelmi Marescalli Comitis Penbroc' Rectoris nostri & Regni nostri fecimus sigillari. Testibus omnibus prenominatis & aliis multis. Datum per manus predictorum Domini Legati & Willelmi Marescalli
Comitis Penbroc' apud Bristollum duodecimo die Novembris. Anno Regni nostri primo.

ISSUE OF NOVEMBER 1217

There are four originals. Printed (from no.8, in many ways the least satisfactory of the originals) Blackstone (1759), pp.37–46 (with facsimile of the seals); *Statutes* (1810), pp.17–19 no.9, and cf. Stubbs, *Select Charters*, pp.340–4; *Guala Letters*, pp.29–31 no.38.

6. Oxford, Bodleian Library MS. Ch. Oxon. Oseney 142b (with seal now ibid. 142b*). Good condition. Approx. 378 x 490 + 35mm, with margins of approx. 17 (left), 10 (top) and 17mm (right). The capital *H* of *Henricus* left blank, no infilling of the final line, restrained majuscule lettering for the first line. Three large holes down the middle of the left hand side of the document as a result of rodent damage whilst folded in the past. A neat chancery-style hand, 66 lines. Sealed *sur double queue*, two thin parchment tags (8mm wide) through two single slits; seal impression of William Marshal the elder, detached, now stored in a separate box as Ch. Oxon. Oseney 142b*, in green wax, legend illegible, apparently taken from the right hand tag. The seal itself, in use by the Marshal from at least the 1190s, is an unimpressive, perhaps deliberately modest affair. Seven other impressions survive: generally in green wax, round, 22mm diameter, equestrian effigy, wielding a sword, legend within the rim of the seal impression, + S(IGILLVM) WILL(ELMI) MARESCAL(I). Left hand seal apparently lost entirely, presumably the seal of the legate Guala, as below no.7. Endorsed: *magna cart(a) r(egis) H(enrici) iiii. ti de libert(atibus) totius regni dup(plicatur)* (s.xiv ex): *li* (s.xvi); *13* (s.xvii); *62* (s.xvii/xviii); various other post medieval endorsements. Almost certainly one of two exemplars stored at Oseney Abbey in Oxfordshire, perhaps both originals first sent to the county of Oxfordshire, or one for Oxfordshire, the other for Berkshire.

**7. Oxford, Bodleian Library MS. Ch. Oxon. Oseney 142c
(with seal now ibid. 142c*).** Good condition. Approx. 410 x
296 + 32mm, with margins of approx. 10 (left), 5 (top) and 10mm
(right). Opens *Henricus*, with an undecorated *H* restricted to
a single line, restrained majuscule lettering for the first line,
infilled at the end so that the final words *aliis multis* are hard
against the right hand margin. Some damp damage leading to
fading but not the loss of lettering. Neat chancery-style hand,
43 lines. Sealed *sur double queue*, two thin parchment tags (8mm
wide) through two single slits, left hand seal cut away and now
stored separately as Ch. Oxon. Oseney 142c*: the seal of the
legate Guala, vesica shaped, dark green wax, a figure standing,
in pontificals, dalmatic and pointed mitre, both hands raised in
blessing with palms facing outwards, legend: SIGILL(UM) <GUALE
T(I)T(ULI)> S(AN)C(T)I <MARTINI PR(ESBITERI)> CARD(INALIS),
stored together with a modern caste of the same. Right hand
seal apparently missing entirely, presumed to be the seal of
William Marshal as above no.6. Endorsed: *Magna carta reg(is)
Henr(ici)* (3 – added s.xvi over an erasure) *de libertate totius regni*
(s.xiii/xiv); *dup(plicatur)* (s.xiv ex); *li* (s.xvi); *14* (s.xvii); *61* (s.xvii/xviii).
Provenance as for no.6, Oseney Abbey, perhaps the exemplar
sent either to Oxfordshire or to Berkshire. Recent investigations
suggest that the scribe of the present charter may have been the
same man who wrote the 1215 Lincoln Magna Carta, above no.3.
As a clerk in the service of Hugh of Wells, bishop of Lincoln, he
could have become involved here given the close involvement
of Bishop Hugh in the publication of the 1217 charter within the
diocese of Lincoln, as revealed by the publication schedule from
April 1218 supplied by RLC, 377b-378.

142c

8. Oxford, Bodleian Library MS. Ch. Glouc. 8. In near perfect condition. Approx. 422 x 490 + 40mm, with margins of approx. 15 (left), 15 (top) and 12mm (right). Opens *Henricus* with decorated capital *H* in the same hand as the remainder of the charter, fairly flamboyant majuscule lettering in the first line, not infilled at the end so that the final line ends three-quarters of the way across the text block. Neat chancery-style hand, 56 lines. Sealed *sur double queue*, two thin parchment tags (8mm) through two single slits; left hand seal of the legate Guala, apparently removed and then replaced back to front, white wax, entirely defaced, presumably as above no.7; right hand, small round equestrian seal of William Marshal the elder in green wax, legend illegible, but as above no.6. Endorsed: *Magna carta caps' xiiii.a de laic' te* (s.xiii, apparently an archival marking from St Peter's Gloucester); *registratur* (s.xiv/xv, another regular Gloucester archival marking); *cart(a) H(enrici) reg(is) de*
libertatibus magne carte H(enrici) reg(is) aui nostri (s.xiv/xv); various post medieval endorsements. Apparently the exemplar stored at St Peter's Gloucester, perhaps originally sent for proclamation in the county of Gloucestershire, and in the 1390s copied into Gloucester Cathedral Library MS. Register A part 1 fos.32v–35v no.82. Belonged to Richard Furney (1694–1753), archdeacon of Surrey and native of Gloucester, schoolmaster at Gloucester Cathedral (1719–24) and a collector of local antiquities, from whose collections it passed to the Bodleian. Gloucester provenance queried by Poole ('Publication', p.451), but surely confirmed by the endorsements and especially by the note of registration, identical to that of no.36 iii, and especially no.42 below which was undoubtedly directed to Gloucester(shire). Peculiarities include the fact that the present text offers a unique version of the sealing clause, distinct from that of nos.6–7, 9 (Poole, 'Publication', p.451).

9. Hereford Cathedral Archives charter no.1516. In near perfect condition. Approx. 305 x 470 + 23mm, with margins of approx. 9 (left), 11 (top) and 5mm (right). A neat chancery-style hand, with a decorated capital *H* for *Henricus* restricted to a single line, restrained majuscule lettering for the first line, no infilling of the final line, 64 lines in all. Two minor tears on the right hand side and a deeper tear in the bottom right hand corner. Originally sealed *sur double queue*, with two slits on the left and right of the foot, 60mm apart. Tags and seal impressions missing, but presumably the seals of William Marshal and the legate Guala, as above nos.6–8. Endorsed: *consuetudines et libertates regnum Anglie edicto per rege(m) et parliamentu(m)* (s.xiv ex); *Copia magne carte* (s.xv med.); brief post medieval endorsement. No indication of provenance, but (despite the survival at Hereford Cathedral of significant numbers of Gloucester Abbey charters) apparently the version originally sent to Herefordshire. © Dean and Chapter of Hereford Cathedral.

ISSUE OF 11 FEBRUARY 1225

There are four surviving originals. Printed (from nos.10, 11, misdated 1224, with facsimile of seal) Blackstone (1759), pp.47–59, 67; (with facsimile from no.10, also noting Blackstone's edition of no.11, then still at Lacock), *Statutes* (1810), pp.22–25 no.11; Bémont, *Chartes*, pp.45–60 no.7; below appendix (from no.13), and cf. Stubbs, *Select Charters*, pp.349–51; Holt, *Magna Carta* (1992), pp.501–11. Only nos.10 and 11 were known to Collins, 'Documents', pp.269–70. Blackstone (1759), pp.xlvi, refers to the possibility of there being two further orginals. The first noticed after James Tyrrell, *The General History of England*, 3 vols (London 1700-4), ii, p.1104, supposedly from Battle Abbey, reported by Tyrrell in the possession of Sir Nathaniel Powel of Ewhurst (d.1707), remains untraced. The other, as noted by Blackstone after Thomas Carte, *A General History of England* (London 1747–55), ii, p.29, supposed to survive at Norwich Cathedral, perhaps represents confusion with a s.xiv cartulary copy, now Norwich, Norfolk Record Office MS. DCN Register 3 fos.84v–90r. Blackstone rightly denied the credentials of another copy of the 1225 charter, now London, Society of Antiquaries MS.544 (first recorded in 1749, in the possession of Charles Lyttelton), to be considered an original rather than a mid-thirteenth-century copy (cf. notes to no.13 below). A further such early copy is enrolled as Durham, University Library Special Collections, Durham Cathedral Muniments Locellus 1.25: mid s.xiii copy of the 1225 Magna Carta and Forest Charter, endorsed with copies of the clerical sentence of 1253 and its confirmation by Pope Innocent IV (below no.37).

10. Durham, University Library Special Collections, Durham Cathedral Muniments 1.2.Reg.2. Good condition. Approx. 369 x 545 + 41mm, with margins of approx. 17 (left), 32 (top) and 14mm (right). Capitalized *H* to *Henricus* with the lettering of both *Henricus* and *Dei* in fairly flamboyant majuscule, the remaining lettering of the first line in restrained majuscule, not infilled at the end. Extensive damp damage to the right hand side of the document, obscuring a section of the text in the bottom right hand corner; several holes in the document elsewhere, possibly the result of rodent damage. Neat chancery-style hand, 65 lines. Sealed *sur double queue* on pink cords with impression of the first great seal of King Henry in green wax, in near perfect condition. Endorsed: *Magna carta H(enrici) regis tercii de libertatibus totius regni* (s. xiii/xiv); *Carta magna Henr(ici) regis III de libertatibus totius …* (s. xiii/xiv); *Tertia prime regalium; I 2e II H(enrici) regalium* (s. xiii/xiv); various postmedieval endorsements. Engraved facsimile by James Basire in *Statutes* (1810), pp.22–5 no.11. Apparently the exemplar sent to Durham. © Dean and Chapter of Durham Cathedral.

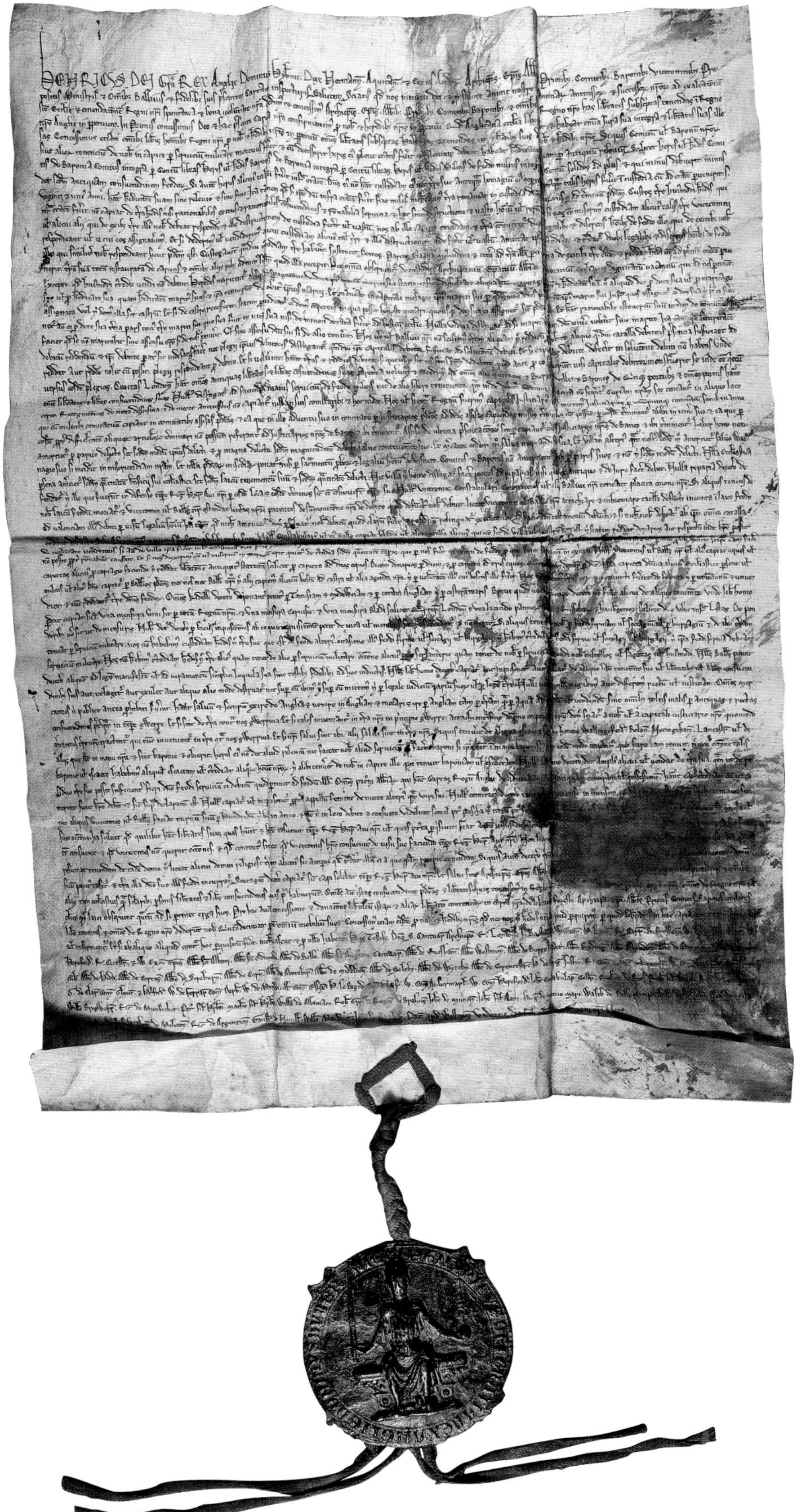

11. London, British Library MS. Additional 46144 (previously Lacock Abbey, Talbot Family, gifted to the British Museum in 1945 by Miss Matilda Theresa Talbot). On permanent public display in the British Library. Near perfect condition. Approx. 300 x 500 + 20mm, with margins of 20 (left), 20 (top) and 20mm (right). Neat chancery-style hand, capital *H* to *Henricus*, with restrained majuscule lettering in the first line, 67 lines in all, not infilled at the end. Sealed *sur double queue* on green cords, impression of the first great seal of Henry III in green wax, chipped and imperfect inside a white silk seal bag. Endorsed: *Hen(rici) reg(is) fil(ii) Ioh(annis) reg(is) de libertatibus et quibusdam consuetudinibus per Angliam constitutis* (s.xiii med); *ex deposito militu(m) Wiltisir'* (s.xiii). Apparently the exemplar of the charter sent into Wiltshire. Deposited at Lacock Abbey for safe custody by the knights or the county community of Wiltshire, perhaps in the time of Ela, countess of Salisbury, who had founded the abbey in 1232 and thereafter served as its abbess 1239–57. Her husband, William Longuespée, earl of Salisbury, had been sheriff of Wiltshire when the charter was issued. Ela herself succeeded him in this office, 1227–8 and 1231–6. Recorded by Blackstone (1759), pp.xlvi–vii, in the possession of John Talbot of Lacock, to whom it had presumably descended from Sir William Sharington, purchaser of the abbey's site in 1540. From John Talbot it passed by descent to the donor, Miss Talbot. © The British Library Board.

HENRICUS DEI GRACIA REX Anglie Dominus [Hibernie Dux Normannie Aquitanie et Comes Andegavie Archiepiscopis Episcopis Abbatibus Prioribus Comitibus Baronibus...]

12. London, The National Archives DL 10/71. Severely damp damaged, with significant portions of the text missing and with considerable modern repairs. Approx. 295 x 535 + 35mm, with margins of 8 (left), 18 (top) and 5mm (right). Written in a chancery-style hand verging towards book hand, restrained majuscule lettering to opening line, including the *H* of *Henricus*, 74 lines in all, not infilled at the end. Three large portions of damp damage with significant loss of text, rebacked and repaired. Sealed *sur double queue* on pink, green/blue cords through three holes, blob of modern plastic encasing fragments of a seal impression now hidden. Mounted in a display box, dorse inaccessible. Provenance unknown, although its presence amongst the Duchy of Lancaster deeds might suggest association with one of the counties in which the Duchy lands were chiefly situated, perhaps Leicestershire, Nottinghamshire/Derbyshire or Lancashire. © National Archives, London.

13. Oxford, Bodleian Library MS. Ch. London 1. Good condition, save for the foot. Approx. 298 x 472mm, originally 298 x 440 + 32mm, with margins of approx. 14 (left), 20 (top) and 12mm (right). Opens *H(enricus) Dei gratia rex*, without decoration, restrained majuscule lettering in the opening line, not infilled at the end. Some water damage to face, with one large patch and one smaller patch of lettering badly faded, the foot and all evidence of sealing trimmed away. Neat chancery-style hand, 72 lines. Apparently originally sealed *sur double queue*, fold and seal entirely cut away, with the bottom of the document torn and more recently repaired. Endorsed: *carta regia de diuersis libertatibus tocius Anglie magnatibus <… conce>ssis* (s.xiii in-med); *Henr(icus) iiii.us* (s.xiii med); *ii.ii* (s.xvi, perhaps an archival mark); various post medieval endorsements, including *K H. 3 confirmation of Magna Charta et(c)* (s.xvii); *11 feb. 9 H. 3* (s.xvii); *63* (s.xvii/xviii). Today stored as a London charter, but with no evidence of provenance. The London/Middlesex section of the Bodleian catalogue of charters, being amongst the last to be listed, was sometimes used as a *pis aller* for documents that would otherwise have been left homeless. One possibility would be that this, like nos.6–7 above, was an Oseney charter, the endorsed number '63' placing it in sequence after above no.7 ('61') and no.6 ('62'). Alternatively, it might be identified as the Magna Carta offered for sale from the estate of the bankrupt Henry Brydges, 2nd Duke of Chandos, as a 'Magna Charta. Vellum. Very ancient': Christopher Cock, *A Catalogue of the Large and Valuable Library of … James Duke of Chandos … 12th of March 1746–7* (London, 1747), p.65 lot 1579, from the library of Cannons, the family house at Little Stanmore in Middlesex. The British Library copy of this catalogue gives the price paid as 3 shillings, one of the three copies in the Bodleian as 3 shillings and sixpence. None of the surviving copies of the sale catalogue so far examined gives the name of the buyer. Even so, it is worth noting that a large collection of manuscripts entered the Bodleian as a result of the Chandos sale, not least via Richard Rawlinson (1690–1755) (N. I. Petrovskaia, 'The Travels of a Quire', *Middle English Texts in Transition*, ed. S. Horobin and L.R. Mooney (Woodbridge 2014), pp.257–8). To extend this chain of speculation even further, both Henry Brydges and his father, James Brydges, the 1st duke, served as MPs for Hereford 1698–1714 and 1727–34. Hereford Cathedral would therefore be one amongst many possible sources. However, the hand of the chief endorsement to the 1225 Bodleian charter has much greater similarity to that of the endorsements from Lincoln (nos.3, 34 i, 35 ii), and the survival of the Lincoln 1225 Forest Charter (no.35 ii) certainly implies that Lincoln once also possessed Magna Carta 1225. However tempting it might be to identify the Chandos charter with the copy of the 1225 charter now belonging to the Society of Antiquaries (MS. 544), this latter was first exhibited by Charles Lyttelton in 1749 as having been 'brought from the Abbey of Halesowen in Shropshire' (*recte* the Lyttelton property at Halesowen, Worcestershire, cf. London, Society of Antiquaries MS. Minute Book VI p.17).

ISSUE OF 14 MARCH 1265

On 14 March 1265, whilst Simon de Montfort governed England, with King Henry III as his prisoner, Magna Carta was confirmed by letters patent of Henry III referring to the dispatch of 'charters and ordinances' under the king's seal, apparently sent into every county as a permanent record (*Documents of the Baronial Movement of Reform and Rebellion 1258–67*, ed. R.E. Treharne and I.J. Sanders (Oxford 1973), pp.312–13 no.42, and cf. *Statutes* (1810), pp.31–2 no.15). There is no surviving single sheet original of this exemplification, but later copies, in the form of charters of inspeximus, dated 14 March 1265, apparently taken from lost exemplars originally sent to the counties of Middlesex, Somerset/Dorset, Herefordshire and perhaps elsewhere, are preserved in the London Guildhall collection of laws, now London BL MS. Cotton Claudius D ii (Statutes etc) fo.128v (138v, 125v) (addressed to Middlesex, with full witness list but reciting only the opening words of the 1225 Magna Carta, s.xiv, also in Cambridge, Corpus Christi College MSS. 70, 258); BL MS. Harley 489 fos.4r–8v (in similar terms, but addressed to Somerset and Dorset and dated 13 March 1265); BL MS. Harley 170 fos.7r–9v (from Reading Abbey); Oxford, Bodleian Library MS. Add. C. 188 fos.1r–5v, and in the register of Bishop Richard Swinfield of Hereford (1282–1317) (Hereford, Herefordshire Record Office MS. AL19/2 fos.105r–6r). At Hereford, Swinfield succeeded Thomas of Cantiloupe, bishop of Hereford (1275–82), who himself, as royal chancellor 1264–5, had been responsible for the Magna Carta reissued in 1265. For the copies and their context, see *Statutes* (1810), 'Table of Contents' no.15; Sophie Ambler, 'Magna Carta: Its Confirmation at Simon de Montfort's Parliament of 1265', *EHR*, cxxx (2015), and the online links: http://magnacarta.cmp. uea.ac.uk/read/feature_of_the_month/Mar_2014 and Dec-2014. David Carpenter has recently established that it was in 1265 (not, as previously supposed, in 1297) that the relief payable by a baron was reduced from £100 to 100 marks, and that an 'earldom' was for the first time treated, within the text, as a hereditary estate.

ISSUE OF 12 OCTOBER 1297

This was the first issue, so far as is known, to be officially enrolled in chancery, a contemporary copy being entered in the Statute Roll of Edward I: London, The National Archives C 74/1. There are four surviving originals. Editions (with facsimile from no.15) *Statutes* (1810), pp.33–6 no.16; (from no.14, with translation) *Sotheby's MC*, pp.24–34; (from no.16, translation only) Nicholas Vincent, *Australia's Magna Carta* (Canberra, Senate of Australia, 2011, 2nd ed. 2015), pp.25–32, and cf. Bémont, *Chartes*, pp.90–1 no.13. For the process of publication, *Sotheby's MC*, pp.36–9.

14. Washington, National Archives, deposited on loan by the owner, Mr David Rubenstein. Repaired and in places rebacked. Approx. 370 x 420 + 32mm, with margins of 10 (left), 28 (top) and 15mm (right). The writing on ruled lines, with faint ruled vertical plumb lines for the margins. The capital *E* of the king's name *Edwardus* decorated and extending down two lines of text. Written throughout in a neat chancery-style hand, in 68 lines of text, the final line extended with a note of warranty *Scowe* (the name of the chancery official, John of Stowe) infilling the line to the right hand margin. Sealed *sur double queue*, using a parchment tag (22mm wide) through a single slit at the foot. On the tag, an impression of the small seal of Edward I, used as the seal of absence by the regency council in England whilst the king was in Flanders 1297–8: natural wax, the central portion of the seal, broken and repaired, various details legible including the letters EDW … , and the small lion or leopard between the king's legs on the obverse side, the king seated in majesty on a bench-like throne, carrying two rods or sceptres, one of which remains topped with a fleur-de-lys device. The reverse of the seal, and the dorse of the document inaccessible inside its modern argon-filled display cabinet. Recorded in photographs, the endorsements: *Magna Carta* (s.xvi/xvii); *25 E(dward) I* (s.xvii) to the left on the dorse: *Magna Carta 25 Ed(ward) I* repeated on the right of the dorse; *1296* (?s.xvii); a nineteenth-century stamp mark of the Brudenell family motto *En Grace Affie* ('On grace depend') with the call number *A.viii.6* written in pen at the centre and repeated in pencil at the foot of the dorse. On the outside of the fold, to the left of the seal tag, the word *Buk'*, denoting that this was the exemplar of the charter sent into Buckinghamshire. On the fold to the right of the seal tag, the words *tradatur Rogero Hodelyn de Neuport (c.1297)*: a unique detail, recording the proclamation of the charter within the county (*Sotheby's MC*, pp.36–9). The exemplar of the charter sent into Buckinghamshire, subsequently owned by the Brudenell family of Deene Park in Northamptonshire, perhaps by descent from a Brudenell sheriff or other royal official in Buckinghamshire, perhaps from the the Chief Justice of Common Pleas, Sir Robert Brudenell (d.1531), perhaps from Sir Robert's son, the antiquary Sir Thomas Brudnell (c.1497–1549), or his descendent, another antiquary, Sir Thomas Brudenell (1578–1663). Deposited after 1920 with other family papers in the Northamptonshire Record Office. Returned before 1975 to Deene Park by the house's owners, Edmund and Marian Brudenell, and displayed on an easel in the Bow Room. Sold in 1983 from Deene Park to the American entrepreneur and two-times presidential candidate, Ross Perot, for a figure reportedly of $1.5 million. Sold by the Perot Foundation at Sotheby's New York, 18 December 2007, to David Rubenstein for $21.3 million. Photo: National Archives, Washington, DC.

15. London, Metropolitan Archives, Corporation of London charter 21. In near-perfect condition. Approx. 538 x 482 + 30mm, with margins of 28 (left), 35 (top) and 30mm (right). A neat chancery-style hand, with the *E* of *Edwardus* decorated, extending down two lines. All told 62 lines, not infilled at the end. Sealed *sur double queue* on pink cords through three holes, large part of seal impression of Edward I's small seal of absence in dark green wax. Endorsed: *magna carta r(egis) H(enrici) de libertatibus Angl(ie) confirmata per dominum r(egem) E(dwardum) patrem regis nunc* (s.xiv in); *in reg(istro) cum littera B* (s.xiv); *carta r(egis) E(dwardi) fil(ii) H(enrici) de confirmatione* (s.xv); *carta magna de libertatibus Angl(ie) exam(inata) … nem indeque confirmari* (s.xv/xvi). On the left of the fold, to the left of the seal cords, *R. de Stard' examinavit* (s.xiii ex); on the right of the fold, to the right of the seal cords *London'* (apparently a contemporary address, s.xiii ex). The word *nota* written in the margin on the left next to the clause relating to the liberties of the city of London, and in the margin on the right next to the clause relating to the standard measure of London. Sewn into the fold is an original writ, sealed *sur simple queue*, tongue and seal impression missing, by which the regency council acting in the name of Edward I, 12 October 1297, commanded the sheriff(s) of London to publish Magna Carta and the Forest Charter. Engraved facsimile by James Basire in *Statutes* (1810), pp.33–6 no.16. The exemplar sent to the City of London. Photo: London Metropolital Archives.

London

16. Canberra, Parliament House. Good condition. Approx. 430mm x 455 + 15mm. A neat chancery-style hand, with the *E* of *Edwardus* decorated, extending down two lines. 69 lines of text. Sealed *sur double queue* on pink and green cords through three holes, central portion of seal impression of Edward I's small seal of absence in natural (white) wax. Mounted, dorse inaccessible. On the fold, to the left of the seal, *com(itatus) Surr'*, and to the right of the seal *exam(inatur)*. The name of the scribe or notary *Iern'* (i.e. the chancery clerk, Hugh of Yarmouth) inserted in the bottom right hand corner of the text block, after the dating clause. The exemplar of the charter sent into the county of Surrey, thereafter apparently preserved in the archives of the nuns of Easebourne Priory in Sussex (perhaps by the sheriff, who was sheriff jointly of Surrey and Sussex), as the pair to the 1297 Forest Charter (below no.39). After the dissolution of the monasteries, by means unknown, by *c*.1900 into the hands of the Louch family, solicitors at Drayton in Somerset, and thereafter, before 1939, again by unknown means, perhaps by accident, to the headmaster and trustees of Bruton School, whence sold in 1952–3 to representatives of the Australian government and the National Library of Australia, for £12,500. Photographs and full discussion of provenance by Nicholas Vincent, in *Australia's Magna Carta* (Canberra, 2011, 2nd ed. 2015).

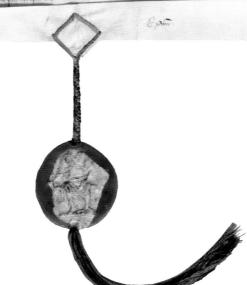

17. London, The National Archives DL 10/197. Good condition, save for three holes in the text, the largest midway down on the left hand side, the result of friction when folded, leading to the loss of half a dozen words. Approx. 445 x 562 + 43mm, with margins of 30 (left), 50 (top) and 27mm (right). A neat chancery-style hand, with the *E* of *Edwardus* decorated, extending down three lines. All told 76 lines, not infilled at the end. Now flattened out and rebacked with modern parchment. Originally sealed *sur double queue*, probably on cords through three holes, central portion of fold with cords and seal impression now lost. Endorsed: *Exam(inatur)* (contemporary chancery marking, s.xiii ex); *magna carta de libertatibus Angl(ie)* (s.xiii/xiv); *7* (s.xvii); *45* (s.xvii/xviii). No indication of provenance, and no writing on the outside of the fold. Association with the Duchy of Lancaster deeds might imply provenance from one or other of the counties in which the duchy estates chiefly lay: perhaps Leicestershire, Nottinghamshire, Derbyshire or Lancashire. © National Archives, London.

ISSUE OF 28 MARCH 1300

This was the last issue, so far as can be established, to have been prepared in the royal chancery for publication under the king's seal. There are seven surviving single-sheet originals, of which the last is best regarded as a contemporary exemplification rather than as a product of the royal chancery. A further original recorded by *Statutes* (1810) ('Table of Contents' no.18) in the possession of the Borough of Appleby in Westmoreland either records a document since lost or represents confusion with some other record, since untraced amongst the Appleby charters, today preserved in the Cumbria Archives at Kendal. Noticed (from 20, 22) Blackstone (1759), p.xlviii. Printed (from the enrolment in the chancery Charter Roll, TNA C 53/86 m.7 (whence *Cal.Chart.R. 1257–1300*, p.483), also noting nos.18–20, 22) *Statutes* (1810), pp.38–41 no.18, and cf. Bémont, *Chartes*, pp.90–1 no.13. For the process of publication, supposedly four times a year henceforth, see *Calendar of the Close Rolls 1296–1302* (London 1906), pp.387–8, 396.

18. London, Metropolitan Archives, Corporation of London charter 23Z. Good condition. Approx. 417 x 453 + 39mm, with margins of approx. 18 (left), 20 (top) and 18mm (left). Neat chancery-style hand, the initial *E* of *Edwardus* decorated and extending down three lines, in all 70 lines. Sealed *sur double queue*, single slit, tag and seal impression missing. Endorsed: *magna carta r(egis) E(dwardi) fil(ii) reg(is) H(enrici) de libertatibus Angl(ie)* (s.xiv in); various post medieval endorsements including stamps from the charter's time in the Public Record Office. On the face, in the left hand margin, a hand pointing to the clause on the liberties of the city of London. On the fold, to the left of the slit: *magna carta de libertatibus Angl(ie) pro civitate London'* (s.xiv in). The exemplar directed to the City of London. Recorded in the possession of the Corporation of London in 1810, but by 1869 reported missing. Rediscovered in 1958 in the Public Record Office where it had perhaps been brought by Thomas Duffus Hardy at the time of his cataloguing of the London city charters and where it had acquired the Public Record Office (now The National Archives) class number E 40/15200. Returned to the Mayor of London by the Master of the Rolls at a banquet held on St George's day (23 April) 1958, cf. correspondence concerning the events of 1958 in London, The National Archives LCO 2/7899. Photo: Metropolitan Archives, London.

19. Durham, University Library Special Collections Durham Cathedral Muniments 2.2.Reg.2. In near perfect condition. Approx. 499 x 583 + 39mm, with margins of approx. 54 (left), 49 (top) and 51mm (right). The *E* of *Edwardus* decorated and extending down seven lines, with restrained majuscule lettering in the first line, not infilled in the final line, the final sentence ending in the left hand third of the document. A small hole close to the extreme right hand edge of the document, but with no loss of lettering. A neat chancery-style hand, 79 lines. Sealed *sur double queue* on a parchment tag (approx. 17mm wide) through a single slit (26mm wide), impression of the great seal of Edward I in natural wax, damaged in the top left hand corner. In the left hand margin *No(ta) confir'* (a Durham archival mark *c.*1415). On the fold: *per dominum I(ohannem) canc(ellarium) do(mi)ni reg(is)* (*c.*1300, contemporary chancery warrant). Endorsed: *Confirmacio magne carte Henrici tercii facta per Edwardum primum filium eiusdem regis* (s. xiv in); *Magna Carta. Edward(o) nobil(i) t(ri)plicat(ur), de libertatibus concess(is) archiepiscopis episcopis comitibus et baronibus abbatibus et prioribus ab Edwardo rege stabili filio regis Henrici tercii* … (s. xv in); *2u. 2e. Reg(alium)* (s. xv in); *Tertia prime regalium* (s. xv); various post medieval endorsements. Apparently the exemplar sent to Durham.
© Dean and Chapter of Durham Cathedral.

20. Oxford, Oriel College Archives EST D 2 B1/1 (formerly D.R. 16C8). Good condition, despite rodent damage to the left and right sides, along earlier folds. Approx. 426 x 430 + 42mm, with margins 32 (left), 40 (top) and 26mm (right). A clear chancery-style hand, with the capital *E* to *Edwardus* extending down four lines with neat pen and ink geometric decoration, 68 lines in all, neatly infilled to the right margin at the end. Sealed *sur double queue* on pink and green cords through three holes, almost perfect impression of the great seal of Edward I in natural wax (115mm in diameter) protected in a tin seal box. Endorsed: *de libertatibus ecclesie Anglicane* (s.xiv in); *C8.8* (s.xvii/xviii). No certain evidence of provenance, but probably from the archives of St Mary's, the University church in Oxford, of which Oriel College has been patron since the college's foundation. © Oriel College, Oxford.

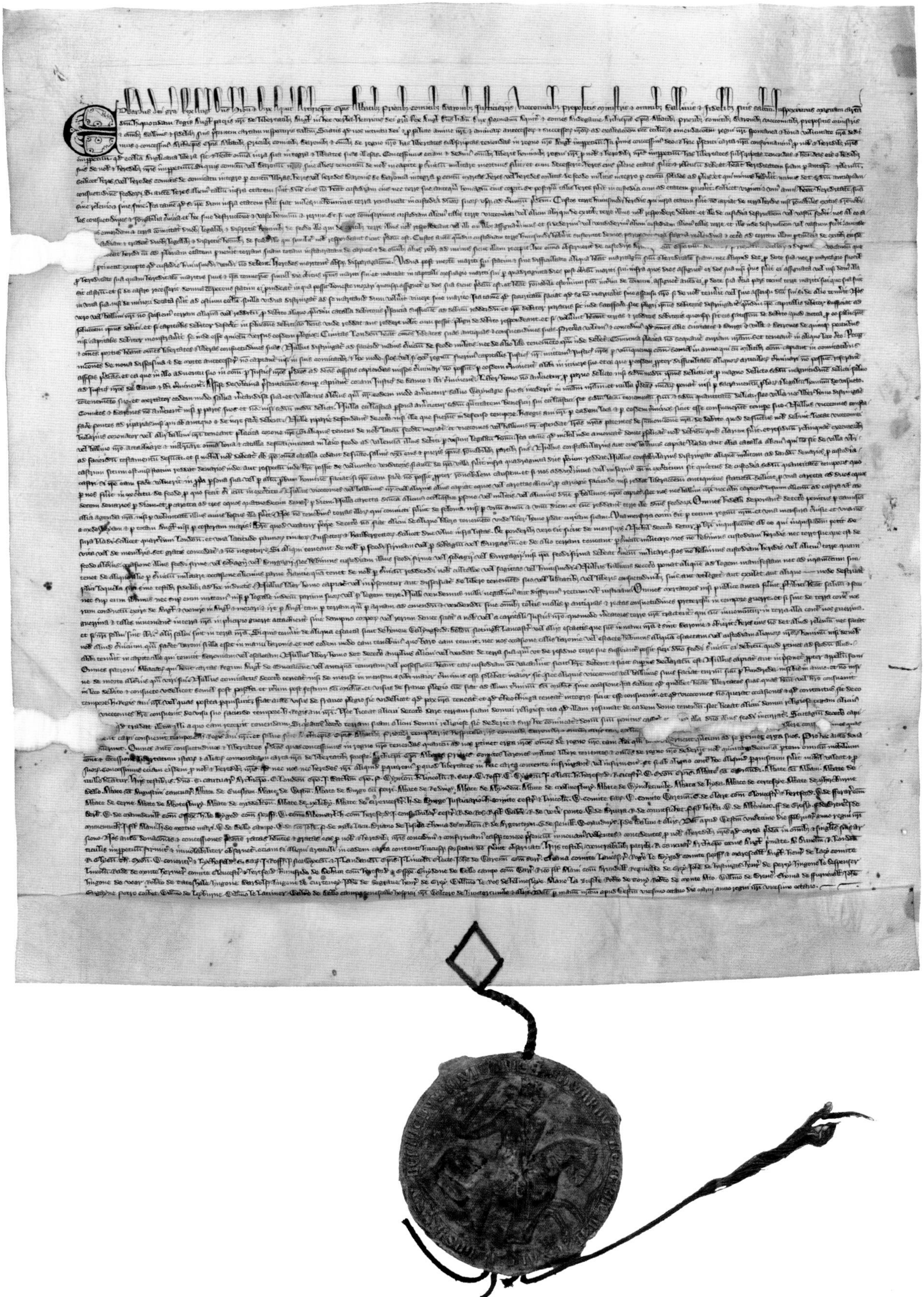

21. Faversham, Faversham Borough Archives. Good condition, save for damp damage to the left hand side of the document. Approx. 591 x 444 + 32mm, with margins of approx. 34 (left), 12 (top) and 36mm (right). Neat chancery-style hand, the capital *E* of *Edwardus* fairly elaborately decorated and extending down three lines, restrained majuscule lettering in the opening line, final line infilled with decorative marking, 58 lines in all. Four patches of severe damp damage on the left hand side of the charter, resulting in the loss of several words; other traces of minor damp damage. Sealed *sur double queue*, parchment tag (a modern replacement, 19mm wide) through a single slit with fragment of medieval parchment tag (13mm wide), impression of the great seal of King Edward I in natural wax stored separately. On the front of the fold to the left of the sealing, *pro baronibus port(us) de Fauresh(a)m'* and on the right hand side *Examinat(ur) per mag(ist)r(u)m Edmundum de London'* (both notes contemporary with the charter itself, s.xiv in). Dorse inaccessible. The exemplar directed to the Cinque Port town of Faversham.
© Faversham Borough Council.

22. Westminster Abbey Muniments LX. Good condition, save for the trimming away of and repair to the foot. Approx. 472 x 492mm, originally 472 x 463 + 29mm, the fold now trimmed away, with margins of approx. 25 (left), 34 (top), 20 (right) and 29mm (foot). Neat chancery-style hand, the capital *E* of *Edwardus* decorated extending down three lines, infilled to the right margin at the end, 63 lines in all. Six holes of varying size in the far left hand section of the charter, obliterating letters and in one case a fairly substantial portion of the text, apparently rodent damage, now repaired and rebacked. Originally sealed *sur double queue* on a parchment tag through a single slit, tag and seal impression missing, and fold trimmed away. Endorsed: *Magna Carta r(egis) Edwardi <de> libertat(ibus) <Ang>lie* (s.xiv/ xv, ?Westminster archival mark); *126* (Westminster archival mark, ?s.xv). According to Blackstone (1759), p.xlviii, the word *Wilts* written across the fold, trimmed away at the time of the charter's mounting, suggesting that this is the charter originally directed to Wiltshire. © Dean and Chapter of Westminster Abbey.

23. Maidstone, Kent Archives Sa/ZBI/46 no.34. A mutilated original, badly damp damaged, with approximately a third of the text now lost. Approx. 420 x 535 + 35mm, with margins of approximately 20 (left), 28 (top) and 15mm (right). Neat chancery-style hand, the initial *E* of *Edwardus* extending down three lines. 82 lines of text in all, not infilled at the end. Fold cut away, originally sealed *sur double queue*, slit for parchment tag, tag and seal impression missing. Mounted, dorse inaccessible. Note on the front (by E. Salisbury, British Museum official who put together the scrap book in which the charter is now stored): *Endorsed Magna Carta de libertatibus et consuetudinibus Anglie. This confirmation was by Edward Ist in the 28th year of his reign* (c.1898). Apparently the version of the charter sent to the Cinque Port town of Sandwich, preserved together with others of the borough's charters in a scrap book assembled c.1898. Rediscovered during research for this present book in December 2014, with considerable media attention thereafter, including *Sunday Times* (8 February 2015) and *Times Literary Supplement* (20 February 2015). © Kent County Council.

24. Oxford, Bodleian Library MS. Ch. Oxon. Oseney 143b (with seal now ibid. 143b*). Good condition, but of uncertain status. Best regarded as a contemporary exemplification rather than as a product of the royal chancery. Approx. 548 x 335 + 37mm, with margins of 30 (left), 23 (top) and 30mm (right). Simple capital letter *E* to *Edwardus*, extending down two lines of text. Peculiar, spidery business hand, 50 lines in all. Blatant corrections and insertions at over a dozen points in the text, the first in line four where *omnia sua iua* has been corrected to *omnia sua iura*. Sealed *sur double queue*, narrow parchment tag (15mm) through 3 slits, seal tag clearly too narrow to carry the great seal of Edward I. Sealed instead with a seal impression, stored separately (as 143b*), oval, single-sided, dark green wax, a mitred figure standing in full pontificals with a book held across his chest in his left hand, and a crozier in his right hand, beneath a decorated arch or doorway, legend (barely legible, due to warping of the wax on the left hand side): S'FR'IS IOH'IS DI GRA … BATIS OSEN … apparently the seal of Abbot John (de Bibury) of Oseney (1297–1317), suggesting that the whole is an Oseney Abbey production rather than a product of the royal chancery, issued in exemplification of the 1300 Magna Carta at some time, perhaps shortly after 28 March 1300. Endorsed: *confirmat(io) reg(is) E(dwardi) primi super magnam cartam de libert(atibus) foreste 2x* (s.xiv ex, either implying association with a related though today untraced 1300 Forest Charter, or more likely citing the references to the Forest Charter within the text itself); *v.v.* (s.xvi); *64* (s.xvii).

[illegible] Prioribus Comitibus Baronibus Justiciariis Vicecomitibus prepositis ministris et omnibus ballivis et fidelibus suis salutem. Inspeximus magnam cartam domini [illegible]

[illegible] Normannie [illegible] et Comes Andegavie Archiepiscopis Episcopis Abbatibus Prioribus Comitibus Baronibus Vicecomitibus prepositis ministris et omnibus ballivis et fidelibus suis presentem cartam inspecturis salutem. [illegible]

[illegible] spontanea et bona voluntate nostra dedimus et concessimus Archiepiscopis Episcopis Abbatibus Prioribus Comitibus Baronibus et omnibus de Regno nostro has [illegible]

[illegible] libertates suas illesas. Concessimus etiam et dedimus omnibus liberis hominibus regni nostri pro nobis et heredibus nostris imperpetuum has libertates subscriptas habendas et tenendas [illegible]

[illegible]

[illegible] concedimus et confirmamus eisque tenore presencium innovamus volentes et concedentes pro nobis et heredibus nostris [illegible]

[illegible] Archiepiscopo [illegible] R. London. [illegible] Exon. [illegible]

[illegible] Comite Gloucestrie et Hertford. Humfrido de Bohun Comite Hereford et Essex. [illegible] de Bello [illegible]

[illegible] Hugone de Curtenay [illegible] Henrico de Grey [illegible] de Ros de Helmeslake. Alano de [illegible]

[illegible] et Waltero de Huntercumbe et aliis. Datum per manum nostram apud Westmonasterium vicesimo octavo die Marcii Anno Regni nostri vicesimo octavo.

143b

This exhausts the listing of known originals of Magna Carta. I have no doubt that others remain to be identified. Scattered sightings continue to be reported. Some can be easily explained. *The Times* of 18 May 1861 (p.12 col.f), for example, reports a Magna Carta in the possession of the late Miss Richardson Currer of Eshton. In reality, the catalogue of the Currer collection (C. J. Stewart, *A Catalogue of the Library Collected by Miss Richardson Currer at Eshton Hall, Craven, Yorkshire* (London 1833), p.73) identifies this as one of the luxurious facsimiles of Magna Carta printed in 1816 by John Whittaker for the Whig politician, George 2nd Earl Spencer. Other such references retain their mystery. A catalogue of manuscripts and books sold on behalf of the (bankrupt) 2nd duke of Chandos (1747) reports the sale of a 'very ancient' Magna Carta on vellum. This may or may not be identifiable with one or other of the charters listed above (for the most promising possibility here see above no.13). In 1759, Blackstone referred to an original of the 1225 Magna Carta, apparently from Battle Abbey, last seen *c.*1700 (see notes on the 1225 charter, preceding nos.10-13 above). In 1873, at the time of the British Museum's acquisition of the Parva Carta of 1237 (below no.36 ii), the Museum was approached by a correspondent claiming to own 'The Magna Carter of England .... it being a heir loom of my family' (BL Department of Western Manuscripts, Correspondence File on Acquisitions, 5 August 1873). Nothing further is reported here, although the spelling ('Magna Carter') and the fact that this correspondent wrote from what seems to have been a London crossing sweeper's cottage, does little to encourage any suspension of disbelief.

RELATED TEXTS

Besides the original exemplars of Magna Carta, there are other original documents whose history is so closely linked to that of the charter that they deserve to be considered as integral elements of the charter's story. These include, in roughly chronological order:

25. The so-called 'Unknown' Charter, preserved in the French royal archives, now the Archives nationales. This consists of a series of clauses, apparently recording negotiations between king and barons, written at the foot of and in the same neat early thirteenth-century hand as a single-sheet copy of the coronation charter of King Henry I (1100–1135), the new clauses headed 'This is the charter of King Henry by which the barons seek liberties, and King John conceded the following'. The document is still referred to as the 'Unknown' charter, even though it was published at least twice in the nineteenth century, first (without proper notice of its significance) in the official catalogue of French national archives in 1863, thereafter (with commentary, but without noting its previous printing) by John Horace Round, in 1893. There is no certain evidence of the means by which this document arrived in France, but the archbishop of Canterbury's brother, Master Simon Langton, has been suggested as a possible conduit: a man close to the negotiations of 1215 and subsequently attached to the service of the future Louis VIII, son of the French king Philip Augustus. Set against this, there is the fact that the version of Henry I's coronation charter recited here, above the text of the 'Unknown' charter, is not the Canterbury or Lambeth version of Henry I's coronation charter that would have been readily available to Archbishop Langton, but more closely related to versions in circulation elsewhere in England from the so-called 'Quadripartitus' family of manuscripts. Several times printed, beginning with *Layettes*, i, pp.34–5 no.34, 423 no.1153, thereafter independently by J.H. Round, 'An Unknown Charter of Liberties', *EHR*, viii (1893), pp.288–94, with responses by J.W. Prothero, Hubert Hall and H.W.C. Davis, *EHR*, ix (1894), pp.117–21, 326–35; xx (1905), pp.719–26. For the standard modern edition and commentary, see Holt, *Magna Carta* (1992), pp.418–24, with photographic facsimiles plates 2–3.

Paris, Archives nationales MS. J655 Angleterre sans date no.31bis. In near perfect condition. Approx. 268 x 256mm, with margins of 7 (left), 10 (top), 2 (right) and 72mm (foot). Written on a single, irregularly shaped sheet of parchment (with one large hole, around which the scribe has arranged his writing), in a clear, almost certainly English business hand not infilled at the end, very similar to that of BL MS. Harley 458 (below no.26). Various corrections and excisions, the first in line 1 where *consilio baron(um) regni nostri Anglie* has been marked to show the omission of *nostri*. Clearly never intended for sealing. The Coronation Charter of Henry I written in 18 lines, the memorandum of John's concessions in a further 10 lines, as two distinct text blocks, the transition marked with the words *Hec est carta regis Henrici per quam barones querunt libertates et hec consequentia concedit rex Ioh(anne)s*. Endorsed: *promittit rex Anglie H(enricus) tenere contenta in ista cedula suis boronis (sic.) et episcopis et aliis* (s.xiv); various post medieval endorsements. For Master Simon Langton as potential transmitter to the French royal archives, see J.W. Baldwin, 'Master Stephen Langton, Future archbishop of Canterbury: The Paris Schools and Magna Carta', *EHR*, cxxiii (2008), pp.811–46, esp. pp.838–46. For an alternative explanation, suggesting that the charter represents negotiations between king and barons, sent to King John in Poitou in 1214 and there intercepted by the French, see L. Riess, 'Zur Vorgeschichte der Magna Charta', *Historische Vierteljahrschrift*, xiii (1910), pp.449–58, reprised in English as 'The Reissue of Henry I's Coronation Charter', *EHR*, xli (1926), pp.321–31, esp.pp.325–6.

26. A bifolium of copies of earlier royal charters of liberties issued in the names of Kings Henry I, Stephen and Henry II, preserved both in their original Latin and in early thirteenth-century Norman-French translations. There can be no certainty here, but it is highly probable that this short dossier formed part of the portfolio of documents carried into negotiations between king and barons prior to the meeting at Runnymede. One possibility is that it was drafted and intended for the use of Stephen Langton, archbishop of Canterbury, purportedly the first person to draw the barons' attention to the significance and the potential uses of Henry I's Coronation Charter as a precedent in their negotiations with the king, perhaps as early as 1213 or 1214. Described, with part reproduced in photographic facsimile, Holt, *Magna Carta* (1992), pp.474–7, plates 4–5. To date, there is no proper edition, in particular of the Norman-French translations.

London, British Library MS. Harley 458. Parchment bifolium, s.xiii in, each folio approx 185 x 295mm, between 39 and 41 lines per page, with ownership signatures of *Brianus Merecroft* (s.xv/xvi) and *pertinet Petro Le Neve al(ia)s Norroy 1704*, i.e. the antiquary and herald Peter Le Neve (1661–1729), Norroy King of Arms.

27. The Articles of the Barons. A set of proposals sealed by the king in token of his agreement and thereafter preserved by one of the parties in attendance at Runnymede either during or at the end of negotiation, the most likely candidate here being Archbishop Langton. Very close to the final text of Magna Carta, although arranged in a different order of clauses, and as two distinct blocks of text, the first listing 'chapters' (*capitula*) which the barons had sought and the king had granted, the second supplying a form of security backed by twenty-five elected barons, ending with a promise by the king to obtain letters from the bishops in support of the baronial insistence that the king obtain no future annulment from the pope. Almost certainly sealed at Runnymede on or shortly after 10 June 1215. Many times printed, first (from a copy in the Canterbury cartulary, now London, Lambeth Palace Library MS. 1212 fos.27v–29v no.30) in David Wilkins' edition of Henry Spelman's 'Codex Veterum Legum', in Wilkins, *Leges Anglo-Saxonicae* (London 1721), pp.356–9. Printed (after the original then belonging to David Mitchell) by Blackstone (1759), 1–9, thereafter as an appendix to the second edition of Allan Ramsay's *Essay on the Constitution of England* (London 1766). Modern editions (after the original, with engraved facsimile) in *Statutes* (1810), pp.6–8 no.6, and *Foedera*, pp.129–30 (with engraving of seal); Bémont, *Chartes*, pp.15–23 no.4; Stubbs, *Select Charters*, pp.284–91. For the standard text, with photographic facsimiles, see Holt, *Magna Carta* (1992), pp.429–40, plates 6–7.

London, British Library MS. Additional 4838. On permanent public display and therefore inaccessible for measurement. Written in a somewhat untidily arranged chancery-style hand, 89 lines, the whole divided into two distinct text blocks. When presented to the British Museum by Philip Earl Stanhope in May 1769, it still preserved a natural wax seal attached on a parchment tag, now stored separately. Sealed *sur double queue*, single slit for a tag and seal impression now stored apart. Endorsed: *articuli magne carte libertatum sub sigillo regis Iohannis* (s.xiii med); *Iohannes xxx* (s.xiii med). This latter is a Lambeth Palace press mark, corresponding to that of the copy of the Articles now Lambeth Palace Library MS.1212 fos.27–29v, proving that the articles were originally stored in the archive of the archbishops of Canterbury, whence removed by Archishop Laud and thence, after Laud's impeachment (18 December 1640) via Bishop Warner of Rochester (d.1666), to Dr John Lee, archdeacon of Rochester, to Lee's younger brother, Colonel Lee (MP for Canterbury

1685–1715) and then to Gilbert Burnet, bishop of Salisbury (d.1715). From Bishop Burnet's son-in-law, David Mitchell (d.1766), the document passed to Mitchell's daughter, Mary, who permitted Allan Ramsay, George III's court painter, to print it, with critical notes, in 1766. Thereafter, purchased by Ramsay acting as agent for Philip Lord Stanhope for 50 guineas (13 May 1769). Presented by Stanhope to the British Museum on or before 26 May 1769. For the transmission, see Collins, 'Documents', pp.234–43, with further correspondence, relating to Ramsay and Stanhope's involvement in the affair, Maidstone, Kent Archives U1590/C34/6; Alastair Smart, *The Life and Art of Allan Ramsay* (London 1952), pp.140–3. © The British Library Board.

28. The letters of King John announcing the Peace made at Runnymede, preserved in the archives of Hereford Cathedral. These letters, dated 20 June, addressed to the sheriff and other royal officials in Gloucestershire, announce the making of a firm peace between king and barons, embodied in a charter (clearly Magna Carta) that was to be read aloud and observed in the counties. The sheriff was to ensure compliance with the oath that Magna Carta demanded be taken to the baronial twenty-five, and the election of twelve knights of the county, at the next meeting of the county court, to enquire into evil customs in accordance with the procedures stipulated in Magna Carta 1215 clause 48. A version of these same letters, there dated 19 June, was copied onto the dorse of the Patent Roll of the royal chancery, followed by memoranda of its dispatch for publication via a mixed collection of bishops, barons and royal clerks. First printed by W.W. Capes, *Charters and Records of Hereford Cathedral* (Hereford, 1908), pp.44–5. Reprinted, more accurately and with full commentary, by Ifor Rowlands, 'The Text and Distribution of the Writ for the Publication of Magna Carta, 1215', *EHR*, cxxiv (2009), pp.1422–31. For the enrolled version, see *RLP*, 180b.

Hereford Cathedral Archives charter no.2256. Good condition. Approx. 153 x 105mm, apparently sealed *sur simple queue*, tongue and seal impression torn away. Addressed to Gloucestershire, and therefore assumed, like other Gloucester charters, to have migrated from St Peter's Abbey Gloucester to Hereford at a later date.

29. The Treaty concerning London, June/July 1215, made as a cyrograph (or two-part writing, one for each party) between the king and thirteen (i.e. a majority) of the twenty-five barons of Magna Carta, agreeing a term to the feast of the Assumption (15 August) during which the barons were to retain the city of London and Archbishop Langton was to take charge of the Tower, pending the fulfilment of arrangements for oaths to be taken to the twenty-five and the enquiry and emendment of evil customs, as laid down in clause 48 and the securities clause of

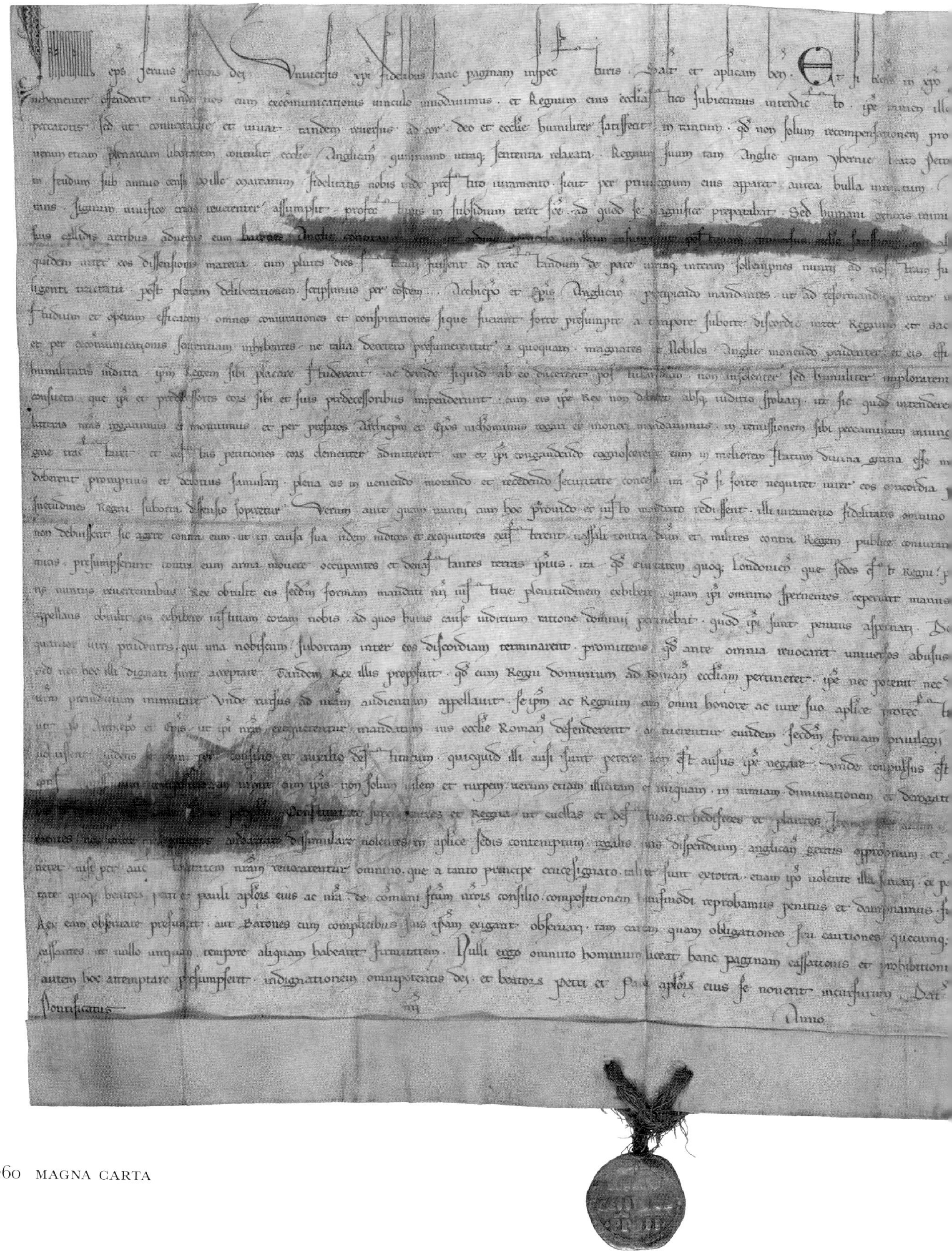

31.

the Runnymede charter. It was the non fulfilment of the terms agreed here, the failure of the barons to surrender London and of the archbishop to deliver up the Tower, that in effect destroyed the peace later that summer. The treaty itself is undated, but is assigned by Holt to *c.*19 June and the field of Runnymede. Printed (from its enrolment on the dorse of the chancery Close Roll, TNA C 54/12 m.27d, also C 54/13 m.27d, cf. *RLC*, i, 268b) *Foedera*, 133, with commentary by H. G. Richardson, 'The Morrow of the Great Charter', *Bulletin of the John Rylands Library*, xxviii (1944), pp.424–5 (with suggested dating to the Oxford Council of 16–23 July), and (with facsimile from the original) by Holt, *Magna Carta* (1992), pp.490–1, plates 10–11 (with commentary at pp.262–6, 486–8, and suggested dating to the field of Runnymede *c.*19 June). The appearance of the enrolled version of this document on the dorse of a membrane of the chancery Close Roll dealing with letters of 11–19 July might suggest a date somewhere between those proposed by Holt (*c.*19 June) and Richardson (in mid to late July).

London, The National Archives C 47/34/1/1. Indented cyrograph. Galled and holed towards the foot, some letters illegible. Endorsed: *conventio inter regem Johannem et barones. Nota (?)signa* (s.xvii); *16 Joh(ann)is* (s.xvii/xviii); *A.D. 1215* (s.xix). Approx. 450 x 115 + 26mm. 9 lines of text. Sealed *sur double queue*, single slits for 11 tags and a further two double slits for tags, all tags and seal impressions now missing. Rebacked, the s.xvii endorsement perhaps suggesting the survival of seals into early-modern times. Provenance, the royal archives, subsequently chancery miscellanea of the Public Record Office/TNA.

30. Letters publishing the papal excommunication of the rebels, preserved in the archives of Canterbury Cathedral, presumably following delivery to Archbishop Stephen Langton. Issued by the king's supporters, Peter des Roches, bishop of Winchester, Simon, abbot of Reading and the papal representative Pandulf. These letters, addressed to Langton from Dover on 5 September 1215 mark a crucial turning point in relations between King John and the rebels, signalling an end to compromise and in effect the king's rejection of the entire settlement agreed at Runnymede. Publishing papal letters of 7 July 1215, issued by the pope after he had received news of the rebel seizure of London but before he had knowledge of Magna Carta, the commissioners hereby pronounced a sentence of excommunication intended to include the leading rebels, the city of London and a series of named clerical supporters, including the bishop of Hereford. First printed by F. M. Powicke, 'The Bull "Miramur Plurimum" and a Letter to Archbishop Stephen Langton, 5 September 1215', *EHR*, xliv (1929), pp.90–93, and thereafter in a critical edition by N. Vincent, *English Episcopal Acta IX: Winchester 1205–1238* (Oxford 1994), pp.82–6 no.100.

Canterbury Cathedral Archives Chartae Antiquae M247.
Good condition. Approx. 275 x 285 + 15mm. Sealed *sur double queue*, slits for three tags, tags and seal impressions all missing. 47 lines, not infilled at the end. Written in an Italianate hand, perhaps by a scribe attached to the household of the papal envoy, Pandulf. Presumably deposited in the Canterbury archive either in 1215 or shortly thereafter.

31. The letters of Pope Innocent III (or 'Papal Bull') declaring Magna Carta annulled, 24 August 1215, surviving as a sealed original in the British Library, still in the royal archives in 1323, thereafter removed, probably by the antiquary Sir Robert Cotton. The king's commitment to Magna Carta was never sincere. Certainly, the barons were concerned from the outset that the king would seek papal annulment. This was duly delivered in papal letters (known from their opening Latin words as the Bull *Etsi karissimus*) at Agnani on 24 August, and published in England by the end of September, by which time civil war had already resumed. Editions by Bémont, *Chartes*, pp.41–4 no.6; *Selected Letters of Pope Innocent III Concerning England (1198–1216)*, ed. C.R. Cheney and W.H. Semple (Edinburgh 1953), pp.212–16 no.82, and cf. C.R. and M.G. Cheney, *The Letters of Pope Innocent III (1198–1216) Concerning England and Wales* (Oxford 1967), pp.170 no.1018; J.E. Sayers, *Original Papal Documents in England and Wales from the Accession of Pope Innocent III to the Death of Pope Benedict XI (1198–1304)* (Oxford 1999), pp.31–2 no.58.

BL MS. Cotton Cleopatra E i fo.155. Good condition. Approx. 498 x 455 + 36mm. Sealed *sur double queue*, lead papal *bulla* (i.e. seal) on red and yellow silk cords. The pope's name *Innocentius* written in capitals, the whole composed in a standard papal chancery hand. No endorsement. At the bottom right hand corner of the plica or fold the letters *JG.* (as a contemporary papal chancery mark). From the king's own archive. Still stored in the royal Exchequer in the 1320s, assumed thereafter purloined by, or for, Sir Robert Cotton, as part of Cotton's wider haul of Magna Carta materials from the royal archives: Collins, 'Documents', 256n., 257, 259n and cf. above p.260. © The British Library Board.

32. A single-sheet copy of the 1215 Magna Carta, now in the Bodleian Library. Written on both sides of a long thin parchment schedule, tapering from left to right at the foot, with holes at the top as if originally intended to hang up on display. Written in an English book hand of the first half of the thirteenth century, but endorsed in such a way to demonstrate that by the eighteenth century it was in Italy. One explanation here might involve the papacy, another the papal legate Guala, via either of whom a copy of the 1215 charter could have found its way across the Alps. To judge from the handwriting, this is not written in a hand of the royal chancery, and therefore cannot have been the copy of the charter that the pope was sent in order to secure

its annulment. Save for a partial and private printing in J.E. Hodgkin, *Rariora* (London 1902), i, p.26, for the most part ignored in the literature on the 1215 Magna Carta, although cf. Collins, 'Documents', pp.258–9.

Oxford, Bodleian Library MS. Lat. hist. a. 1 (P). 122 x 635mm, with writing down the entire face and ending two thirds of the way down the dorse. Some water damage to the text at the front and back, and some holes, but the text itself legible throughout. Endorsed on the back: *1298 16 Guigno* (s.xvii); *1298 papa Innon' 3a 16 Guigno* (s.xvii); at the head of the dorse *xxvii* (?s.xiv); *privilegias regni Anglice* (s.xvi/xvii); *Privilegii concessi a l(ohanne) rege de Inghilterra … regno d'Inghilterra* (s.xvii/xviii). Gifted in 1926 from the collection of John Eliot Hodgkin, engineer and antiquary, son of the Quaker barrister, John Hodgkin (1800–1875) and elder brother of Thomas Hodgkin (1831–1913), the historian of early medieval Italy, having earlier been offered for sale, 22 April 1914 and 11 April 1919 (as noted by Collins, 'Documents', 258n.). David Carpenter, who has collated the text, notes minor variants from the standard version in clauses 2 (omitting the baronial as opposed to the earl or the knight's relief), 12 (where aids are to be assessed by the king in person, not by 'common counsel', and where there is a slip, as occasionally elsewhere, into the first person singular), 48 (where the word 'deleantur' is replaced by 'emendetur', a variant that makes this version closer to the text of the Articles of the Barons), and the dating clause (which gives 16 rather than 15 June).

33 (i and ii). Two single sheet copies of the 1216 Magna Carta, today stored in the same series as the 'Unknown' charter, in the French National Archives. As with the 'Unknown' charter (above no.25), a link has been suggested between these documents and the activities of Master Simon Langton, an adherent both of the rebel barons and of Louis of France during the civil war of 1215–17. One of these two copies involves a full recital, with address and witness list, of the 1216 Magna Carta; the other recites merely the substantive terms of the charter, without the king's title or the address. The script of these copies could be English or northern French, but is otherwise unidentified. Their association with Simon Langton remains entirely speculative. That they were acquired by Louis during his time in England before 1217 remains highly probable. No facsimiles have been printed, and no proper attempt as yet made to collate both copies against the unique single-sheet original of the charter. Printed in *Layettes*, i, pp.434–7 no.1194 (from i, noting principal variants from ii).

i. Paris, Archives nationales J655 Angleterre sans date no.11. Good condition. Approx. 424 x 258mm, with margins of approx. 1 (left), 10 (top) and 33mm (foot), no margin to the right. Full recital of the text, beginning *Henricus*, 44 lines, carefully infilled at the end to the right hand edge of the parchment.

Written in an unlined and somewhat straggling business hand, perhaps northern French rather than English. Not prepared for sealing. Endorsed: *transcriptum e(st) quibusdam statut(is) regni Angl(ie) regni Henrici reg(is) Angl(ie) anno i.* (s.xiv/xv); various post medieval endorsements. For discussion of provenance, see J. W. Baldwin, 'Master Stephen Langton, Future Archbishop of Canterbury: The Paris Schools and Magna Carta', *EHR*, cxxiii (2008), pp.838–46. Text distinct in minor details from above no.5.

ii. Paris, Archives nationales J655 Angleterre sans date no.31.

Good condition. Approx. 452 x 294mm, with margins of 1 (left), 18 (top) and 55mm (foot), no margin to the right. Written in 36 lines of a straggling northern French business hand similar to, but not the same as that of the other copy (no.33 i) but here opening without the titles and address *In primis concessisse Deo et hac presenti carta nostra confirmasse*, with some corrections and insertions over the line, including in the passage just quoted the correction of *presente* to *presenti*. Never prepared for sealing. Endorsed: *in quod rotulo quedam consuetudines Angl(ie) que videntur <pertinere> ad consuetudines Normannie* (s.xiv, cf. below no.48); various post medieval endorsements, including a note by Léopold Delisle (s.xix) that the present copy is very similar to that listed above no.34 i, from which David Carpenter has now established that it is copied.

34 (i and ii). The Forest Charter of 6 November 1217, of which there are two surviving single-sheet originals, at Durham and Lincoln. Issuing Magna Carta in June 1215, King John had promised in due course that he would issue provisions for those who dwelt within the royal forest – vast tracts of land extending into most of the counties of England – in which, until then, it had been the king's arbitrary authority rather than the laws of the realm that had chiefly operated. The resulting Forest Charter, issued at the same time as Magna Carta in November 1217, was intended both to restrict the royal forests to the geographical limits set during the twelfth century, removing any land newly afforested, and to offer protection to the rights of those who dwelt within such areas, in order to defend them against the arbitrary exercise of royal authority. From 1217 onwards, the reissue of Magna Carta was invariably accompanied by the reissue of the Forest Charter, so that the two texts are to be seen as twin elements of a phenomena known to contemporaries as 'the charters' or 'the charters of liberties'. From 1217 onwards, the format and diplomatic of the surviving originals of the Forest Charter is thus of great significance to our understanding of the format and diplomatic of Magna Carta. Printed (from the 1300 inspeximus by Edward I (below nos.41 i, iv) Blackstone (1759), pp.60–7; (from ii, with engraved facsimile by James Basire) *Statutes* (1810), pp.20–1 no.10; Bémont, *Chartes*, pp.64–70 no.8; Stubbs, *Select Charters*, pp.344–8, and cf. *Guala Letters*, p.31 no.39. Falsely attributed to King John by the chronicler Matthew Paris, whence *Foedera*, p.133.

32.

i. Lincoln, Lincolnshire Archives MS. Dean and Chapter of Lincoln A1/1/46. Good condition. Approx. 331 x 301 + 29mm, with margins of approx. 14 (left), 16 (top) and 13mm (right). The *H* of *Henricus* left blank, restrained majuscule lettering in the final line, infilled in the final line so that *aliis multis* is hard against the right hand margin. Neat chancery-style hand, 41 lines. Damaged at the top left hand corner and in the extreme left hand side, obliterating sections of the text. Some minor brown staining. Neat chancery-style hand, 41 lines. Sealed *sur double queue*, one thin seal tag (9mm wide) through a single slit on the left hand side, the seal tag on the right missing with only the slit remaining. On the surviving tag, the seal of the legate Guala in dark green wax, defaced, but presumably as above no.7. Endorsed: *Carta de foresta sub sigillo episcopi* (s.xiv); *libertates* … (faint and mostly illegible, s.xiv); various post medieval endorsements. Apparently the exemplar sent to Lincoln.

ii. Durham, University Library Special Collections, Durham Cathedral Muniments 1.2.Reg.4. Lower third of the document badly damaged. Approx. 338 x 400 + 26mm, with margins of approx. 17 (left), 22 (top) and 13mm (right). The *H* of *Henricus* occupies one line and is undecorated, restrained majuscule lettering in the first line, not infilled in the final line (the sentence ending almost halfway across the document). Neat chancery-style hand, 48 lines. Substantial damage to the lower third of the document, substantial sections of text missing. Sealed *sur double queue*, but only the extreme left hand section of the fold now survives, with one thin parchment tag (11mm wide) through a single slit. The seal of the legate Guala in green wax on the surviving tag, as above no.7. Endorsed *C(arta) general(is) tocius regni et p(rim)o de forestis signata sigillata G(uale) legati et W(illelmi) comit(is)* (s. xiii in); … *ista carta postea fuit sigillata apud Westm' cum magno sigillo eiusdem H(enrici) reg(is) III XI die Februar' anno regni sui nono* (s. xiv in); *Henr(icus) ter(tius)* (s. xiv ex); *Transcribed Sept. 1806 T. E. Tomlins W. Illingworth* (s. xix). Printed with engraved facsimile in *Statutes* (1810). Apparentlty the exemplar sent to Durham.

35 (i–iv). The Forest Charter of 11 February 1225, of which there are four surviving originals. Printed (from i, with missing passages supplied from a Durham Cathedral cartulary) *Statutes* (1810), pp.26–7 no.12; Holt, *Magna Carta* (1992), pp.512–17.

i. Durham, University Library Special Collections Durham Cathedral Muniments 1.2.Reg.5. Good condition. Approx. 335 x 352 + 57mm, with margins of approx. 17 (left), 27 (top) and 20mm (right). The first five letters of *Henricus* are missing, but both *Henricus* and *Dei* were originally written in fairly flamboyant majuscule lettering, with restrained majuscule lettering for the remainder of the first line. Not infilled in the final line (the line ending in the first third of the space). Extensive damage to the

left and right hand sides of the document, obliterating substantial sections of the text. A neat chancery-style hand, 41 lines. Sealed *sur double queue* on pink cords with impression of the first great seal of King Henry III in green wax, in good condition. Endorsed: *<Carta ge>n(er)alis totius regni de forestis … reg(is) III* (s. xiii in); one other medieval endorsement very faded; *Transcribed Sept 1806 T. E. Tomlins W. Illingworth* (s.xix). Apparently the exemplar sent to Durham.

ii. Lincoln, Lincolnshire Archives MS. Dean and Chapter A1/1/47. Good condition. Approx. 329 x 216 + 26mm, with margins of approx. 9 (left), 10 (top) and 8mm (left). The *H* of *Henricus* is capitalized, occupying one line, with restrained majuscule lettering in the first line, not infilled to the end of the final line. Damp damage to the top left hand corner and to the middle lower third of the document; the entire right hand side of the foot has been torn away obliterating an extensive section of the text (some twenty-one words); two small holes. A neat chancery-style hand, 42 lines. Originally sealed *sur double queue*, part of the fold and slit for seal tag torn, tag and seal impression missing. Endorsed: *Libertates concesse per Hen(ricum) r(egem) . III .* (s. xiii ex); *XVI* (s. xiii ex); *H III* (s. xiii ex); various post medieval endorsements. Apparently the exemplar sent to Lincoln.

iii. BL Additional Charter 24712. Good condition. Approx. 352 x 292 + 48mm, with margins of approx. 7 (left), 5 (top) and 8mm (right). Neat, slightly fussy chancery-style hand, majuscule *H* to *Henricus*, 36 lines, not infilled at the end. Sealed *sur double queue* on pink or brown and white cords through 3 holes, impression of the great seal of Henry III in green wax within a linen seal bag. Endorsed: *carta de foresta* (s.xvi); various post medieval endorsements. Acquired by the British Museum in 1875 from R.E. Cain for £16. Cain, in correspondence (10 August 1875), claimed to have recovered it in 1865 from waste paper sold from the stock of an unnamed lithographer, disposed of via the sale room of Cutten and Davis of Bassinghall Street, London (just behind the London Guildhall). Acquired from the purchaser, Edwin Joseph Pennell of Lambeth, by Cain in lieu of 4 shillings owed in wages.

iv. Cambridge University Library MS. EDC/1/B/30. Approx. 345 x 278 + 40mm, with margins of 15 (left), 10 (top) and 8mm (right). Sealed *sur double queue*, pink, white and blue cords through 3 holes, seal impression in good condition in natural wax varnished green. The whole in excellent state of preservation. Written in a neat chancery-style hand. The *H* of *Henricus* omitted for decoration not completed, not infilled in final line. Endorsed: *carta Henrici reg(is) de foresta* (s.xiii); *A.i.i.* (s.xiii). The second of the endorsements is an Ely Cathedral press mark, suggesting that this was in the Cathedral archives from a very early date. Perhaps the exemplar sent to Cambridgeshire, or alternatively to the bishop and cathedral of Ely, certainly stored at Ely thereafter.

Henricus Dei gra Rex Angl Dns Hybn Dux Norm et Aquit Com Andeg Omnibz xpi fidelibz psentem cartam inspectis sal. Sciatis q intuitu dei et p salute anime nostre et Animab Ancessor et heredu nostror ad exaltacoem sce ecclie et emendacone Regni nostr concessim et hac carta nostra confirmauim Archiepis Epis Abbibz Prioribz Comitibz Baronibz militibz libis hoimbz et omnibz de Regno nostro Anglie omes libtates et libtas consuetudines conteneal in cartis nostris quas eisdem fidelibz nostris fieri fecim Cum minores essem etatis Scilicet tam in magna carta nra qm in Carta nra de foresta. Et volum et concedim p nob et heredibz nostris qd pfati fideles nostr et successores et heredes eor habeant et teneant in ppetuu omes libtates et libtas consuetudines pdcas. Non obstance eo qd pdce carte confecte fuerint Cum minores essem etatis. Hiis testibz. Dns Cantuar, de nepabilibz patrbz. O Archiepo Cantuar. p Wyncon. J Bathon. et Dunolm. R Londin W Karl W Exon R Sarr W Elyen R Lme R Hereford A Couentr et Lychefeld Epis. W Valenc et Wygorn elctis. R Com et Cornub et Pictau J Com Cestr et Hunt edon J Com Line Constabul Cestr G Marescall Com Pembr. W Com de Ferrar W Com Warenn W Com Lanc W Com Essex et Hereford Symone de Monteforti Will Longesp Will de Ferrar Will de Veley Ric de Percy et ro de Mumfichet Will et lo Joh Byset Gilbto de Umfranuill Will de Lancastr Will de Cantilupo Walt de Clifford Joh Monem Rad de mortuo Mari Will Maudut Rog La Zuch Elud de Vallibz Gilbto Basset et Allys. Dat p manu venerabilis patr R Cycestr epi cancellarii nostr apd Westmonaster xxbiij die Januar Anno Regni nostr Vicesimo primo.

Gloster 10.ª

36.iii

36 (i–iii). The 'Parva Carta' of 28 January 1237, of which at least three originals survive. These take the form of a confirmation by Henry III in charter form but without any recital of either Magna Carta or the Forest Charter, of 'the liberties and free customs granted by us … either in the great charter (*magna carta*) or in our charter of the Forest'. This was accompanied by the renewal of the sentences of excommunication passed against violators of the charters in 1225 (*Councils and Synods*, i, pp.205–7). Printed (from iii, with facsimile of the seal) Blackstone (1759), pp.68–9; (from iii, with facsimile from the enrolment in the Charter Roll 21 Henry III, TNA C 53/30 m.7, whence *Cal.Chart.R. 1226–57*, pp.225–6) *Statutes* (1810), p.28 no.13, and cf. Collins, 'Documents', pp.269–70.

i. London, British Library MS. Cotton Vespasian F xiii fo.17.

Good condition. Approx. 178 x 110 + 30mm, with narrow margins of 3 (left), 2 (top) and 2mm (right), neatly infilled to the right hand margin at the end, 15 lines in all. Neat chancery-style hand, capital *H* for *H(enricus)*. Sealed *sur double queue*, slit for tag, tag and seal impression missing. Endorsed: *confirmatio H(enrici) r(egis) general(is) ecclesiasticis et laycis viris tocius Anglie* (s.xiii ex); *iiii.* (s.xiv); *ii.g* (s.xiv/xv). Provenance before Sir Robert Cotton unknown.

ii. London, British Library Additional Charter 19826.
Good condition. Approx. 202 x 209 + 50mm, with margins of 15 (left), 35 (top) and 10mm (right), not infilled in the final line. Rounded, slightly archaic hand, but probably a chancery production, capitalized *H* to the initial word *Henricus*, 19 lines of text. Sealed *sur double queue*, single slit through an exceptionally generous fold, tag and seal impression now missing, tag replaced with a modern piece of parchment. Endorsed: *conf(irmatio) reg(is) Henr(ici) iiii.ti de libertate totius regni et de libertate foreste* (s.xiii/xiv); *kk* (s.xv); various post medieval endorsements. A hole cut into the top margin, perhaps for filing, remains of a parchment guard apparently from previous binding into a book. Acquired by the British Museum 12 July 1873, from the collections of the earl of Winchilsea, previously deposited in the Albert Memorial Museum at Exeter, ultimately from the antiquary, Sir Christopher Hatton (1605–70). Hatton's collecting was omnivorous, but certainly included extensive acquisitions from Worcester Cathedral.

iii. Oxford, Bodleian Library MS. Ch. Glouc. 10a (with seal now ibid. 10a*).
Good condition. Approx. 170 x 163 + 40mm, with margins of 8 (left), 25 (top) and 10mm (right). Rounded chancery hand with capital *H* of *Henricus* much as above no.36 ii. 20 lines of text, last line not infilled. Sealed *sur double queue*, pink cords through three holes, impression of the first great seal of Henry III in dark green wax. Endorsed: *confirmatio reg(is) de libertatibus Angl(ie) caps' xiiii.a.* (s.xiii med); *de laicis tenuris* (s.xiii/xiv); *registratur* (s.xiv/xv); various post medieval endorsements. As with nos.8, 42, archived at St Peter's Gloucester during the Middle Ages (cf. Gloucester Cathedral Library MS. Register A part 1 fo.45r–v no.90) and therefore, presumably, the original intended for transmission to Gloucestershire. Belonged to the Gloucestershire antiquary Richard Furney (1694–1753).

37 (i and ii). The clerical sentence against infringements of Magna Carta and the Forest Charter, 13 May 1253, which survives in two single-sheet originals and a great multitude of later copies. Issued in Parliament before the king and magnates by Boniface of Savoy, archbishop of Canterbury and thirteen other bishops, this was pronounced against all who made attacks upon the Church or who violated 'the liberties and free customs contained in the charter of common liberties (i.e. Magna Carta) and the charter of the forest(s)'. This was of significance, not only on Magna Carta's path from law to totem, but as the spur to the pope to confirm this sentence, and thereby demand obedience to Magna Carta. Innocent IV's letters of 30 September 1254 were themselves confirmed four years later by Pope Alexander IV. The general sentence against violators of the charters was renewed by successive archbishops of Canterbury. Meanwhile, in publishing the sentence of May 1253 and the papal confirmation of September 1254, the English bishops were instructed to ensure that it was expounded in public by officials, archdeacons and deans in shires, hundreds and other places, 'distinctly and lucidly in the English and French languages' ('Burton Annals', in *Annales Monastici*, i, pp.320–2; Cambridge, University Library MS. EDC 1/B/95 (R(ichard of Gravesend) dean of Lincoln to W(illiam of Kilkenny) bishop-elect of Ely, 12 May 1255, requiring publication *distincte et dilucide in lingua Anglicana et Gallicana*). This supplies our first certain reference to sentences, associated with Magna Carta, being expounded in English as well as in Latin and French. Several times printed, including *Foedera*, pp.289 (from i); Bémont, *Chartes*, pp.71–4 no.9; *English Episcopal Acta 35: Hereford 1234–1275*, ed. Julia Barrow (Oxford 2009), pp.43–7 no.43, listing at least thirty-five later copies in monastic cartularies or other manuscripts, and cf. *Councils and Synods*, i, pp.474–9; David Carpenter, 'Magna Carta 1253: The Ambitions of the Church and the Divisions within the Realm', *Historical Research*, lxxxvi (2013), pp.179–90.

i. Wells Cathedral Muniments D.& C. Charter 84.
Good condition. Approx. 297 x 98 + 25mm. Endorsed: *excommunicatio generalis in venientes contra libertates contentas in magna carta libertatum Anglie et de foresta* (s.xiv); various post medieval endorsements, including one by the commissioners who compiled *Statutes* (1810), dated *4 August 1806*. Originally sealed *sur double queue*, with single slits for 14 tags and seal impressions, tags still present, only one surviving seal fragment, unidentified, in green wax, on the second of the tags. Presumably the version of the sentence sent for proclamation at Wells.

Edwardus dei gra Rex Angl dominus Hibn & Dux Aquitann omnibz ad quos presentes lree puenint salut. Sciatis qd cum nos magnam cartam dni H. quondam Regis Angl patris nostri de libertatibz Anglie vna cum carta de fforesta concesserimus & confirmauerimus. Ac innouauerimus per cartam nostram preceperimus qd qd carte ille in omnibz suis articulis teneantur & firmiter obseruentur: Volumus & concedimus p nobis & heredibus nostris qd si que statuta fuerint contraria dicte carte vel alicui articulo in eadem carte contento: ea de comuni consilio regni nostri modo debito emendentur vel etiam adnullentur. In cuius rei testimonium has litteras nostras fieri fecimus patentes. Teste meipo Apud Lincolniam quartodecimo die ffebruarii Anno regni nostri vicessimo nono

Gloucestr

26.

42.

ii. BL MS. Additional Charter 75748. Badly rubbed on the left hand side, galled and illegible in parts. Approx. 332 x 119 + 21mm. Endorsed: *Pro … carte etc sententia exco(mmunicationis) contra viol(atores) Magn(e) Cart(e) lata per archiepiscopum et suos suffraganeos* (s.xv/xvi); *excommunicatio v … contra libertates* (s.xvi); various post medieval endorsments. Originally sealed *sur double queue*, with single slits for 14 tags and seal impressions, nine tags still present, with fragments or impressions of the seals of the bishops of London, Lincoln, Worcester, Hereford and (probably) Exeter. Seals described by Barrow. Provenance unknown before its arrival in the collections of Sir Thomas Phillipps (1792–1872) (Phillipps MS. 27568), whence purchased by the BL at Sotheby's London, 14 June 1971.

38. The supposed reissue of Magna Carta 1252–3. In 1253, the archbishop of Canterbury and other bishops solemnly confirmed Magna Carta and the Forest Charter in a public ceremony of excommunication (above no.37). It has been assumed a document which survives in a peculiar and unexplained state in the British Library, is an original Magna Carta issued by King Henry III, dated 11 February 1252. As printed in *Statutes* (1810), pp.28–31 no.14, it has previously been cited as a 1252 or 1253 confirmation of the 1225 Magna Carta, associated with the public excommunication of 1253. In fact, the text it recites is a hybrid, confusing elements of the 1217 Magna Carta with that of 1225, reminiscent in various ways of the hybrid text that came to be accepted by the chroniclers of St Albans – Roger of Wendover and Matthew Paris – as a result, in part of confusion between the various issues, in part in order that the chroniclers could deliberately manipulate the historical record. Although presented as an original written on a single sheet, the sheet itself already had holes and faults at the time of writing that would have been entirely unacceptable to the royal chancery. The date of the text, 11 February at Westminster, appears to be borrowed from the 1225 charter, although here amended to the 36th rather than the 11th year of the reign (1252 rather than 1225). The witness list which precedes this dating clause (*Hiis testibus domino B(onefacio) Cant' archiepiscopo, G. London', Iohanne Bathon', R. Witthon', R. Lincoln', R. Saresbur' et aliis episcopis, abbatibus, prior(ibus), comit(ibus), baron(ibus), militibus et ceteris*) is both garbled and irregular, and once again appears to represent a fairly crude and unsuccessful attempt to adapt the witnesses of the 1225 charter to the circumstances of the early 1250s. For the confusions sown at St Albans, see J.C. Holt, 'The St Albans Chroniclers and Magna Carta', *Transactions of the Royal Historical Society*, 5th series xiv (1964), pp.67–88.

London, British Library MS. Cotton Augustus ii.51. Good condition. Approx. 246 x 483mm, at one time folded in four from top to bottom, now rebacked. Neat business hand, opening with a capital *H* for *Henr(icus)* (itself not a standard chancery abbreviation), 83 lines in all. No indication of sealing. No medieval endorsements. To be compared to the St Albans copy of the 1225 charter associated with Matthew Paris' book of *Additamenta* in BL MS. Cotton Nero D i fo.199v, sometimes described as an 'original' 1253 reissue of the 1225 charter, but in reality a single sheet copy of the 1225 charter neither intended nor suitable for sealing. For further commentary here, see S. Reynolds, 'Magna Carta 1297 and the Legal Use of Literacy', *Bulletin of the Institute of Historical Research*, lxii (1989), pp.239–40, and cf. Collins, 'Documents', p.272, accepting this as an authentic original. Provenance, presumably St Albans Abbey.

39. The Forest Charter of 12 October 1297, of which there is a single surviving original in the British Library, once stored in the archives of Easebourne Priory in Sussex and thence one of nineteen Easebourne Priory charters donated to the British Library by Francis Quekett Louch on 16 June 1905. Apparently the version of the charter that was intended for proclamation within the county of Surrey, itself administered in the thirteenth century by a sheriff who also served the county of Sussex. Discovered and upgraded from its previous status as a 'copy' only in September 2007. Not printed, either in text or in facsimile, with *Statutes* (1810), 'Table of Contents', declaring there to be no known original of the 1297 Forest Charter. A key document in understanding the diplomatic, sealing and script of the 1297 Magna Carta, and of the provenance of the particular exemplar of the 1297 Magna Carta now in Canberra (above no.16), which clearly originated in the same archive. Cf. *Australia's Magna Carta* (Canberra, Senate of Australia, 2011, 2nd ed. 2015).

London, British Library Additional Charter 53712. Good condition. Approx. 400 x 335 + 43mm, with margins 20 (left), 35 (top) and 20mm (right). Chancery-style hand, undecorated capital letter *E* to *Edwardus*. Infilled at the end with the name of the chancery official placed after the date, *lern'*, apparently for 'Hugh of Yarmouth', the same clerk whose name appears in the Canberra 1297 Magna Carta. 49 lines of text. Sealed *sur double queue* on pink and green cords through four holes, fragment of a double-sided seal impression in natural wax, the same small seal of Edward I described in detail as attached to the 1297 Magna Carta. Contemporary address and chancery marking on the outside of the fold, to the left and right of the cords: *Surr' … Exam(inatur)*. Endorsed: *carte foreste* (s.xv); *relating to Eastborne Priory* (s.xviii); various post medieval endorsements. Presented to the British Museum in 1905 by Francis Quekett Louch. Apparently the copy of the Forest Charter directed to the county of Surrey, twin to the Surrey Magna Carta of 1297 now in Canberra, above no.16, with similar provenance, via the nuns of Easebourne Priory to the Louch family solicitors firm.

40. The so-called 'Confirmatio Cartarum', first agreed on 10 October, ratified by Edward I on 5 November 1297, a French text agreeing to the reissue of Magna Carta and the Forest Charter, undertaking that they be published by the king's justices, sheriffs and officials in each county and city, with sealed originals to be deposited in every cathedral church, there to be publicly read twice a year. The version of this undertaking, issued by Edward's eldest son and his councillors at London, 10 October 1297, is known only from copies on the Statute Roll (TNA C 74/1 m.38), whence Blackstone (1759), pp.80–2; *Statutes* (1810), part 2 p.123; Stubbs, *Select Charters*, pp.490–3 (with translation), and from what appears to be a contemporary copy or draft (TNA E 175/1/11, cf. Prestwich, *Documents*, pp.158–60 no.155). The confirmation by Edward I himself, issued at Ghent on 5 November 1300, survives in the collections of Sir Robert Cotton, whence printed *Statutes* (1810), pp.37–8 no.17. In general, see J.G. Edwards, '"Confirmatio Cartarum" and Baronial Grievances in 1297', *EHR*, lviii (1943), pp.147–71, 273–300; H. Rothwell, 'The Confirmation of the Charters, 1297', *EHR*, lx (1945), p.16–35, 177–91, 300–15; idem, 'Edward I and the Struggle for the Charters, 1297–1305', *Studies in Medieval History Presented to Frederick Maurice Powicke*, ed. R.W. Hunt and others (Oxford 1948), pp.319–32; Prestwich, *Documents*.

BL MS. Cotton Charter vii.9. Good condition, despite the Cotton fire of 1731. Approx. 428 x 135mm. Cropped, foot cut away, sealing details and seal impression lost. Mounted, dorse in part inaccessible, various post-medieval endorsements. Printed by Bémont, *Chartes*, pp.96–8 no.14. For the background, Prestwich, *Documents*; Prestwich, *Edward I*, pp.427–30, 518–19. Provenance before Sir Robert Cotton unknown.

41 (i–vi). The Forest Charter of 28 March 1300, of which there are five surviving originals in Durham, Eton, London and Oxford, and a mutilated fragment from a fifth, in the archives of the town of Sandwich. Printed (from i, iv) Blackstone (1759), pp.60–7; from the enrolment in the chancery Charter Roll 28 Edward I, TNA C 53/86 m.6 (whence *Cal.Chart.R. 1257–1300*, p.483) *Statutes* (1810), pp.42–4 no.19.

i. Durham, University Library Special Collections Durham Cathedral Muniments 2.2.Reg.8. In near perfect condition. Approx. 330 x 450 + 37mm, with margins of approx. 21 (right), 37 (top) and 14mm (right). The E of *Edwardus* decorated extending down five lines, with restrained majuscule lettering in the first line, not infilled in the final line. A neat chancery-style hand, 62 lines. Sealed *sur double queue* on a thin parchment tag (24mm) through a single slit, impression of the great seal of Edward I in natural wax. On the fold: *per dominum I(ohannem) canc(ellarium) do(mi)ni reg(is)* (c.1300, contemporary chancery warrant). Presumably the exemplar sent to Durham.

ii. London, British Library Harley Charter 43.D.6. In near perfect condition. Approx. 362 x 342 + 43mm, with margins of approx. 30 (left), 20 (top) and 20mm (right). Capital *E* of *Edwardus*

extending down five lines of text with pen and ink geometric decoration. Written in a neat chancery-style hand, 58 lines. Sealed *sur double queue*, green and white cords through 3 holes, impression of Edward I's great seal in dark green wax, damaged and repaired. Endorsed: *de foresta* (s.xiv); various post medieval endorsements. No indication of provenance. Sewn into the fold is a schedule written on a single sheet of parchment in the same or a very similar chancery-style hand to the body of the text, a copy of letters patent of Edward I, 27 May 1306 (yr.34), described as a statute on the forests.

iii. London, British Library Additional Charter 19831. In near perfect condition. Approx. 505 x 267 + 35mm, with margins of approx. 30 (left), 30 (top) and 25mm (right). Capital *E* of *Edwardus* extending down three lines of text with pen and ink geometric decoration. Written in a neat chancery-style hand, 37 lines. Sealed *sur double queue*, parchment tag through 3 slits, traces of green wax on the tag. Endorsed: *confirmatio r(egis) E(dwardi) primi super magnam cartam de libertat(ibus) foreste* 2 (s.xiv/xv) *vv.* (s.xiv/xv); various post medieval endorsements. Provenance unknown, although from the same source as above no.36 ii, via Sir Christopher Hatton.

iv. Oxford, Oriel College Archives EST A 1/6. Approx. 375 x 340 + 32mm, with margins of approx. 32 (left) and 25mm (right). Capital *E* of *Edwardus* undecorated. Written in a neat chancery-style hand, 52 lines. Sealed *sur double queue*, red and green cords through four holes, fine seal impression in natural wax. Endorsed: *carta de libertatibus foreste Anglie* (s.xiv); 5 (s.xiv Oriel listing, corresponding to the fifth box in the the 1397 list of college muniments). Provenance, almost certainly as for the 1300 Magna Carta at Oriel (above no.20), from the archives of St Mary's, the University church in Oxford.

v. Maidstone, Kent Archives Sa/ZBI/46 no.33. A mutilated fragment. So badly damp damaged by the time of mounting (c.1898) that it survives as four separate pieces of parchment, today glued onto a single sheet of backing cloth, but misaligned. The individual pieces 245 x 100, 185 x 120, 120 x 130, and 230 x 180mm. Margins 34 (left), 10 (top) and 27mm (right). Fold entirely cut away, originally sealed *sur double queue*, seal impression missing. As presently arranged on the backing sheet, 50 lines of text, but the present arrangement of the pieces is jumbled. Neat chancery-style hand, with the decorated initial *E* of *Edwardus* extending down three lines of text. Dorse inaccessible. Presumably the exemplar sent to the Cinque Port town of Sandwich, companion to no.23 above.

vi. Eton College MS. 284. In near perfect condition. Approx. 325 x 312 + 20mm. Decorated E of Edwardus stretching down four lines, 51 lines in all. Sealed *sur double queue repli redoublé*, parchment tag through a single slit, impression of the great seal in natural wax, damaged at the foot. Endorsed: *Magna Charta r(egis) Edwardi primi de libertatibus forest(e)* (s.xiv/xv); *de forest.* (s.xiii); *A.i.i.* (s.xiii).. Stored with a note on provenance c.1743, claiming that the charter was found by Robert Bygrave at Hackney in 1743 amongst writings of 'the ancient family of Shordiche'. Presented by Bygrave to Sir Edward Walpole (1706-1784), who in turn presented it to his brother Horace (1717-1797). In 1774, listed amongst the most treasured items in the library of Horace Walpole at Strawberry Hill. Later presented by Horace Walpole to Eton College. Cf. *Horatio Walpole's Strawberry Hill*, ed. M. Snodin (New Haven 2009), pp.244, 292 no.80, as drawn to my attention by Rowan Watson. Bygrave was presumably the one-time Clerk of the Papers of the Fleet Prison, author of *A Case of Mr Bygrave* (London 1729), demanding compensation following the deprivation of the late Warden of the Fleet (cf. TNA C 11/765/1). The provenance here remains untraced before 1743, although the association with the notoriously corrupt Fleet Prison might well suggest a connection to the archives either of Middlesex or of the City of London. 'Shoredich' in this context may imply not a real family name but a byword for destitution. Horace Walpole himself reports, jokingly, in October 1756 hanging Magna Carta (probably in the 1750 print by Vertue) and the death warrant of Charles I on either side of his bed at Strawberry Hill (The Yale Edition of *Horace Walpole's Correspondence*, ed. W.S. Lewis and others, 48 vols (New Haven 1937-83), pp.ix, 197, and cf. x, 141, 158 for further jokes over 'a scrap of Magna Charta', like Cromwell's codpiece, or William III's cravat, a relic to be treasured by any self-respecting Whig).

The so-called 'Articuli super cartas' of 1300, offered an additional series of undertakings, again issued in French, forced upon the king, not only agreeing to the confirmation of Magna Carta and the Forest Charter, themselves to be publicly proclaimed four times a year, but accepting further limitations on the king's authority so that three knights were to be elected in each shire to hear complaints against infringers of the charters. Printed (with translation, from the enrolment in the chancery Statute Roll, TNA C 74/1 m.35) *Statutes* (1810), pp.136–41; Bémont, *Chartes*, pp.99–108 no.15. Cf. Prestwich, *Edward I*, pp.522–7, 547–8. No original is known to survive. Nonetheless, see:

42. Letters Patent of Edward I, 14 February 1301, issued in the aftermath of a Parliament held at Lincoln, acknowledging the king's renewal of Magna Carta and the Charter of the Forests as granted by Henry III, ordering their enforcement, and promising amendment and annulment 'with the common counsel of the realm' of anything decreed against the charters. Known from a single surviging original, apparently from Gloucester Abbey. Printed Blackstone (1759), pp.85–7; *Statutes* (1810), p.44 no.20; Bémont, *Chartes*, pp.109 no.16, and cf. Prestwich, *Edward I*, 525–6.

Oxford, Bodleian Library MS. Ch. Glouc. 26. Good condition. Approx. 244 x 68 + 33mm. Sealed *sur double queue*, parchment tag through a single slit, fine impression of the great seal of Edward I in white wax. Endorsed: *confirmacio E. reg(is) de libertatibus Anglie et foreste Registratur* (s.xiv); various post medieval endorsements. On the outside of the fold, to the right of the tag *Gloucestr'* (contemporary address). Presumably the exemplar once stored at St Peter's Abbey Gloucester, and duly copied into Gloucester Cathedral Library MS. Register A part 1 fo.41r no.85. As with above nos.8, 36 iii, presumably from the collections of the Gloucester antiquary Richard Furney (1694–1753).

43. Letters of Pope Clement V, 29 December 1305, claiming to annul the charters extracted from Edward I by force when he was in Flanders. This represents a last ditch stand by royal proctors to permit the king to wriggle out not only of the 'Articles on the Charters' of 1300 but, should he so wish, from the more general promises to uphold Magna Carta. The annulment of Magna Carta was never a practical possibility. The pope's letters were nonetheless used by Edward I to undermine his commitment both to the the 'Confirmatio Cartarum' of 1297 (above no.40), the document to which they explicitly refer, and also to the Articles of 1300, that the pope does not himself mention. The letters were kept in the royal archives from which they found their way into the possession of Sir Robert Cotton. Printed (apparently from a lost original in the Public Records) *Foedera*, I part ii, 978; Bémont, *Chartes*, pp.110–12 no.17, and cf. Collins, 'Documents', p.274; P.N.R. Zutshi, *Original Papal Letters in England, 1305–1415* (Vatican City 1990), p.10 no.16, at p.xxxiii n.101 arguing that the surviving original is a duplicate, pair to the exemplar seen by Rymer in the Exchequer and thence printed in *Foedera*. For the bull's (non) enforcement, see Prestwich, *Edward I*, pp.547–8.

London, British Library, MS. Cotton Vespasian E i fos.266–7. Original papal bull, known from its opening words as *Regalis devotionis integritas*. Cropped for purposes of binding. Endorsed with a taxation mark (showing payment for issue), and an archival endorsement *Bulla Clementis … concessio … in cartis … de forest … mo* (s.xiv). Long post medieval abstract in English on the face of the document (s.xvii). Sealed *sur double queue*, two holes for cords, lead bulla missing. Provenance the royal archives, whence acquired by Sir Robert Cotton.

This exhausts the 'original' evidences for the first century of Magna Carta, or at least those evidences that have thus far been brought to light. There are also various secondary texts or copies that have been used by historians to throw further light upon the charter's genesis and development. For example:

44. A List naming the twenty-five barons of Magna Carta whose appointment as conservators of Magna Carta formed so crucial and controversial an element of the 1215 charter. Lambeth Palace MS. 371 fo.56v, whence C. R. Cheney, 'The Twenty Five Barons of Magna Carta', *Bulletin of the John Rylands Library*, l (1968), pp.280–307.

45. A copy of the 1215 Magna Carta, preserved in an English legal manuscript now in California (San Marino, Huntington Library MS. HM 25782), discovered by Vivian Galbraith and assumed to be derived from an earlier stage of negotiations than the eventual originals of the charter, here with the reliefs payable by earls and barons set at distinct levels of £100 and 100 marks, in accordance with the Articles of the Barons, but not with the eventual charter of 1215, and with this copy of the charter granted at Windsor rather than at Runnymede. Cf. V. H. Galbraith, 'A Draft of Magna Carta (1215)', *Proceedings of the British Academy*, liii (1967), pp.345–60; Carpenter, *Magna Carta* (2015), pp.19–21, 343–7, and the detailed list of copies and variants, several of them closer to the variants in the present text than to the canonical version of Magna Carta 1215, posted by David Carpenter on the Magna Carta website: http://magnacarta.cmp.uea.ac.uk

46. An exemplification of the 1215 Magna Carta under the seal of the arcbhbishop of Canterbury and other bishops, generally known as the 'Letters Testimonial', delivered to the royal Treasury and thence, in the reign of Edward II, copied into the Red Book of the Exchequer (London, The National Archives E 164/2 fos.234r–236v), whence printed from Henry Spelman, 'Codex Veterum Legum', in Wilkins, *Leges Anglo-Saxonicae* (London 1721), pp.373–6. Noted by Blackstone (1759), pp.10–24. Had the original of these 'Letters Testimonial' survived it would deserve to rank as perhaps the closest that we might claim to come to an 'original text' of the 1215 Magna Carta (Collins, 'Documents', pp.248–58, correcting Poole, 'Publication', p.449, with a partial edition in *Acta Stephani Langton Cantuariensis archiepiscopi A.D. 1207–1228*, ed. Kathleen Major, Canterbury and York Society I (1950), p.24 no.16). For the baronial twenty-five and others of their letters, see H. G. Richardson, 'The Morrow of the Great Charter', *Bulletin of the John Rylands Library*, xxviii (1944), pp.422–43; xxix (1945), pp.184–200; Nicholas Vincent, 'The Twenty-Five Barons of Magna Carta: An Augustinian Echo?',

Rulership and Rebellion in the Anglo-Norman World, c.1066–c.1216: Essays in Honour of Professor Edmund King, ed. Paul Dalton and David Luscombe (Farnham 2015).

47. A French translation of the 1215 Magna Carta, first printed by J.C. Holt, suggesting that the charter was promulgated not only in Latin but in French and possibly in the English vernacular spoken by the majority of the king's subjects. Preserved in the cartulary of the hospital of St-Gilles at Pont-Audemer in Normandy (Rouen, Bibliothèque municipale MS.1232), and in all likelihood drafted on the basis of the version of the 1215 charter sent into the county of Hampshire. Cf. J.C. Holt, 'A Vernacular-French Text of Magna Carta 1215', *EHR*, lxxxix (1974), pp.346–64.

48. A version of the 1225 Magna Carta, in Latin but closely associated with Normandy, preserved in various French manuscripts from the late thirteenth century onwards (including Paris, Bibliothèque nationale MSS. Latin 11034 fos.13v–15r; Latin 4651 fos.61v–63r; Latin 1597B fos.151r–154v; Latin 11033 fos.67r–69r). Attributed to King Henry II (1154–89) rather than to Henry III (1216–72), being anachronistically redrafted as a charter of liberties granted not to England and the English but to Normandy and the Normans. The intention, apparently, was to persuade the kings of France that the Normans, before 1204 subjects of the Plantagenet kings, had received liberties and immunities from their former sovereigns which it was the obligation of successive French kings to uphold. First noticed in modern times by John Horace Round, 'Note on Magna Carta', *EHR*, ix (1894), p.541, with further commentary by Nicholas Vincent, *Magna Carta: A Very Short Introduction* (Oxford 2012), pp.88–9, and Vincent (forthcoming), and cf. the endorsement to above no.33 ii.

49. The version of the 1216 Magna Carta sent into Ireland, duly (but falsely) modified so as to apply to both the English and the Irish Church, is known only from its copying into the so-called 'Red Book of the Exchequer of Dublin', a manuscript destroyed together with the rest of Ireland's medieval public records during the Irish civil war in 1922, but printed before its destruction, and otherwise known from seventeenth-century copies of the Red Book (now Armagh Public Library MSS. KH.II.1, and KH.II.24, and cf. R.D. Edwards, 'Magna Carta Hiberniae', *Essays and Studies Presented to Professor Eoin MacNeil, D.LITT., on the Occasion of his Seventieth Birthday*, ed. J. Ryan (Dublin 1940), pp.307–18; H.G. Richardson, 'Magna Carta Hiberniae', *Irish Historical Studies*, iii (1942–3), pp.31–3).

As the unearthing of such texts reveals, the history of Magna Carta has continued to evolve over the past century. Further discoveries no doubt remain to be made.

comiti vel alicui alii qui de exitibus terre illius nobis debeat respondere et ille destructionem de custodia fecerit vel vastum, nos ab illo capiemus emendam, et terra committatur duobus legalibus et discretis hominibus de feodo illo

qui de exitibus nobis respondeant vel ei cui eos assignaverimus. Et si dederimus vel vendiderimus alicui custodiam alicuius talis terre et ille destructionem inde fecerit vel vastum, amittat ipsam custodiam et tradatur duobus legalibus

et discretis hominibus de feodo illo qui similiter nobis respondeant sicut predictum est. Custos autem quamdiu custodiam terre habuerit, sustentet domos, parcos, vivaria, stagna, molendina et cetera ad terram illam pertinentia de exitibus terre

et reddat heredi cum ad plenam etatem pervenerit terram suam totam instauratam de carrucis et de omnibus aliis rebus, ad minus secundum quod illam recepit. Hec omnia observentur de custodiis archiepiscopatuum, episcopatuum, abbatiarum, prioratuum,

ecclesiarum et dignitatum vacantium que ad nos pertinent, excepto quod custodie huiusmodi vendi non debent. Heredes maritentur absque disparagatione. Vidua post mortem mariti sui statim et sine difficultate aliqua habeat maritagium

suum et hereditatem suam, nec aliquid det pro dote sua vel pro maritagio suo vel hereditate sua, quam hereditatem maritus suus et ipsa tenuerunt die obitus ipsius mariti, et maneat in capitali mesagio mariti

sui per quadraginta dies post obitum ipsius mariti, infra quos assignetur ei dos sua, nisi prius fuerit ei assignata vel nisi domus illa sit castrum; et si de castro recesserit, statim provideatur ei domus competens in qua possit

honeste morari quousque dos sua ei assignetur secundum quod predictum est, et habeat rationabile estoverium suum interim de communi. Assignetur autem ei pro dote sua tertia pars totius terre mariti sui que sua fuit in vita sua, nisi de minori

dotata fuerit ad hostium ecclesie. Nulla vidua distringatur ad se maritandam dum voluerit vivere sine marito, ita tamen quod securitatem faciat quod se non maritabit sine assensu nostro, si de nobis tenuerit, vel sine assensu domini sui

de quo tenuerit. Nos vero vel ballivi nostri non seisiemus terram aliquam nec redditum pro debito aliquo quamdiu catalla debitoris presentia sufficiant ad debitum reddendum et ipse debitor paratus sit inde satisfacere. Nec plegii ipsius

debitoris distringantur quamdiu ipse capitalis debitor sufficiat ad solutionem debiti. Et si capitalis debitor defecerit in solutione debiti, non habens unde reddat, aut reddere nolit cum possit, plegii respondeant pro debito. Et si voluerint,

habeant terras et redditus debitoris quousque sit eis satisfactum de debito quod ante pro eo solverint, nisi capitalis debitor monstraverit se inde esse quietum versus eosdem plegios. Civitas London' habeat omnes antiquas libertates et

consuetudines suas. Preterea volumus et concedimus quod omnes alie civitates et burgi et ville et barones de quinque portubus et omnes portus habeant omnes libertates et liberas consuetudines suas. Nullus distringatur ad faciendum

maius servitium de feodo militis nec de alio libero tenemento quam inde debetur. Communia placita non sequantur curiam nostram, sed teneantur in aliquo loco certo. Recognitiones [illegible] disseisina et de morte antecessoris non capiantur

nisi in suis comitatibus, et hoc modo. Nos vel si extra regnum fuerimus capitalis iusticiarius noster mittemus iusticiarios per unumquemque comitatum semel in anno [illegible] comitatuum capiant in comitatibus assisas predictas,

et ea que in illo adventu suo in comitatu per iusticiarios predictos ad dictas assisas capiendas missos terminari non possunt, per eosdem terminentur alibi in itinere [illegible] aliquorum difficultatem ter-

minari non possunt, referantur ad iusticiarios nostros de banco et ibi terminentur. Assise de ultima presentatione semper capiantur coram iusticiariis de banco [illegible] pro parvo delicto nisi secundum modum

ipsius delicti, et pro magno delicto secundum magnitudinem delicti, salvo contenemento suo, et mercator eodem modo salva mercandisa sua [illegible] si inciderit

in misericordiam nostram. Et nulla predictarum misericordiarum ponatur nisi per sacramentum proborum et legalium hominum de visneto. Comites et [illegible] Nulla ecclesiastica persona

amercietur secundum quantitatem beneficii sui ecclesiastici, sed secundum laicum tenementum suum et secundum quantitatem delicti. Nec villa [illegible] de iure facere debet. Nulla

riparia de cetero defendatur nisi ille que fuerunt in defenso tempore H. regis avi nostri per eadem loca et eosdem terminos [illegible] Constabularii, coronatores vel alii ballivi

nostri teneant placita corone nostre. Si aliquis tenens de nobis laicum feodum moriatur et vicecomes vel ballivus noster ostendat [illegible] debuit, liceat vicecomiti

vel ballivo nostro attachiare et inbreviare catalla defuncti inventa in laico feodo ad valentiam illius debiti per visum [illegible] inde amoveatur [illegible] nobis debitum quod clarum fuerit,

et residuum relinquatur executoribus ad faciendum testamentum defuncti; et si nichil nobis debeatur ab ipso, omnia catalla cedant [illegible] et pueris suis rationabilibus partibus suis. Nullus constabularius vel eius

ballivus capiat blada vel alia catalla alicuius qui non sit de villa ubi castrum situm est nisi statim inde reddat denarios [illegible] de voluntate venditoris. Si autem de villa ipsa fuerit, infra quadra-

ginta dies pretium reddat. Nullus constabularius distringat aliquem militem ad dandum denarios pro custodia castri si ipse eam [illegible] vel per alium probum hominem si ipse eam facere non possit propter ra-

tionabilem causam. Et si nos duxerimus eum vel miserimus in exercitum, erit quietus de custodia secundum quantitatem temporis quo per nos fuerit [illegible] pro quo fecit servitium in exercitu. Nullus vicecomes vel ballivus noster vel alius

capiat equos vel carettas alicuius pro cariagio faciendo nisi reddat liberationem antiquitus statutam, scilicet pro caretta [illegible] decem denarios per diem, et pro caretta ad tres equos quatuordecim denarios

per diem. Nulla caretta alicuius ecclesiastice persone vel militis vel alicuius domine capiatur per ballivos predictos. Nec nos nec ballivi nostri nec [illegible] capiemus alienum boscum ad castra vel alia agenda nostra nisi per voluntatem illius

cuius boscus ille fuerit. Nos non tenebimus terras eorum qui convicti fuerint de felonia nisi per unum annum et unum diem, et tunc reddantur terre dominis feodorum. Omnes kidelli de cetero deponantur penitus per Tamisiam et

Medeweiam et per totam Angliam nisi per costeram maris. Breve quod vocatur precipe de cetero non fiat alicui de aliquo tenemento unde liber homo perdat curiam suam. Una mensura vini sit per totum regnum nostrum et una mensura

cervisie et una mensura bladi, scilicet quarterium London', et una latitudo pannorum tinctorum et russettorum et haubergettorum, scilicet due ulne infra listas. De ponderibus vero sit ut de mensuris. Nichil

detur de cetero pro brevi inquisitionis ab eo qui inquisitionem petit de vita vel membris, sed gratis concedatur et non negetur. Si aliquis teneat de nobis per feodifirmam vel per socagium vel per burgagium et de alio

teneat terram per servitium militare, nos non habebimus custodiam heredis nec terre sue que est de feodo alterius occasione illius feodifirme vel socagii vel burgagii. Nec habebimus custodiam illius feodi-

firme vel socagii vel burgagii nisi ipsa feodifirma debeat servitium militare. Nos non habebimus custodiam heredis [illegible] terre alicuius quam tenet de alio per servitium militare occasione alicuius parve serianterie quam tenet

de nobis per servitium reddendi nobis cultellos vel sagittas vel huiusmodi. Nullus ballivus ponat de cetero aliquem ad legem manifestam nec ad [illegible] simplici loquela sua sine testibus fidelibus ad hoc inductis. Nullus liber

homo capiatur vel inprisonetur aut disseisiatur de libero tenemento suo vel libertatibus vel liberis consuetudinibus suis aut utlagetur aut exuletur aut aliquo alio modo destruatur, nec super eum ibimus nec super eum mittemus

nisi per legale iudicium parium suorum vel per legem terre. Nulli vendemus, nulli negabimus aut differemus rectum vel iustitiam. Omnes mercatores nisi publice antea prohibiti fuerint habeant salvum et securum exire de Anglia et

venire in Angliam et morari et ire per Angliam tam per terram quam per aquam ad emendum vel vendendum sine omnibus toltis malis per antiquas et [illegible] consuetudines preterquam in tempore guerre. Et si sint de terra contra nos

guerrina et si tales inveniantur in terra nostra in principio guerre, attachientur sine dampno corporum vel rerum donec sciatur a nobis vel a [illegible] iusticiario nostro quomodo mercatores terre nostre tractentur qui tunc invenientur in

terra contra nos guerrina; et si nostri salvi sint ibi, alii salvi sint in terra nostra. Si quis tenuerit de aliqua escaeta sicut de honore [illegible] Bolonie, Notingham, Lancastrie vel de aliis escaetis que sunt in

manu nostra et sint baronie, et obierit, heres eius non det aliud relevium nec faciat nobis aliud servitium quam faceret baroni [illegible] esset in manu baronis; et nos eodem modo eam tenebimus quo baro eam tenuit. Nec

nos occasione talis baronie vel escaete habebimus aliquam escaetam vel custodiam aliquorum hominum nostrorum nisi alibi tenuerint de nobis in capite, ille qui tenuit baroniam vel escaetam. Nullus liber homo de cetero det ampli-

us alicui vel vendat de terra sua quam ut de residuo terre sue possit sufficienter fieri domino feodi servitium ei debitum quod pertinet ad feodum illud. Omnes patroni abbatiarum qui habent cartas regum Anglie de advocatione vel

antiquam tenuram vel possessionem habeant earum custodiam cum vacaverint, sicut habere debent et sicut supra declaratum est. Nullus capiatur vel inprisonetur propter appellum femine de morte alterius quam viri sui. Nullus comitatus de cetero

teneatur nisi de mense in mensem, et ubi maior terminus esse solebat, maior sit. Nec aliquis vicecomes vel ballivus suus faciat turnum suum per hundredum nisi bis in anno et non nisi in loco debito et consueto, videlicet semel post

Pascha et iterum post festum sancti Michaelis. Et visus de franco plegio tunc fiat ad illum terminum sancti Michaelis sine occasione, ita scilicet quod quilibet habeat libertates suas quas habuit et habere consuevit tempore H. regis avi nostri vel quas

postea perquisivit. Fiat autem visus de franco plegio sic, videlicet quod pax nostra teneatur et quod tethinga integra sit sicut esse consuevit, et quod vicecomes non querat occasiones, et quod contentus sit de eo quod vicecomes habere

consuevit de visu suo faciendo tempore H. regis avi nostri. Non liceat alicui de cetero dare terram suam alicui domui religiose ita quod illam resumat tenendam de eadem domo, nec liceat alicui domui religiose

terram alicuius sic accipere quod tradat illam ei a quo ipsam recepit tenendam. Si quis autem de cetero terram suam alicui domui religiose sic dederit et super hoc convincatur, donum suum penitus cassetur et terra illa domino suo illius feodi in-

curratur. Scutagium de cetero capiatur sicut capi consuevit tempore H. regis avi nostri. Et salve sint archiepiscopis, episcopis, abbatibus, prioribus, templariis, hospitalariis, comitibus, baronibus et omnibus aliis tam ecclesiasticis

quam secularibus personis libertates et libere consuetudines quas prius habuerunt. Omnes autem istas consuetudines predictas et libertates quas concessimus in regno nostro tenendas quantum ad nos pertinet erga nostros, omnes de regno nostro tam

clerici quam laici observent quantum ad se pertinet erga suos. Pro hac autem concessione et donatione libertatum istarum et aliarum contentarum in carta nostra de libertatibus foreste, archiepiscopi, episcopi, abbates, priores, comites, barones,

milites et libere tenentes et omnes de regno nostro dederunt nobis quintamdecimam partem omnium mobilium suorum. Concessimus autem eisdem pro nobis et heredibus nostris quod nec nos nec heredes nostri aliquid perquiremus per quod libertates in hac carta con-

tente infringantur vel infirmentur; et si ab aliquo aliquid contra hoc perquisitum fuerit, nichil valeat et pro nullo habeatur. Hiis testibus domino S. Cantuar' archiepiscopo, E. London', I. Bathon', P. Winton', H. Linc', R. Sar', B.

Roff', W. Wigorn', I. Elien', H. Hereford', R. Cicestr', W. Exon' episcopis, abbate sancti Edmundi, abbate sancti Albani, abbate de Bello, abbate sancti Augustini Cantuar', abbate de Eveshan', abbate de Westmon', abbate de Burgo

sancti Petri, abbate Radingens', abbate de Abbendon', abbate de Malmesbir', abbate de Winchecumb', abbate de Hida, abbate de Certes', abbate de Sireburn', abbate de Cerne, abbate de Abbotebir', abbate de Middelton', abbate de

Selebi, abbate de Wyteby, abbate de Cirencestr', H. de Burgo iusticiario Anglie, R. comite Cestr' et Linc', W. comite Sar', G. de Clare comite Glouc' et Hertford', W. de Ferrariis comite Derby, W. de Mandevill'

comite Essex', H. le Bigod comite Norf', W. comite Albemarl', H. comite Hereford', I. de Lasci constabulario Cestr', Roberto de Ros, Roberto filio Walteri, Roberto de Veteri Ponte, [illegible]

[illegible] de Munfichet [illegible]

CHAPTER 9

The 1225 Magna Carta

TEXT AND TRANSLATION

Oxford, Bodleian Library MS. Ch. London 1

Above no.13

The numbering of the clauses below follows that of Bishop Stubbs and thence of the modern authorities, including Holt. The English translation is a fairly free one, newly adapted for this particular version. The Bodleian original supplies an accurate text, with the exception of a single word ('conductum') missing in c.30. Letters within brackets below <> are illegible in the original as a result of staining and damp damage, supplied from the edition of the Durham version (above no.10) printed in *Statutes* (1810), pp.22–5 no.11.

TEXT

H(enricus) Dei gratia rex Angl(ie), dominus Hybern(ie), dux Norm(annie) et Aquit(annie), comes Andeg(auie) archiepiscopis, episcopis, abbatibus, prioribus, comitibus, baronibus, vicecomitibus, prepositis, ministris et omnibus ball(iu)is et fidelibus suis presentem cartam inspecturis salutem. Sciatis quod nos intuitu Dei et pro salute anime nostre et animarum an(te)cessorum et successorum nostrorum, ad exaltacionem sancte ecclesie et emendationem regni nostri, spontanea et bona voluntate nostra dedimus et concessimus archiepiscopis, episcopis, comitibus, baronibus et omnibus de regno nostro has libertates subscriptas tenendas in regno nostro Angl(ie) in perpetuum.

(1) In primis concessimus Deo et hac presenti carta nostra confirmauimus pro nob(is) et heredibus nostris in perpetuum quod Anglicana ecclesia libera sit et habeat iura sua integra et omnes libertates suas illesas. Concessimus etiam et dedimus omnibus liberis hominibus regni nostri pro nob(is) et heredibus nostris in perpetuum omnes libertates subscriptas habendas et tenendas eis et heredibus suis de nobis et heredibus nostris.

(2) Si quis comitum vel baronum nostrorum siue aliorum de nob(is) tenencium in capite per seruicium militare mortuus fuerit, et cum decesserit heres eius plene etatis fuerit et releuium debeat, h(abe)at hereditatem suam per antiquum releuium, scilicet heres vel heredes comitis de baronia comitis integra per centum libras, heres vel heredes baronis de baronia integra per centum libras, heres vel heredes militis de feodo militis integro per centum solidos ad plus, et qui minus debuerit minus det,

secundum antiquam consuetudinem feodorum.

(3) Si au(tem) heres alicuius talium fuerit infra etatem, dominus eius non habeat custodiam eius nec terre sue an(te)quam homagium eius ceperit, et postquam talis heres fuerit in custodia, cum ad etatem peruenerit, scilicet viginti et unius anni, h(abe)at hereditatem suam sine releuio et sine fine, ita t(ame)n quod si ipse dum infra etatem fuerit fiat miles nich(il)ominus terra remaneat in custodia dominorum suorum usque ad predictum terminum.

(4) Custos autem huiusmodi heredis qui infra etatem fuerit non capiat de terra heredis nisi r(ati)onabiles exitus et r(ati)onabiles consuetudines et r(ati)onabilia seruicia, et hoc sine destructione et vasto hominum vel rerum. Et si nos commiserimus custodiam alicuius talis terre vicecomiti vel alicui alii qui de exitibus terre illius nobis debeat respondere, et ille destructionem de custodia fecerit vel vastum, nos ab illo capiemus emendam, et terra committatur duobus legalibus et discretis hominibus de feodo illo qui de exitibus nobis respondeant, vel ei cui eos assignauerimus. Et si dederimus vel vendiderimus alicui custodiam alicuius tal(is) terre et ille destructionem inde fecerit vel vastum, amittat ipsam custodiam et tradatur duobus legalibus et discretis hominibus de feodo illo qui similiter nobis respondeant sicut predictum est.

(5) Custos autem, quamdiu custodiam terre habuerit, sustentet domos, parcos, viuaria, molendina et cetera ad terram illam pertinentia de exitibus terre eiusdem, et reddat heredi cum ad plenam etatem peruenerit terram suam totam instauratam de carrucis et de omnibus aliis rebus adminus secundum quod illam recepit. Hec

omnia obseruentur de custodiis archiepiscopatuum, episcopatuum, abb(at)iarum, prioratuum, ecclesiarum et dignitatum vacantium que ad nos pertinent, excepto quod custodie huiusmodi vendi non debent.

(6) Heredes maritentur absque disparagatione.

(7) Vidua post mortem mariti sui statim et sine difficultate aliqua h(abe)at maritagium suum et hereditatem suam, nec aliquid det pro dote sua vel maritagio suo vel hereditate sua quam hereditatem maritus suus et ipsa tenuerunt die obitus ipsius mariti, et maneat in capitali mesuagio mariti sui per quadraginta dies post obitum ipsius mariti, infra quos assignetur ei dos sua nisi prius fuerit ei assignata vel nisi domus illa sit castrum, et si de castro recesserit, statim prouideatur ei domus competens in qua possit honeste morari quousque dos sua ei assignetur secundum quod predictum est, et habeat rationabile estouerium suum interim de communi. Assignetur au(tem) ei pro dote sua tercia pars tocius terre mariti sui que sua fuit in vita sua, nisi de minori dotata fuit ad hostium ecclesie. Nulla vidua distringatur ad se maritandam dum voluerit viuere sine marito, ita t(ame)n quod securitatem faciat quod se non maritabit s(i)n(e) assensu nostro si de nob(is) tenuerit vel s(i)n(e) assensu domini sui si de alio tenuerit.

(8) Nos vero vel ball(iu)i nostri non saisiemus terram aliquam nec redditum pro debito aliquo quamdiu catalla debitoris presentia sufficiunt ad debitum reddendum et ipse debitor paratus sit inde satisfacere, nec plegii ipsius debitoris distringantur quamdiu ipse capital(is) debitor sufficiat ad solutionem ipsius debiti. Et si capital(is) debitor defecerit in solutione debiti, non habens un(de) reddat, aut reddere nolit cum possit, plegii respondeant pro debito, et si voluerint h(abe)ant terras et redditus debitoris quousque sit eis satisfactum de debito quod ante pro eo soluerunt, nisi capital(is) debitor monstrauerit se inde esse quietum versus eosdem plegios.

(9) Ciuitas Lond' h(abe)at omnes antiquas libertates et liberas consuetudines suas. Preterea volumus et concedimus quod omnes alie ciuitates et burgi et ville et barones de Quinque Portubus et omnes portus h(abe)ant omnes libertates et liberas consuetudines suas.

(10) Nullus distringatur ad faciendum maius seruicium de feodo militis nec de alio libero tenemento quam inde debetur.

(11) Communia placita non sequantur curiam nostram sed teneantur in aliquo loco certo.

(12) Recogni<ciones de no>ua dissaisina et de morte antecessoris non capiantur nisi in suis comitatibus et hoc modo. Nos vel, si extra regnum fuerimus, capital(is) iusticiarius noster mittemus iusticiarios per unumquemque comitatum semel in anno, <qui cum militibus> comitatuum capiant in comitatibus assisas predictas, et ea que in illo aduentu suo in comitatu per iusticiar(ios) predictos ad dictas assisas capiendas missos terminari non possunt, per eosdem terminentur alibi in itinere suo,

<et ea que per eosdem propter> difficultatem aliquorum articulorum terminari non possunt, referantur ad iusticiar(os) nostros de Banco et ibi terminentur.

(13) Assise de ultima present(aci)o(n)e semper capiantur coram iustic(iis) de Banco et <ibi terminentur>.

(14) <Liber homo non> amercietur pro paruo delicto nisi secundum modum ipsius delicti, et pro magno delicto secundum magnitudinem delicti, saluo contenemento suo, et mercator eodem modo salua mercandisa sua, et vill<anus alterius quam noster eodem modo amer>cietur saluo waynagio suo si inciderit in misericordiam nostram. Et nulla predictarum misericordiarum ponatur nisi per sacramentum proborum et leg(alium) hominum de visneto. Comites et b<arones non amercientur nisi per pares suos et non nisi> secundum modum delicti. Nulla ecclesiastica persona amercietur secundum quantitatem beneficii sui ecclesiastici sed secundum laicum tenementum suum et secundum quantitatem delicti.

(15) Nec villa ne<c homo distringatur facere pontes ad riparias nisi qui ab an>tiquo et de iure facere debet.

(16) Nulle riparia decetero defendatur nisi ille que fuerunt in defenso tempore H(enrici) regis aui nostri per eadem loca et eosdem terminos <sicut esse consueuerunt> tempore suo.

(17) Nullus vicecomes, constabularius, coronatores vel alii ball(iu)i nostri teneant placita corone nostre.

(18) Si aliquis tenens de nob(is) laicum feodum moriatur et vic(ecomes) vel ball(iuu)s noster ostendat l<itteras nostras patentes de summonicione> nostra de debito quod defunctus nob(is) debuit, liceat vicec(omi)ti vel ball(iu)o nostro attachiare et inbreuiare catalla defuncti inuenta in laico feodo ad valentiam illius debiti per visum <leg(alium) hominum, ita tamen quod n>ich(il) inde amoueatur donec persoluatur nob(is) debitum quod clarum fuerit, et residuum relinquatur executoribus ad faciendum testamentum defuncti, et si nich(il) debeatur nob(is) ab ipso, omnia catalla cedant d<efuncto, saluis uxori eius> et pueris suis r(ati)onabilibus partibus suis.

(19) Nullus constabularius vel eius ball(iu)us capiat blada vel alia catalla alicuius qui non sit de villa ubi castrum situm est, nisi statim reddat denar(ios) <inde aut respectum inde habere> possit de voluntate venditoris. Si autem de villa ipsa fuerit, infra quadraginta dies precium reddat.

(20) Nullus constabularius distringat aliquem militem ad dand(um) denar(ios) pro custodia castri si ipse eam facere <voluerit in propria per>sona sua vel per alium probum hominem faciat si ipse eam facere non possit propter r(ati)onabilem causam. Et si nos duxerimus eum vel miserimus in excercitum, erit quietus de custodia secundum quantitatem temporis quo per nos fuerit <in excercitu, de feod>o pro quo fecit seruicium in excercitu.

(21) Nullus vicecomes vel ball(iuu)s noster vel alius capiat equos vel carettas alicuius pro cariagio faciendo nisi reddat liberat(i)o(ne)m antiquitus statutam, scilicet pro <caretta

ad duos e>quos decem denar(ios) per diem, et pro caretta
ad tres equos quatuordecim denar(ios) per diem. Nulla
caretta alicuius ecclesiastice persone vel militis vel alicuius
d(omi)ne capiatur per ball(iuo)s predictos nec nos nec
ball(iu)i nostri nec alii capiemus alienum boscum ad
castra vel alia agenda nostra nisi per voluntatem illius
cuius boscus ille fuerit.

(22) Nos non tenebimus terras eorum qui conuicti fuerint
de felonia nisi per unum annum et unum diem, et tunc
reddantur terre d(omi)nis feodorum.

(23) Omnes kidelli decetero deponantur penitus per
Tamisyam et Medeweyam et per totam Angl(iam) nisi per
costeram maris.

(24) Breue quod vocatur precipe decetero non fiat alicui
de aliquo libero tenemento un(de) liber h(om)o perdat
curiam suam.

(25) Una mensura vini sit per totum regnum nostrum et
una mensura ceruisie et una mensura bladi, scilicet
quarter(ium) Lond(oniensem), et una latitudo pannorum
tinctorum et russettorum et haubergettorum, scilicet due
ulne infra listas. De ponderibus vero sit sicut de mensuris.

(26) Nich(il) detur decetero pro breui inquisitionis ab eo
qui inquisitionem petit de vita vel membris, sed gratis
concedatur et non negetur.

(27) Si aliquis teneat de nob(is) per feodi firmam vel soccagium
vel burgagium et de alio teneat terram per seruicium
militare, nos non habebimus custodiam heredis nec terre
sue que est de feodo alterius occasione illius feodifirme
vel soccagii vel burgagii nec habebimus custodiam illius
feodifirme vel soccagii vel burgagii nisi ipsa feodifirma
debeat seruicium militare. Nos non habebimus custodiam
heredis vel terre alicuius quam tenet de alio per seruicium
militare occ(asi)one alicuius parue seriantie quam tenet
de nob(is) per seruicium reddendi nobis cultellos vel
sagittas vel huiusmodi.

(28) Nullus ball(iuu)s ponat decetero aliq(uem) ad legem
manifestam nec ad iuramentum simplici loquela sua sine
testibus fidelibus ad hoc inductis.

(29) Nullus liber homo capiatur vel imprisonetur aut
dissaisiatur de libero tenemento suo vel libertatibus vel
liberis consuetudinibus suis aut utlagetur aut exuletur
aut aliquo alio modo destruatur nec super eum ibimus
nec super eum mittemus nisi per legale iudicium parium
suorum vel per legem terre. Nulli vendemus, nulli
negabimus aut differemus rectum vel iusticiam.

(30) Omnes mercatores, nisi puplice antea prohibiti fuerint,
h(abe)ant saluum et securum [conductum]exire de
Anglia et venire in Angl(iam) et morari et ire per
Angliam tam per terram quam per aquam ad emendum
et vendendum sine omnibus toltis malis per antiquas et
rectas consuetudines preterquam in tempore guerre, et
si sint de terra contra nos guerrina et si tales inueniantur
in terra nostra in principio guerre, attachientur sine
dampno corporum vel rerum donec sciatur a nob(is) vel

a capitali iustic(iario) nostro quomodo mercatores terre
nostre tractentur qui tunc inveniantur in terra contra nos
guerrina, et si nostri salui sint ibi, alii salui sint in terra
nostra.

(31) Si quis tenuerit de aliqua eschaeta sicut de honore
<Wali>ngeford', Bolon', Notingham', Lancastr' vel de
aliis escaetis que sunt in manu nostra et sint baronie et
obierit, heres eius non det aliud releuium nec faciet nob(is)
aliud seruicium quam faceret baroni si illa esset in manu
baronis, et nos eodem modo eam tenebimus quo baro
eam tenuit, nec nos occ(asi)one tal(is) baronie vel eschaete
h(ab)ebimus aliquam eschaetam vel custodiam aliquorum
hominum nostrorum nisi alibi tenuerit de nob(is) in capite
ille qui tenuit baroniam vel eschaetam.

(32) Nullus liber homo decetero det amplius alicui vel vendat
de terra sua quam ut de residuo terre sue possit sufficienter
fieri domino feodi seruicium ei debitum quod pertinet ad
feodum illud.

(33) Omnes patroni abb(at)iarum qui h(abe)nt cartas
regum Angl(ie) de aduocatione vel antiquam tenuram
vel poss(ession)em h(abe)ant earum custodiam cum
vacauerint sic(ut) habere debent et sic(ut) sup(erius)
declaratum est.

(34) Nullus capiatur aut imprisonetur propter appellum femine
de morte alterius quam viri sui.

(35) Nullus comitatus decetero teneatur nisi de mense in
mensem, et ubi maior terminus esse solebat, maior sit,
nec aliquis vicecomes vel ball(iuu)s suus faciat turnum
suum per hundredum nisi bis in anno et non nisi in
loco debito et consueto, videlicet semel post Pasch(a) et
iterum post festum sancti Mich(aelis), et visus de franco
plegio tunc fiat ad illum terminum sancti Mich(aelis) sine
occ(asi)one, ita scilicet quod quilibet h(abe)at libertates
suas quas habuit vel habere consueuit tempore H(enrici)
reg(is) aui nostri vel quas postea perquisiuit. Fiat au(tem)
visus de franco plegio sic, videlicet quod pax nostra
teneatur et quod thethinga integra sit sicut esse consueuit,
et quod vicecomes non querat occ(asi)ones, et quod
contentus sit de eo quod vicecomes habere consueuit de
visu suo faciendo tempore H(enrici) reg(is) aui nostri.

(36) Nec liceat alicui decetero dare terram suam alicui domui
religiose ita quod illam resumat tenendam de eadem
domo, nec liceat alicui domui religiose terram alicuius sic
accipere quod tradat eam illi a quo eam recepit tenendam.
Si quis au(tem) decetero terram suam alicui domui
religiose sic dederit et super hoc conuincatur, donum
suum penitus cassetur et terra illa d(omi)no illius feodi
incurratur.

(37) Scutagium decetero capiatur sicut capi consueuit tempore
H(enrici) reg(is) aui nostri, et salue sint archiepiscopis,
ep(iscop)is, abb(at)ibus, prioribus, Templar(iis),
Hospitalar(iis), comitibus, baronibus et omnibus aliis tam
eccl(es)iast(ic)is personis quam secularibus libertates et
libere consuetudines quas prius habuerunt.

Omnes autem consuetudines predictas et libertates quas concessimus in regno nostro tenendas quantum ad nos pertinet erga nostros, omnes de regno nostro tam clerici quam laici observent quantum ad se pertinet erga suos. Pro hac autem concessione et donatione libertatum istarum et aliarum contentarum in carta nostra de libertatibus foreste, archiepiscopi, episcopi, abb(at)es, priores, comites, barones, milites et libere tenentes et omnes de regno nostro dederunt nob(is) quintamdecimam partem omnium mobilium suorum. Concessimus au(tem) eisdem pro nob(is) et heredibus nostris quod nec nos nec heredes nostri aliquid perquiremus per quod libertates in hac carta contente infringantur vel infirmentur, et si ab aliquo aliquid contra hoc perquisitum fuerit, nich(il) valeat et pro nullo habeatur. Hiis testibus: domino S(tephano) Cantuar(iensi) archiepiscopo, E(ustachio) Lond(oniensi), I(ocelino) Bathon(ensi), P(etro) Winton(iensi), H(ugone) Linc(olniensi), R(icardo) Sarr(esberiensi), B(enedicto) Roff(ensi), W(illelmo) Wigorn(iensi), I(ohanne) Elyens(i), H(ugone) Hereford(ensi), R(anulfo) Cicestr(ensi), W(illelmo) Exon(iensi) episcopis, abbate Sancti Eadmundi, abbate Sancti Albani, abbate de Bello, abbate Sancti Augustini Cantuar(iensi), abbate de Euesham, abbate de Westmon(asterio), abbate de Burgo Sancti Petri, abbate de Rading(ensi), abbate de Abendon(ensi), abbate de Malmesbir', abbate de Winchecumb', abbate de Hyda, abbate de Certes(eye), abbate de Sireburn', abbate de Cern', abbate de Abbotesbir', abbate de Middelton', abbate de Seleby, abbate de Witeby, abbate de Cyrencestr', H(uberto) de Burg' iustic(iario) Angl(ie), R(anulfo) comite Cestr(ensi) et Linc(olniensi), W(illelmo) comite Sarr', G(ilberto) de Clare com(ite) Glouc(estrensi) et Hertford(ensi), W(illelmo) de Ferrariis comite Derby, W(illelmo) de Maundeuill' com(ite) Essex', H(ugone) le Bigot com(ite) Norf', W(illelmo) com(ite) Albemarl', H(umfrido) comit(e) de Heref(ordensi), I(ohanne) de Lascy constab(u)lar(io) Cestr(ensi), Roberto de Ros, R(oberto) fil(io) Walteri, Roberto de Veteriponte, Will(elm)o de Briwer', Ric(ardo) de Munfichet, Petro fil(io) Hereberti, Math(e)o fil(io) Hereberti, Will(elm)o de Albiniaco, Roberto Gresley, Reg(inaldo) de Braos', Ioh(ann)e de Monem', Ioh(ann)e fil(io) Alani, Hugone de Mortuomari, Waltero de Bello Campo. Will(elm)o de Sancto Ioh(ann)e, Petro de Malo Lacu, Brian(o) de Insula, Thom(a) de Muleton', Ric(ardo) de Arg<entein', Galfrido de> Neuill', Will(elm)o Mauduit, Ioh(ann)e de Baalun. Dat' apud Westm(onasterium) xi°. die Febr(uarii) anno regni nostri nono.

TRANSLATION

Henry by the grace of God king of England, lord of Ireland, duke of Normandy and Aquitaine, count of Anjou sends greetings to his archbishops, bishops, abbots, priors, earls, barons, sheriffs, reeves, ministers and all his bailiffs and faithful men inspecting the present charter. Know that we, at the prompting of God and for the health of our soul and the souls of our ancestors and successors, for the glory of holy Church and the improvement of our realm, freely and out of our good will have given and granted to the archbishops, bishops, earls, barons and all of our realm these liberties written below to hold in our realm of England in perpetuity.

(1) In the first place we grant to God and confirm by this our present charter for ourselves and our heirs in perpetuity that the English Church is to be free and to have its rights fully and all its liberties unimpeded. We furthermore grant and give to all the free men of our realm for ourselves and our heirs in perpetuity all the liberties written below to have and to hold to them and their heirs from us and our heirs.

(2) If any of our earls or barons, or anyone else holding from us in chief by military service should die, and should his heir be of full age and owe relief, the heir is to have his inheritance for the ancient relief, namely the heir or heirs of an earl for the whole barony of an earl £100, the heir or heirs of a baron for a whole barony £100, the heir or heirs of a knight for a whole knight's fee 100 shillings at most, and he who owes less will give less, according to the ancient custom of fees.

(3) If, however, the heir of such a person be under age, his lord is not to have custody of him and his land until he has taken homage from the heir, and after such an heir has been in custody, when he comes of age, namely at twenty-one years old, he is to have his inheritance without relief and without fine, saving that if, whilst under age, he is made a knight, his land will nonetheless remain in the custody of his lords until the aforesaid term.

(4) The keeper, however, of such an heir who is under age is only to take reasonable receipts from the heir's land and reasonable customs and reasonable services, and this without destruction or waste of men or things. And if we assign custody of any such land to a sheriff or to anyone else who should answer to us for the issues, and such a person should commit destruction of the custody or waste, we will take recompense from him and the land will be assigned to two law-worthy and discreet men of that fee who will answer to us or to the person to whom we assign such issues. And if we give or sell to anyone custody of any such land and that person commits destruction or waste, he is to lose that custody which is to be assigned to two law-worthy and discreet men of that fee who similarly will answer to us as is aforesaid.

(5) The keeper, for as long as he has the custody of the land, is to maintain the houses, parks, fishponds, mills and other things pertaining to that land from the issues of the same land, and he will restore to the heir, when the heir comes to full age, all his land stocked with ploughs and all other things in at least the same condition as when he received it. All these things are to be observed in the custodies of archbishoprics, bishoprics, abbeys, priories, churches and vacant offices which pertain to us, save that such custodies ought not to be sold.

(6) Heirs are to be married without disparagement.

(7) A widow, after the death of her husband, is immediately and without any difficulty to have her marriage portion and her inheritance, nor is she to pay anything for her dower or her marriage portion or for her inheritance which her husband and she held on the day of her husband's death, and she shall remain in the chief dwelling place of her husband for forty days after her husband's death, within which time her dower will be assigned her if it has not already been assigned and unless that house is a castle, and if it is a castle which she leaves, then a suitable house will immediately be provided for her in which she may properly dwell until her dower is assigned to her in accordance with what is aforesaid, and in the meantime she is to have her reasonable maintenance (*estouerium*) from the common property. As dower she will be assigned the third part of all the lands of her husband which were his during his lifetime, save when she was dowered with less at the church door. No widow shall be distrained to marry for so long as she wishes to live without a husband, provided that she gives surety that she will not marry without our assent if she holds of us, or without the assent of her lord, if she holds of another.

(8) Neither we nor our bailiffs will seize any land or rent for any debt, so long as the existing chattels of the debtor suffice for the repayment of the debt and so long as the debtor is ready to pay the debt, nor will the debtor's guarantors be distrained for so long as the principal debtor is able to pay the debt; and should the principal debtor default in his payment of the debt, not having the means to repay it, or should he refuse to pay it despite being able to do so, the guarantors will answer for the debt and, if they wish, they are to have the lands and rents of the debtor until they are repaid the debt that previously they paid on behalf of the debtor, unless the principal debtor can show that he is quit in respect to these guarantors.

(9) The city of London is to have its ancient liberties and free customs. Moreover we wish and grant that all other cities and boroughs and vills and the barons of the Cinque Ports and all ports are to have all their liberties and free customs.

(10) No-one is to be distrained to do more service for a knight's fee or for any other free tenement than is due from it.

(11) Common pleas are not to follow our court but are to be held in a certain fixed place.

(12) Recognisances of novel disseisin and of mort d'ancestor are not to be taken save in their particular counties and in the following way. We or, should we be outside the realm, our chief justiciar, will send justices once a year through each county, so that, together with the knights of the counties, that may take the aforesaid assizes in the counties; and those (assizes) that cannot be completed in that visitation of the county by our aforesaid justices assigned to take the said assizes are to be completed elsewhere by the justices in their visitation; and those that cannot be completed by them on account of the difficulty of various articles (of law) are to be referred to our justices of the Bench and completed there.

(13) Assizes of darrein presentment are always to be taken before our justices of the Bench and are to be completed there.

(14) A freeman is not to be amerced for a small offence save in accordance with the manner of the offence, and for a major offence according to its magnitude, saving his sufficiency (*salvo contenemento suo*), and a merchant likewise, saving his merchandise, and any villain other than one of our own is to be amerced in the same way, saving his necessity (*salvo waynagio*) should he fall into our mercy, and none of the aforesaid amercements is to be imposed save by the oath of honest and law-worthy men of the neighbourhood. Earls and barons are not to be amerced save by their peers and only in accordance with the manner of their offence. No clergyman is to be amerced according to the value of his ecclesiastical benefice, but according to his lay tenement and the degree of his wrongdoing.

(15) No town or man is to be distrained to make bridges or bank works save for those that ought to do so of old and by right.

(16) No bank works of any sort are to be kept up save for those that were in defense in the time of King H(enry II) our grandfather and in the same places and on the same terms as was customary in his time.

(17) No sheriff, constable, coroners or any others of our bailiffs are to hold pleas of our crown.

(18) If anyone holding a lay fee from us should die, and our sheriff or bailiff shows our letters patent containing our summons for a debt that the dead man owed us, our sheriff or bailiff is permitted to attach and enroll all the goods and chattels of the dead man found in lay fee, to the value of the said debt, by view of law-worthy men, so that nothing is to be removed thence until the debt that remains is paid to us, and the remainder is to be released to the executors to discharge the will of the dead man, and if nothing is owed to us from such a person, all the chattels are to pass to the (use of) the dead man, saving to the dead man's wife and children their reasonable portions.

(19) No constable or his bailiff is to take corn or other chattels from anyone who is not themselves of a vill where a castle is built, unless the constable or his bailiff immediately offers money in payment of obtains a respite by the wish of the seller. If the person whose corn or chattels are taken is

of such a vill, then the constable or his bailiff is to pay the purchase price within forty days.

(20) No constable is to distrain any knight to give money for castle guard if the knight is willing to do such guard in person or by proxy of any other honest man, should the knight be prevented from doing so by just cause. And if we take or send such a knight into the army, he is to be quit of (castle) guard in accordance with the length of time the we have him in the army for the fee for which he has done service in the army.

(21) No sheriff or bailiff of ours or anyone else is to take anyone's horses or carts to perform carriage work, unless he renders the payment customarily due, namely for a two-horse cart ten pence per day, and for a three-horse cart fourteen pence per day. No demesne cart belonging to any churchman or knight or any lady is to be taken by the aforesaid bailiffs, nor will we or our bailiffs or anyone else take someone else's timber for a castle or any other of our business save by the will of he to whom the wood belongs.

(22) We shall not hold the lands of those convicted of felony save for a year and a day, whereafter such land is to be restored to the lords of the fees.

(23) All fish weirs (*kidelli*) on the Thames and the Medway and throughout England are to be entirely dismantled, save on the sea coast.

(24) The writ called 'praecipe' is not to be issued to anyone in respect to any free tenement in such a way that a free man might lose his court.

(25) There is to be a single measure for wine throughout our realm, and a single measure for ale, and a single measure for corn, that is to say the London quarter, and a single breadth for dyed cloth, russets, and haberjects, that is to say two yards within the lists. And it shall be the same for weights as for measures.

(26) Henceforth there is to be nothing given for a writ of inquest from the person seeking an inquest of life or members, but such a writ is to be given freely and is not to be denied.

(27) If any persons hold from us at fee farm or in socage or burgage, and hold land from another by knight service, we are not, by virtue of such a fee farm or socage or burgage, to have custody of the heir or their land which pertains to another's fee, nor are we to have custody of such a fee farm or socage or burgage unless this fee farm owes knight service. We are not to have the custody of an heir or of any land which is held from another by knight service on the pretext of some small serjeanty held from us by service of rendering us knives or arrows or suchlike things.

(28) No bailiff is henceforth to put any man on his open law or on oath simply by virtue of his spoken word, without reliable witnesses being produced for the same.

(29) No free man is to be taken or imprisoned or disseised of his free tenement or of his liberties or free customs, or outlawed or exiled or in any other way ruined, nor will we go against such a man or send against him save by lawful judgement of his peers or by the law of the land. To no-one shall we sell or deny of delay right or justice.

(30) All merchants, unless they have been previously and publicly forbidden, are to have safe and secure [conduct] in leaving and coming to England and in staying and going through England both by land and by water to buy and to sell, without any evil exactions, according to the ancient and right customs, save in time of war, and if they should be from a land at war against us and be found in our land at the beginning of the war, they are to be attached without damage to their bodies or goods until it is known by us or our chief justiciar in what way the merchants of our land are treated who at such a time are found in the land that is at war with us, and if our merchants are safe there, the other merchants are to be safe in our land.

(31) If anyone dies holding of any escheat such as the honour of Wallingford, Boulogne, Nottingham, Lancaster or of other escheats which are in our hands and which are baronies, his heir is not to give any other relief or render any other service to us that would not have been rendered to the baron if the barony were still held by a baron, and we shall hold such things in the same way as the baron held them, nor, on account of such a barony or escheat, are we to have the escheat or custody of any of our men unless the man who held the barony or the escheat held elsewhere from us in chief.

(32) No free man is henceforth to give or sell any more of his land to anyone, unless the residue of his land is sufficient to render due service to the lord of the fee as pertains to that fee.

(33) All patrons of abbeys which have charters of the kings of England over advowson or ancient tenure or possession are to have the custody of such abbeys when they fall vacant just as they ought to have and as is declared above.

(34) No-one is to be taken or imprisoned on the appeal of woman for the death of anyone save for the death of that woman's husband.

(35) No county court is to be held save from month to month, and where the greater term used to be held, nor will any sheriff or his bailiff make his tourn through the hundred save for twice a year and only in the place that is due and customary, namely once after Easter and again after Michaelmas, and the view of frankpledge is to be taken at the Michaelmas term without exception, in such a way that every man is to have his liberties which he had or used to have in the time of King H(enry II) my grandfather or which he has acquired since. The view of frankpledge is to be taken so that our peace be held and so that the tithing is to be held entire as it used to be, and so that the sheriff does not seek exceptions but remains content with that which the sheriff used to have in taking the view in the time of King H(enry) our grandfather.

(36) Nor is it permitted to anyone to give his land to any religious house in such a way that he receives it back from

such a house to hold, nor is it permitted to any religious house to accept the land of anyone in such way that the land is restored to the person from whom it was received to hold. If anyone henceforth gives his land in such a way to any religious house and is convicted of the same, the gift is to be entirely quashed and such land is to revert to the lord of that fee.

(37)   Scutage furthermore is to be taken as it used to be in the time of King H(enry) our grandfather, and all liberties and free customs shall be preserved to archbishops, bishops, abbots, priors, Templars, Hospitallers, earls, barons and all others, both ecclesiastical and secular persons, just as they formerly had.

All these aforesaid customs and liberties which we have granted to be held in our realm in so far as pertains to us are to be observed by all of our realm, both clergy and laity, in so far as pertains to them in respect to their own men.

For this gift and grant of these liberties and of others contained in our charter over the liberties of the forest, the archbishops, bishops, abbots, priors, earls, barons, knights, free holders and all of our realm have given us a fifteenth part of all their movable goods. Moreover we grant to them for us and our heirs that neither we nor our heirs will seek anything by which the liberties contained in this charter might be infringed or damaged, and should anything be obtained from anyone against this it is to count for nothing and to be held as nothing. With these witnesses: the lord S(tephen) archbishop of Canterbury, E(ustace) bishop of London, J(ocelin) bishop of Bath, P(eter) bishop of Winchester, H(ugh) bishop of Lincoln, R(ichard) bishop of Salisbury, B(enedict) bishop of Rochester, W(illiam) bishop of Worcester, J(ohn) bishop of Ely, H(ugh) bishop of Hereford, R(anulf) bishop of Chichester, W(illiam) bishop of Exeter, the abbot of (Bury) St Edmunds, the abbot of St Albans, the abbot of Battle, the abbot of St Augustine's Canterbury, the abbot of Evesham, the abbot of Westminster, the abbot of Peterborough, the abbot of Reading, the abbot of Abingdon, the abbot of Malmesbury, the abbot of Winchcombe, the abbot of Hyde (Winchester), the abbot of Chertsey, the abbot of Sherborne, the abbot of Cerne, the abbot of Abbotsbury, the abbot of Milton (Abbas), the abbot of Selby, the abbot of Whitby, the abbot of Cirencester, H(ubert) de Burgh the justiciar of England, R(anulf) earl of Chester and Lincoln, W(illiam) earl of Salisbury, G(ilbert) de Clare earl of Gloucester and Hertford, W(illiam) de Ferrers earl of Derby, W(illiam) de Mandeville earl of Essex, H(ugh) Bigod earl of Norfolk, W(illiam) earl Aumale, H(umphrey) earl of Hereford, J(ohn) de Lacy constable of Chester, Robert de Ros, R(obert) fitz Walter, Robert de Vieuxpont, W(illiam) Brewer, R(ichard) de Montfiquet, P(eter) fitz Herbert, Matthew fitz Herbert, W(illiam) de Aubigné, Robert Grelley, Reginald de Braose, John of Monmouth, John fitz Alan, Hugh de Mortemer, Walter de Beauchamp, William de St John, Peter de Maulay, Brian de Lisle, Thomas of Moulton, Richard de Arg<entan, Geoffrey de> Neville, W(illiam) Mauduit, John de Baalon and others. Given at Westminster on the eleventh day of February in the ninth year of our reign.

GENEALOGY OF THE KINGS OF ENGLAND, 1066–1377

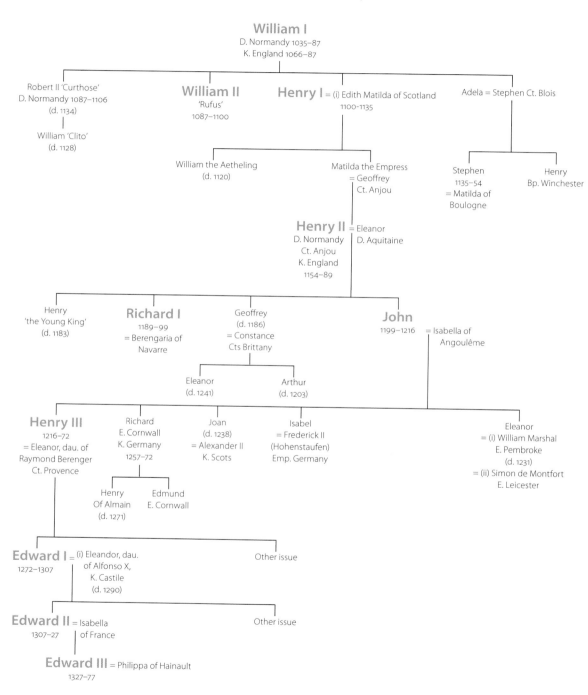

William I
D. Normandy 1035–87
K. England 1066–87

Robert II 'Curthose'
D. Normandy 1087–1106
(d. 1134)

William 'Clito'
(d. 1128)

William II
'Rufus'
1087–1100

Henry I = (i) Edith Matilda of Scotland
1100–1135

Adela = Stephen Ct. Blois

William the Aetheling
(d. 1120)

Matilda the Empress
= Geoffrey
Ct. Anjou

Stephen
1135–54
= Matilda of
Boulogne

Henry
Bp. Winchester

Henry II = Eleanor
D. Normandy   D. Aquitaine
Ct. Anjou
K. England
1154–89

Henry
'the Young King'
(d. 1183)

Richard I
1189–99
= Berengaria of
Navarre

Geoffrey
(d. 1186)
= Constance
Cts Brittany

John
1199–1216 = Isabella of
Angoulême

Eleanor
(d. 1241)

Arthur
(d. 1203)

Henry III
1216–72
= Eleanor, dau. of
Raymond Berenger
Ct. Provence

Richard
E. Cornwall
K. Germany
1257–72

Joan
(d. 1238)
= Alexander II
K. Scots

Isabel
= Frederick II
(Hohenstaufen)
Emp. Germany

Eleanor
= (i) William Marshal
E. Pembroke
(d. 1231)
= (ii) Simon de Montfort
E. Leicester

Henry
Of Almain
(d. 1271)

Edmund
E. Cornwall

Edward I = (i) Eleandor, dau.
1272–1307   of Alfonso X,
K. Castile
(d. 1290)

Other issue

Edward II = Isabella
1307–27   of France

Other issue

Edward III = Philippa of Hainault
1327–77

LIST OF ABBREVIATIONS

Annales Monastici	*Annales Monastici*, ed. H.R. Luard, 5 vols (London 1864-9)
Bémont, Charles	*Chartes de libertés anglaises* (Paris 1892)
BL	London, British Library
Blackstone, William	*The Great Charter and Charter of the Forest with Other Authentic Instruments* (Oxford 1759), reissued in a second, revised edition as *Law Tracts*, ii (Oxford 1762)
Carpenter, David	*Magna Carta* (London 2015)
Cal. Chart. R.	*Calendar of the Charter Rolls*, 6 vols (London 1903–27)
Close Rolls	*Close Rolls of the Reign of Henry III*, 14 vols (London 1902–38)
Collins, A.J.	'The Documents of the Great Charter of 1215', *Proceedings of the British Academy*, xxxiv (1948), 233–79
Councils and Synods	*Councils and Synods with Other Documents relating to the English Church II: A.D. 1205–1313*, ed. F.M. Powicke and C.R. Cheney, 2 vols (Oxford 1964)
EHR	*English Historical Review*
Foedera	*Foedera, Conventiones, Litterae et cujuscumque generis acta publica*, ed. T.Rymer, New Edition, vol.I part i, ed. A. Clark and F.Holbrooke (London 1816)
Fox, J(ohn) C(harles)	'The Originals of the Great Charter', *EHR*, xxxix (1924), 321–36
Guala Letters	*The Letters and Charters of Cardinal Guala Bicchieri Papal Legate in England 1216–1218*, ed. N. Vincent, Canterbury and York Society lxxxiii (1996)
Holt, J(ames) C.	*Magna Carta*, 2nd ed. (Cambridge 1992)
Layettes	*Layettes du Trésor des Chartes*, ed. A. Teulet and others, 5 vols (Paris 1863-1909),
Patent Rolls	*Patent Rolls 1216–1232*, 2 vols (London 1901-3)
Poole, R(eginald) L(ane)	The Publication of Great Charters by the English Kings', *EHR*, xxviii (1913), 444–53
Prestwich, Michael	*Documents Illustrating the Crisis of 1297–8 in England*, Camden Society 4th series 24 (London 1980) *Edward I* (London 1988)
RLC	*Rotuli Litterarum Clausarum*, ed. T. D. Hardy, 2 vols (1833–44)
RLP	*Rotuli Litterarum Patentium*, ed. T.D. Hardy (London 1835)
Sotheby's MC	*The Magna Carta*, Sotheby's Sale Catalogue (by Nicholas Vincent) (New York, 18 December 2007)
Statutes (1810)	*The Statutes of the Realm Printed by Command of His Majesty King George III*, vol. 1, Record Commission (London 1810)
Stubbs, William	*Select Charters and Other Illustrations of English Constitutional History*, 9th ed., by H.W.C. Davis (Oxford 1921)
TNA	London, The National Archives

GLOSSARY

Attachment (cc.18, 30): the legal procedure by which property is seized to ensure enforcement of a judgment

Baron/barony (cc.2, 31 etc): the holder/landholding of a lord holding directly of king as a tenant in chief (i.e. without intermediary lord between landholder and king)

Burgage (c.27): form of tenure enjoyed by a burgess (i.e. townsman), generally in return for a fixed annual rent

Coroner (c.17): local knight, since the 1190s entrusted with enquiries into homicides and other suspicious deaths

Common pleas (c.11): legal actions between subject and subject that did not directly concern the king, held before the law court in Westminster known as the 'Bench' or 'Common Bench'

Darrein presentment (c.13): a legal procedure for the recovery of the patronage of churches to which the litigant claims the right of presentation

Demesne (c.21): the land retained in a lord's direct possession, when the rest of his estate was 'farmed' (i.e. rented) out to knights or lesser men

Disseise/disseisin (cc.12, 29): the forced dispossession of property

Distrain/distraint (cc.7-8): forced seizure of property in lieu of unpaid rent or other debt

Escheat (c.31): a landholding that has reverted to its overlord for lack of heirs within the tenant family

Fish weirs (c.33): large traps, essentially a network of wooden staves sunk in rivers, into which fish swim but from which they cannot escape

Forest (final clause): land not necessarily wooded but set aside for the king's hunt under special law intended to protect game animals and their habitat

Haberject (c.25): a type of cloth, probably of mixed colour

Hundred (c.35): an administrative unit of land into which the shire or county was divided

Justiciar (cc.12, 30): the king's chief law officer, responsible for the working of the king's law courts

Mort d'ancestor (c.12): a legal procedure for the recovery of land rightfully inherited

Novel disseisin (c.12): a legal procedure for the recovery of land recently seized

Pleas of the crown (c.17): certain categories of legal procedure, involving such offences as murder, homicide, rape and arson, reserved for hearing in the royal as opposed to manor courts or the courts of lesser lords

Praecipe (c.24): a standard legal writ, sent by the king to the sheriff, ordering him to 'command' (i.e. from the Latin verb 'praecipere') a lord to transfer a case from his own court to that of the king

Relief (c.2, 3, 31): the payment to the king owed by a knight or baron for succession to his inherited lands

Russets (c.25): reddish brown cloth

Scutage (c.37): a money payment made in lieu of personal military service (literally 'shield money')

Serjeanty (c.27): landholding in return for service, often for performance of a regular duty such as keeping a lord's falcons, polishing his weapons etc

Sheriff (cc.4, 17, 18, 35 etc): the 'shire reeve' (in Latin the 'vicecomes' or 'vice-earl') acting as the king's principal officer, generally one for each English county

Socage (c.27): form of tenure enjoyed by a 'soke man', generally in return for a fixed annual rent

Tourn (c.35): court held by a sheriff, often for the sheriff's personal profit

Vill (cc.9, 19): a settlement, usually a small town, usually below the status of a borough

Villein (c.14): an unfree tenant, i.e. a peasant or 'serf', bonded to his or her land

Writ (cc.24, 26): a letter or other written instruction, required to initiate legal action in the king's court

Yards within the lists (c.25): specified distance from one edge of a piece of cloth to its opposite edge

BIBLIOGRAPHY

Armitage, D., *The Ideological Origins of the British Empire*, Cambridge University Press, Cambridge, 2000.

Baker, J., *English Legal Manuscripts in the United States of America,* 2 vols, Selden Society, London, 1985–90.

Baker, J., *A Catalogue of English Legal Manuscripts in Cambridge University Library*, Boydell, Woodbridge, 1996.

Baker, J., *English Legal Manuscripts*, 2 vols, Zug 1975–8.

Bishop, T.A.M., *Scriptores Regis,* Oxford University Press, Oxford, 1961.

Bond, M.F. (ed.), *The Seventh Centenary of Simon de Montfort's Parliament 1265–1965: An Account of the Commemorative Ceremonies and a Historical Narrative*, Her Majesties Stationary Office, London, 1965.

Brand, P., 'English Thirteenth Century Legislation', in Romano, A. (ed.), *Colendi iustitiam et iura condendo. Federico II legislatore del Regno di Sicilia nell'Europa del Ducento*, Rome, 1997.

Brand, P., *Kings, Barons and Justices: the Making and Enforcement of Legislation in Thirteenth-Century England*, Cambridge University Press, Cambridge, 2004.

Brand, P., 'Henry II and the Creation of the English Common Law', in Harper-Bill, C., and N. Vincent (eds.), *Henry II: New Interpretations*, Boydell, Woodbridge, 2007.

Carpenter, D., *The Minority of Henry III*, Methuen, London, 1990.

Carpenter, D., *The Reign of Henry III*, A&C Black, London, 1996.

Carpenter, D., '"In Testimonium Factorum Brevium": The Beginnings of the English Chancery Rolls', in Vincent, N. (ed.), *Records, Administration and Aristocratic Society in the Anglo-Norman Realm: Papers Commemorating the 800th Anniversary of King John's Loss of Normandy*, Boydell, Woodbridge, 2009.

Carpenter, D., *Magna Carta*, Penguin Classics, London, 2015.

Church, S. (ed.), *King John: New Interpretations*, Boydell Press, Woodbridge, 1999.

Clanchy, M.T., *From Memory to Written Record*, Wiley-Blackwell, London, 1979, 3rd ed. Chichester, 2013.

Collins, A.J., 'The Documents of the Great Charter of 1215', *Proceedings of the British Academy* 34, 1948, pp.233–79.

Crouch, D., *Tournament*, Hambledon, London, 2005.

Fox, J.C., 'The originals of the Great Charter of 1215', *English Historical Review*, 39, 1924.

Greene, J.P., *Exclusionary Empire: English Liberty Overseas, 1600–1900*, Cambridge University Press, Cambridge, 2009.

Hershey, A.H., *Drawings and Sketches in the Plea Rolls of the English Royal Courts, c.1200–1300*, List and Index Society Special Series 31, 2002.

Holt, J.C. 'The St Albans Chroniclers and Magna Carta', *Transactions of the Royal Historical Society*, 5th series 14, 1964.

Holt, J.C., 'The Assizes of Henry II: the texts', in Bullough, D. A., and R.L Storey, *The Study of Medieval Records: Essays in honour of Kathleen Major*, Oxford University Press, Oxford, 1971.

Holt, J.C., *The Northerners*, Oxford University Press, Oxford, 1961, 2nd ed. 1992.

Holt, J.C., *Magna Carta*, Cambridge University Press, Cambridge, 1965, 2nd ed. 1992, 3rd. ed. forthcoming 2015.

Howard, A.E. Dick, *The Road from Runnymede: Magna Carta and Constitutionalism in America,* University of Virginia Press, Charlottesville, 1968.

Hudson, J., *The Oxford History of the Laws of England*. Volume II: 871–1216, Oxford University Press, Oxford, 2012.

Hyams, P., *Rancor and Reconciliation in Medieval England*, Cornell University Press, Ithaca, 2003.

Lees-Milne, J., *Ancestral Voices*, Chatto & Windus, London, 1974.

Lees-Milne, J., *Prophesying Peace*, Chatto & Windus, London, 1977.

Lees-Milne, J., *Caves of Ice*, Chatto & Windus, London, 1983.

Loengard, J.S. (ed.), *Magna Carta and the England of King John*, Boydell Press, Woodbridge, 2010.Linebaugh, P., *The Magna Carta Manifesto: Liberties and Commons for All*, University of California Press, Berkeley, 2008.

Maddicott, J.R., 'Magna Carta and the Local Community, 1215–1259', *Past and Present*, 102, 1984, pp.25–65.

Maddicott, J.R., *The Origins of the English Parliament, 924–1327*, Oxford University Press, Oxford, 2010.

Malden, H.E. (ed.), *Magna Carta Commemoration Essays*, Royal Historical Society, London, 1917.

McDowell, G.L., *The Language of Law and the Foundations of American Constitutionalism*, Cambridge University Press, Cambridge, 2010.

O'Brien, B., *God's Peace and King's Peace: The Laws of Edward the Confessor*, University of Pennsylvania Press, Philadelphia, 1999.

O'Brien, B., 'Pre-Conquest Laws and Legislators in the Twelfth Century', in Brett, M., and D.A. Woodman (eds.), *The Long Twelfth-Century View of the Anglo-Saxon Past*, Farnham, 2015.

Otte, T., '"The Shrine at Sulgrave": The Preservation of the Washington Ancestral Home as an "English Mount Vernon" and Transatlantic Relations', in Hall, M. (ed.), *Towards World Heritage: International Origins of the Preservation Movement, 1870–1930*, Ashgate, Farnham, 2011.

Painter, S., *The Reign of King John*, Johns Hopkins University Press, Baltimore, 1949.

Pallister, A., *Magna Carta: The Heritage of Liberty*, Oxford University Press, Oxford, 1971.

Plucknett, T.F.T., *Legislation of Edward I*, Oxford University Press, Oxford, 1949.

Poole, R.L., 'The Publication of Great Charters by the English Kings', *English Historical Review*, 28, 1913, pp.444–53.

Powicke, F.M., and C.R. Cheney (ed.), *Councils and Synods with Other Documents Relating to the English Church: II (A.D. 1205–1313)*, 2 vols, Oxford University Press, Oxford, 1964.

Richardson, H.G., 'The Early Statutes', *Law Quarterly Review*, 50, 1934, pp.201–23, 540–71.

Rowlands, I., 'The Text and Distribution of the Writ for the Publication of Magna Carta, 1215', *English Historical Review*, 124, 2009.

Saul, N., *For Honour and Fame: Chivalry in England, 1066–1500*, Pimlico, London, 2011.

Shalev, E., *Rome Reborn on Western Shores: Historical Imagination and the Creation of the American Republic*, University of Virginia Press, Charlottesville, 2009.

Talbot, M., *My Life and Lacock Abbey*, George Allen and Unwin, London, 1956.

Thompson, F., *Magna Carta: Its Role in the Making of the English Constitution, 1300–1629*, University of Minnesota Press, Minneapolis, 1948.

Thompson, F., *The First Century of Magna Carta*, University of Minnesota Press, Minneapolis, 1925.

Turner, R.V., *King John*, Longman, London, 1994.

Vincent, N., 'Why 1199? Bureaucracy and Enrolment under John and his Contemporaries', in Jobson, A. (ed.), *English Government in the Thirteenth Century*, Boydell, Woodbridge, 2004.

Vincent, N., *The Magna Carta*, Sotheby's Sale Catalogue, New York, 18 December 2007.

Vincent, N., *Magna Carta: A Very Short Introduction*, Oxford University Press, Oxford, 2012.

Vincent, N., 'The Great Lost Library of England's Medieval Kings? Royal Use and Ownership of Books, 1066–1272', in Doyle, K., and S. McKendrick (eds.), *1000 Years of Royal Books and Manuscripts*, British Library, London, 2013.

Vincent, N., *Australia's Magna Carta,* Canberra, Senate of Australia, 2011, 2nd ed. 2015.

Vincent, N. (ed.), *Magna Carta: The Foundation of Freedom, 1215–2015*, Third Millennium Publishing, London, 2015.

Vincent, N., 'Magna Carta and the "English Historical Review"', *English Historical Review*, 120, 2015.

Vincent, N., 'Scribes in the Chancery of Henry II, King of England 1154–1189', in Hermand, X., J-F Nieus and É. Renard (eds.), *Le scribe d'archive dans l'Occident médiéval : formations, carrières, réseaux. Actes du colloque international de Namur, 2–4 mai 2012*, Turnhout, 2015.

Vincent, N., 'The Seals of King Henry II and his Court' in Schofield, P.R. (ed.), *Seals and their Context in the Middle Ages*, Oxford University Press, Oxford, 2015.

Wake, J., *The Brudenells of Deene*, Cassell & Company, London 1953, 2nd ed. 1954.

Warren, W.L., *King John*, Yale University Press, London, 1961.

Warren, W.L., 'Painter's "King John" – Forty Years On', *Haskins Society Journal*, I, 1989, pp.1–9.

White, G., *The Magna Carta of Cheshire*, Cheshire Local History Association, Chester, 2015.

Wormald, P., *The Making of English Law: King Alfred to the Twelfth Century*, Wiley Blackwell, Oxford, 1999.

INDEX OF MANUSCRIPTS

(Covering the census, above pp.206-71)

INDEX OF PERSONS, PLACES AND SUBJECTS